"What will you do with your thousand pounds
O Lincoln City FC?
Will you try to renovate your grounds
Or spend it on the spree?
Have you decided to get new players
Your own League place to raise?
To go up football's 'golden stairs'
And win support and praise?
Or shall you just stay where you are
And leave the team depleted?
From every chance your own team bar
And by others all defeated?"

Past Imperfect

The Story of Lincoln City F.C.

by Brian Halford

With a Foreword by John Inverdale

The Parrs Wood Press
<u>MANCHESTER</u>

First Published 2000

THE PARRS WOOD PRESS
St Wilfrid's Enterprise Centre
Royce Road, Manchester, M15 5BJ

© Brian Halford 2000

ISBN: 1 903158 04 4

This book was produced by Andrew Searle, Bob Wells and Ruth Heritage of The Parrs Wood Press and Printed in Great Britain by:

Fretwell Print and Design
Healey Works
Goulbourne Street
Keighley
West Yorkshire BD21 1 PZ

ACKNOWLEDGEMENTS

MANY PEOPLE have been helpful to me in compiling this book and it would be invidious to try to list them in anything other than alphabetical order. The level of interest and hospitality, not to mention the tea and biscuits, with which I have been greeted has been much appreciated. Without exception, everyone I have approached has been receptive and helpful.

Clearly, a plot as long and diverse as the history of a professional football club includes a cast of thousands. There will always be people to whom the author could have spoken but to whom he didn't, due to pressures of time, get round. I hope everybody mentioned in these pages gets a fair crack of the whip. Similarly, I have made great efforts to ensure all the facts are right but there are more facts here than you could a shake a stick at and if one or two errors have slipped through the net, then I apologise. Anyone who spots an error is very welcome, if they see me in a Lincoln pub, to come over and point it out, so long as you start the conversation with the magic words: "What are you drinking ?"

***

Thanks to:

Chris Ashton, George and Doreen Ashton, Brian Baldam, John Beck, Mike Berry, Gilbert Blades, Mary Bonner, Phil Booth, Barry Clements, Geoff Davey, Frank Eccleshare, Jon Finch, Kerry France, Andy Graver, Kevin Halford, Nick Harrison, Chris Harte, Ruth Heritage, Maurice Hodson, John Inverdale, John and Anna Kennedy, Lyndsay Jubb, Clair Lait, Edward Lee, Bert Linnecor, Jerry Lonsdale, Bert Loxley, Russell Kirk, Colin Murphy, Donald Nannestad, Ian Nannestad, Steve Naylor, Pete Norton, Phil O'Farrell, John Reames, Andrew Searle, Phil Stant, Colin Summerton, Bernard Stewart, Graham Taylor, Dave Thomas, Peter Upton, Peter Washbourn, Bob Wells, Alan Wilson, Monica Withers, the Lincolnshire Echo, Lincolnshire County Council's Library Service and the Local Studies Collection at Lincoln Central Library, courtesy of Lincolnshire County Council, Education and Cultural Services Directorate.

BIBLIOGRAPHY

Lincolnshire Echo
Lincolnshire Gazette
Lincolnshire Chronicle
Rothman Football Yearbook
Wisden Cricketers Almanack
Some Recollections of Former Players of Lincoln City - Ernest Pullein
The Official History of Lincoln City - Donald and Ian Nannestad
Who's Who of Lincoln City, 1892 to1995 - Donald and Ian Nannestad
100 Seasons of League Football - Bryon Butler
Notts County: The Official History, 1862 to1995 - Tony Brown
Tottenham Hotspur: The Official History, 1882 to 1997 - Phil Soar
Coventry City: A Complete Record, 1883 to 1991 - Rod Dean
Rejected F.C. (Volume One) - Dave Twydell

To Mum

CONTENTS

FOREWORD

by John Inverdale

DECEMBER 18, 1982. Never forget it. My flat on Spring Hill, which had been certified by the UN as the coldest in the world, had just reached new levels of unbearability. All three bars of the electric fire were on full blast and still failing to lift the room temperature above freezing. Lincoln City were playing Bournemouth that day. Absolutely no chance of the match being on, surely.

Rang the fount of all knowledge, BBC Radio Lincolnshire. Game still going ahead. Decide not to walk down to Sincil Bank. Socks not thick enough. Take car. Heater not working in car. Lincoln looks like Moscow. Cold and grey. Park car somewhere. Not sure where. Never was a hot soup and a sausage roll so eagerly devoured. Game starts. Lincoln win 9-0. That's NINE. Harry Redknapp's first game in charge of Bournemouth doesn't bode well for the rest of his managerial career. Lincoln nailed on for promotion now, even though the season is barely half over. Decide to have a beer. And another one. And another one.

Leave car near Sincil Bank. Fall over repeatedly climbing Steep Hill. Nothing to do with drink. Just freezing, icy conditions. Start wondering how Radio Lincolnshire will cover the Imps when they graduate to the then Second Division. Sweet dreams.

December 19, 1982. Even colder than day before and have run down in track-suit to bring car back. Car lost. Car stolen ? Jog round every street in vicinity of Sincil Bank. It's nowhere to be found. About to ring police when spy it at junction about 200 yards ahead. What a relief. Try to put key in door. Lock frozen. Start kicking car (intelligent). Getting nowhere fast when lady in dressing gown opens front door of house nearby to ask me what I'm doing. Tells me she's ringing the police because I'm trying to steal a car. Protest that it's my car. She says if it was my car I'd be in it by now. Ask her to try to open lock. "What, me in my dressing gown ?" she says.

Persuade her to put phone down when she's half-way through dialling 999. If you could boil a kettle for me, I could unfreeze the lock and drive off, I say. Grudgingly, she agrees. Pour boiling water on lock. Open door. Get in car. Car won't start. Slam hand on steering wheel (even more intelligent). Go back to woman in dressing gown. Can I borrow phone to ring mate to come and tow me away ?

So all these years later, when I think of the Imps, I think of Colin Murphy and the unbelievably long answers he used to give to very simple questions. But more than anything else I think of that amazing game, and the OHT 17F, a Cortina Mark II, and all the hassle it caused me. (You never forget your first car number plate). Unlike my Cortina, which a short while afterwards disappeared to that great scrap-heap in the sky, LCFC continues in varying degrees of rude health, a club within a community that would only fully appreciate what it means to have a League club in their midst when someone takes it away from them. So many sides in the lower divisions, year on year, seem to be staring the executioner in the face, but it's imperative for English football that they survive. Here's to good fortune for Lincoln City in the next Millennium and beyond. The Imps, and clubs like them, are the heart and soul of the game in this country.

1.
Coming together

MOMENTOUS things occur in pubs. Important decisions are taken. Historic events set in motion. Far-reaching plots are hatched. People fall in love, sometimes at first sight. Inspiration blossoms - Nikolai Gogol wrote the best bits of Dead Souls in a smoky bar.

But perhaps the most significant event ever to unfold inside a public house occurred in the Monson Arms, High Street, Lincoln, in 1884. On July 5, 1884, a warm, musty evening, inside that tavern, the air thick with excitement, beer fumes and cigar smoke, into existence sprang Lincoln City Football Club.

Footballs had been kicked around Lincoln, like the rest of England, with increasing vigour for several decades. Established in public schools in the middle of the century, the sport spread quickly as pupils left those schools only to find, as they matured, that they still harboured the desire to send in 25-yard ripsnorters or dismantle winger's ankles with wild and free sliding-tackles.

When, in 1870, football arrived in the curriculum of Lincoln's schools, the seeds of passion for the sport in the city were planted. Dozens of teams quickly took root: teams rather than clubs for they were vaguely organised, driven more by the desire for leisure than competition.

That soon changed. Competitive juices foamed and boiled and the Lincolnshire County Cup was founded in 1881. When a team from Spilsby, a rural settlement out east on the Wolds, won it for the first three years, Lincoln was stung. Could the county's principal city not muster a football team to beat this tiny village?

During Autumn 1883 Lincoln was dominated by talk of creating one senior football club to represent the city. A big majority of football enthusiasts were in favour, but the two most important clubs differed.

Lincoln Lindum, based at the Wragby Road ground on which sport is still played today, didn't like the way football was going. They wanted to stay casual and amateur. But Lincoln Rovers, from their much less well-equipped London Road home, were more in tune with the popular view. That was: "Let's build the best team we can to bring the County Cup to Lincoln."

That mission triggered the meeting at the Monson Arms. As a humid night enveloped the pub, much ale was sunk, Lincoln Rovers disbanded and into life, all new and shiny and full of hope, burst Lincoln City. The principal driving forces were local businessmen William Mortimer, Sharpley Bainbridge and John Henry ("Jack") Strawson.

Mortimer, an architect by profession, was the real prime mover. As chairman of Lincoln Rovers he saw the way the wind was blowing a year earlier. Along with Strawson, club secretary, he steered through Rovers' annual meeting a motion that only association rules fixtures would be played in the future. Football was burgeoning. Rugby was out. A decade earlier, Mortimer had played cricket for Lincolnshire but football had become his consuming passion. In civic life, business and sport, he was used to achieving his goals. Bringing the County Cup to Lincoln was now his goal.

Bainbridge was a city councillor and prominent businessmen who had inherited control of the family drapery's store in High Street. A magistrate and former goalkeeper, with an impressive property in Lindum Road, he delegated many of his business duties to make room for his love of sport. His passion for football was combined with running a stable of steeplechasers and several coops of racing pigeons.

Vital though Bainbridge and Mortimer were to the football club's creation, it was Strawson who was to become the first great figure in Lincoln City's history. Born into a farming family in the tiny village of East Firsby, eight miles north of Lincoln, he might have spent his whole life tilling and planting had the family not relocated to the "big city" when Jack was still a toddler. They opened Strawson's Dining Rooms, a cafe on High Street.

Jack served in the tearooms but, from infancy, ate, drank and slept football. He joined Rovers and played centre-forward without great distinction but by his early twenties, his talent for organisation and administration was already clear. At 22, he became Rovers' secretary and continued that office when Rovers became City. It was the start of a 35-year association with the club.

These three men bound together the rampant interest in this exciting new sport and translated it into Lincoln City FC. Football was snowballing - though not without opposition. Plenty of brawls, assaults and arrests stemmed from ill-controlled matches and many clergymen despised a pastime which drew aggression from participants and spectators.

Sunday school teachers from Blaenau Ffestiniog, a village at the foot of Mount Snowdon, came right down off the fence. Football, they raged, was "positively wicked" and "surrounded by evil influences." They appealed to Christian people everywhere to "help stamp out the moral contagion of football playing."

Most Lincoln folk did not see it that way and, happily for Lincoln City, those that didn't included local brewer Robert Dawber. A shy man who stayed largely remote from public life, Dawber was a generous benefactor to causes which captured his interest. He was hugely wealthy, having expanded the business he founded in 1826 to include two breweries, supplying 60 pubs in the county. A former Rovers footballer, he required little courting by Bainbridge and Mortimer to add City to his favoured causes. Dawber donated land adjoining one of his breweries for a pitch. The John O'Gaunts ground had a perfect central location, just a hefty goal-kick over Sincil Drain from where the Sincil Bank stadium exists today.

On Saturday October 4, 1884, Lincoln City took the field for the first time. Sleaford Town visited John O'Gaunts and, after the game kicked off 20 minutes late to allow the large crowd in, were beaten 9-1. George Hallam scored City's first ever goal and went on to complete the first hat-trick. City's players wore "beautiful red velvet caps crowned with big golden tassels" and a shot from City right winger Clement Newsum broke the crossbar. Nottingham Forest visited a week later. This time the kick-off was delayed an hour due to Forest's train arriving late. Forest, despite sending a second team, were fitter and faster and won 4-2.

The "Cits" first competitive game came next. Boston Excelsior arrived for a County Cup tie and were hammered 11-0 with Edwin Teesdale junior, another Rovers refugee, scoring four. Like most of the early players, Teesdale was a local man with a public school background. Of the first generation City players, almost all had strong local connections. That would soon change.

Interest was huge and, after a 4-0 second round win over Lincoln Albion, more than 500 supporters accompanied City to the next County Cup tie, away to Horncastle Town. The trail ended there with a 3-0 defeat and the first assault on the FA Cup - apart from those two tournaments all matches were friendlies - was terminated 1-0 by Grimsby. Strawson umpired the game and showed his integrity by ruling out an apparent City equaliser for offside.

It was an encouraging first season. Of 26 games, City won 14, drew three and lost nine, scoring 83 goals and conceding 38. The rising passion for football was illustrated by 7,000 people flocking to Lindum's ground to watch Grantham beat Gainsborough 1-0 in the County Cup final. "The oldest inhabitant never saw such a sight," reported the Lincolnshire Chronicle. "The referee's whistle sounded play followed by a tremendous roar which never ceased until the fateful 90 minutes had sped by." Even without the ludicrous media hype of a century later, football had immediately burrowed itself deep into the English psyche.

For City's second campaign, Dawber financed ground improvements. The John O'Gaunts pitch was relaid and a paved path laid to it from new, spacious dressing rooms. With the Football Association relaxing rules on professionalism, cash was also channelled into importing players.

Lincoln looked to Lancashire, where committee member James West was well-connected. In came four players, most significantly former Blackburn

Rovers half-back Joe Duckworth who also took on coaching duties. Season-tickets, at two shillings each, sold well even though the itinerary was haphazard with fixtures unreliable and kick-off times reliant on railway timetables.

A failed train could mean no match while other games were aborted if darkness fell early. A football ground was also not the safest environment, particularly at derby games. Boston Town pledged never to visit Lincoln again after eight of their players were assaulted by Lincoln Ramblers' supporters. Following a visit to John O'Gaunts, Gainsborough Trinity's executive stated: "We dare not send a team to Lincoln, fearing the spectators." Incidents like these, along with the emergence of gambling, helped to convince many clergymen that football was, indeed, evil.

To many men, however, locked into the drudgery of factories and foundries, it offered precious catharsis. It also injected some success - or at least some hope of success - into lives of hardship and routine. Lincoln City's first whiff of success, accompanied by bitter controversy, arrived in the Spring of 1886.

City beat Lincoln Albion and the fading Spilsby, both 4-0, and Brigg Ancholme 7-0 to reach the County Cup semi-final. A visit to Grimsby Town was the reward. Temporary stands were set up at Clee Park to accommodate a 7,000 crowd, including 1,600 who travelled up on three trains from Lincoln. A titanic tussle ended 1-1. Grimsby wanted to play extra time. Lincoln refused, on the grounds that it was almost totally dark.

Rancorous exchanges followed. Grimsby appealed to the Lincolnshire FA who voted 15-3 to disqualify Lincoln. City took the matter to the English FA. When their verdict was due, more than 800 supporters gathered at the city's historic Stonebow to await the telegram. Umbrellas, hats and handkerchieves were hurled into the air when the FA's reply ordered the semi-final to be replayed. But Grimsby, the cads, refused. They ignored the governing body and all letters and telegrams from Lincoln stating that the replay would be on April 10. Sure enough, on April 10, Grimsby didn't show up. Lincoln waited 10 minutes beyond kick-off time then walked the ball into the net and claimed the game before Notts Rangers, brought along just in case, took the field for a friendly.

After that farce, Grimsby again took the matter to the Lincolnshire FA who again defied their parent association and backed the Mariners. Grimsby went through to the final where they lifted the cup after a 1-0 win over Lincoln Lindum. The Lincs FA was called before the English FA to explain why it had defied Daddy. A valuable lesson - sort out the rules at the start - was learned by all and years of ill-feeling between the two clubs involved were launched.

City's horizons broadened in 1886/7. There were friendlies away to Aston Villa and at home to Birmingham Excelsior, Sheffield Club and Oswaldthwistle.

Still the only competitive matches were in the two cups - but now came success the club had been craving. The FA Cup brought a promising run which saw Middlesbrough and Gainsborough Trinity beaten before a 3-0 defeat to Glasgow Rangers at Kinning Park, much City's longest trip yet. In the County Cup, however, promise was fulfilled. Lincoln got their mitts on the hallowed trophy.

The first round pitted them against Lindum, still stubbornly amateur, whom they trounced 5-0. Grimsby Humber Rovers (5-0), Gainsborough (5-2) and Grantham Victoria (5-0) were vanquished to earn a place in the final against - guess who - Grimsby Town. In red-and-white striped droves, City's fans travelled to Gainsborough's Northolme ground to see the sides slug out a 2-2 draw. Three weeks passed before the replay, again at Gainsborough. In the interim, talk in Lincoln and Grimsby was of little else. Even Lincoln Town Council's shocking assertion that bathers in the River Witham were "not behaving with proper decorum" took second billing.

Before another packed crowd, it was Lincoln who held their nerve to record a 2-0 win. The mighty Duckworth dominated at the back while Billy Gregson and Jimmy Slater scored late in each half. When the team's train rolled back into Lincoln at 10pm a jubilant crowd was there to greet them. They partied late into the night. Mortimer's mission had been accomplished and the club's raison d'etre fulfilled.

With the County Cup lifted and a record of 31 wins from 41 games compiled, the ale flowed at an end-of-season banquet in the Oddfellows Hall. Cheers were loudest when the cup was passed to Dawber and Bainbridge who grinned broadly, hitched up their trousers and took mighty swigs. Edwin Teesdale, captain, claimed that no City side ever took the field with more determination while Bainbridge headed for the moral high ground. "The City club," he purred, "was formed to enable men, working men particularly, when they had borne the burden and heat of a hard week's work, to be able to go into the City football ground and enjoy two hours healthy recreation." The club officers preened themselves. Within months they would be defending themselves.

During the summer of 1887 turnstiles were fitted at the north end of John O'Gaunts to ease admission for anticipated bigger crowds. But when the previous campaign's progress failed to bridge the summer and opposition declined to roll over, supporters soon started to grumble. Those grumbles grew when, in November, an FA Cup 2-0 exit at Grimsby, was followed two days later by a 5-1 friendly defeat at Sheffield Wednesday's Olive Grove ground.

"The players aren't fit enough," argued the fans. The committee bore the brunt of criticism and a special meeting was called for December 12 to discuss "the constitution of the team, past work and future management." Two days before this meeting, supporters' dissent came to a head. City were beaten 6-1 at home by West Brom and full-back Herbert Simpson had what, 110 years on, would be termed a 'mare. He got so much stick from the crowd that at one point he refused to tackle and let the Throstles' winger pass by. The supporters howled.

At the meeting, fitness was called into question but not just the fitness of the players. Was a committee of self-elected grandees really fit to run a football team? Accountable only to themselves, they picked the side during Tuesday night soirees at Bainbridge's house. While the debt owed by the club to its founders was colossal, many supporters - grafting their socks off for a pittance in the foundries - had an intrinsic distrust of business owners. They were quick to voice it. Where, they asked, was the football expertise ?

The Lincolnshire Gazette sided with the fans. "The team will never be able to do full justice to themselves," it announced, "until greater interest is taken in them individually by those in authority. If the committee are unable or unwilling to devote more of their time to the players, the sooner they make way the better." Yer workers, however, had little clout and the committee, the previous season's success still fresh in their minds at least, continued.

Though the team-selection process was redolent of a village side, plenty of adventure was shown in the fixture list. Glasgow Clyde, Bolton Wanderers, Sheffield Wednesday and London Strollers were now among the opposition. But, more exotic though these fixtures were, they were still just friendlies. Those competitive juices still boiled and foamed, unsatisfied.

Clubs all over the country felt the same and Autumn 1888 brought the creation of a 12-strong one-division Football League. Below that elite, a plethora of more regional organisations formed. Lincoln joined the Combination. The ever-generous Dawber again upgraded the ground, a small grandstand now put in place. Strawson's contacts in the north led to enlistment of a clutch of players from Scotland and the north-east of England for the new challenge.

But the Combination era, as eras go, was short and scruffy. It was poorly organised with members differing on many key issues and after one season, during which City won six of 14 matches, collapsed. Next, Lincoln joined the Midland League. A less ambitious structure, it offered moderate opposition - the likes of Warwick County, Derby Midland, Derby Junction and Stavely - but was more regionally based, and therefore more economic.

Lincoln liked it, especially, because they won it. A 10-2 victory over Leek secured the title by early April for a side bolstered by the addition, for the first time, of a trainer. Four of the Scottish signings - Quinten Neil from Queens Park, Harry Millar from Airdrie, Humphrey Barbour from Third Lanark and Hugh McPhee from Hibernian - played major parts in the title triumph.

The season also lifted City's national profile by pitting them against two of the founding giants of the Football League. In the FA Cup, after knocking out Notts Olympic, Notts Rangers, Gainsborough Trinity and Chester, they got the plummest of plum draws: a visit to cup-holders Preston North End.

Preston were miles ahead in the race for the First Division championship and widely acknowledged as "the best team in the world". "The Invincibles". Certainly they were a test and three-quarters for Lincoln. On an afternoon of torrential rain City were well-beaten but limited the score to a respectable 4-0. Their subsequent protest at the match going ahead because "all round each goal for fully 30 yards was nothing but cesspools" was rejected by the FA and labelled sour-grapes by the "best team in the world."

Late-season saw City enter another prestigious arena for the first time: the spacious grandeur of Wolverhampton Wanderers' Molineux home. Lincoln lost an exciting friendly 4-3 but acquitted themselves well and felt pride that Wolves judged them worthy of a fixture.

Sixteen victories from 20 Midland League games secured the championship by nine points. So where next ? The landscape of English football was still, below the 12-strong Football League, shifting every year. Despite an invitation to join the Football Alliance, which offered more accomplished opposition, City chose to defend the Midland League title. They soon regretted it. The standard was poor and the football uninspiring. A 1-0 final victory over Gainsborough secured the County Cup for the second time but interest in that competition was already waning fast. The national picture was assuming priority.

With an eye on being in prime position if the Football League expanded to a Second Division, Lincoln, having finished third in the Midland League, quit to join the Alliance. It promised by far the most exciting fixture list so far. During the summer, anticipation among supporters was high but again they were annoyed by the committee. Almost no information about club business, including the fixture list and transfers, was made public.

Details of the Tuesday night conclaves chez Sharpley were sketchy. Only when the season started with a couple of friendlies against Grimsby did it emerge that goalkeeper Jack Robinson, a firm favourite and cornerstone of the team, had departed to Derby County. Two young goalkeepers - Bennett from Grantham Rovers and Parsons from Derby-based St Lukes - had been brought in. Quality player out, rookies in: a precedent much followed by City during the next century.

With Parsons in goal, City's Alliance existence started well enough. Two goals from Dundee-born Isaac Moore helped them to a 3-0 home win in their first ever meeting with Ardwick (soon to become Manchester City). Plenty of other first acquaintances followed including Small Heath and Newton Heath (Birmingham City and Manchester United).

Newton Heath administered Lincoln's heaviest defeat yet - a 10-1 demolition in front of 6,000 people in Manchester. The step up in class brought other heavy beatings: 7-2 at Sheffield Wednesday and 6-1 defeats at Grimsby Town and Burton Swifts and at home to Newton Heath. The fixture list also spread south with a 3-1 friendly defeat to Royal Arsenal at Plumstead. A challenging but fascinating season ended with Lincoln ninth out of 12 in the Alliance, having lost half their 22 matches.

It was only a question of time before the Football League expanded. For the 1892/93 season, it did. A Second Division was formed, Lincoln applied to join and were accepted. It was their fourth different League in six seasons - but this was the big one. On to the national stage - along with Ardwick, Bootle, Burton Swifts, Burslem Port Vale, Crewe Alexandra, Darwen, Grimsby Town, Northwich Victoria, Sheffield United, Small Heath and Walsall Town Swifts - they stepped.

Lincoln City in the Football League ! Mortimer, Bainbridge, and Strawson marched, arm in arm, down High Street to the Monson Arms. They strode triumphantly in and took turns to aim their bowler hats at the antlers on the moose's head on the wall. Full glasses were thrust into their hands and the three wise men joined in loudly as the assembled rabble sent raucous chants of "Here we go, here we go, here we go" echoing round the ancient beams and rafters.

Well, perhaps not. But little old Lincoln were heading for the big time.

2.
Rolling in the mud

JACK Strawson slept soundly on the night of Lincoln City's acceptance into the Football League. The sleep of an excited, but calm and intelligent man.

A new era awaited. He knew there was much to be done. Much to achieve. Football was growing, shifting: a cultural eruption from which the landscape was far from settled. The Football League was a world still fresh and unknown, offering new challenges and limitless possibilities. And Lincoln were in on it.

The League had been an immediate success. Crowds were high and publicity heavy. Preston North End, Everton and Sunderland had shared the early championship titles and already these clubs carried great fame, charisma and wealth. They paid their players, it was whispered, 50 shillings per week ! For Lincoln to mix it with them would bring true acceptance into the Big League, never mind the Football League.

The League had operated with just a single division for four years. Twelve-strong for three seasons, it grew to 14 in 1891 and, with many clubs interested in joining, the only sensible option was to add another division in 1892. To gain a place in the Second Division was a proud achievement for Lincoln. A place in the First Division - well that would be really something. Now, just one good season......

City got busy planning for their new adventure. Two colossal blows - one self- inflicted, the other tragically unexpected - lurked round the corner.

The self-inflicted wound was administered straight away, though the pain came later. City's committee agreed to double the players' wages, a highly generous gesture toward a team which had just finished in the bottom four of the Alliance.

Cash was also poured into recruiting players. Goalkeeper Billy Gresham was signed from Gainsborough. Full-back Charles Coulton arrived from Birmingham St Georges for whom he had recently lined up against City in the Alliance. Half-back Robert Cameron and inside-left James Kelly were enticed south from Glasgow. These transfer and signing-on fees plus, for Cameron and

Kelly, relocation expenses, allied to a soaring wage-bill throughout the squad, set a financial time-bomb ticking.

City's Football League life began at Bramall Lane with a 4-2 defeat to Sheffield United. Travel arrangements were still erratic. Lincoln arrived late for that match as they did for their second fixture, a 4-1 defeat at Small Heath. For their third game - at home to Sheffield United - they managed to arrive on time, and celebrated with a 1-0 win. Cameron scored the winner, his second goal in three games, but that was the zenith of his City career. Failure to score regularly saw him drift back into midfield, then out of the side, then soon back to Scotland, his £18 signing on fee and subsequent wages hardly money well spent.

By October, Lincoln had sunk to the bottom of Division Two. The adventure was more combat with hostile seas than leisure cruise. The committee had learned a basic lesson. Doubling players' wages does not make them twice as good players. The realisation dawned that some experience of football helps in running a football club. In November, City appointed former Welsh international Bob Roberts, as player-coach. Roberts, with 10 games for Wales and many more in Division One for Bolton and Preston behind him, had experience coming out of his ears. His mission was to lift City clear of the bottom four who, in May, would have to apply for re-election.

Under Roberts there was an improvement. City scored in every league game, led by Gainsborough-born right-winger Frank Smallman who hit 17 goals in 22 games including four (Lincoln's first Football League hat-trick) in a 5-1 home win over Burton Swifts. Further 5-1 home victories against Northwich Victoria and Bootle engineered a position from which one point from their last two matches would ensure City's final placing above that bottom four. But they lost 4-1 at Bootle and 3-1 at Ardwick.

So, first time up, Lincoln had to seek their fellow League members' approval for another season. Strawson wielded his renowned oratory and re-election was a formality. And ninth out of 12, with Crewe, Port Vale and Walsall below them, was not that bad. By now the County Cup had become almost insignificant. Lincoln got a bye straight to the final which they lost 4-0 to Gainsborough.

During the summer, Roberts departed. He had done a creditable job but, as well as experience coming out of his ears, there was often also ale. The gregarious Welshman liked a pint or twelve and survived two suspensions by the club committee during the season, but their patience was stretched as his on-field influence deteriorated with his fitness. Roberts' hungover display in a 5-0 FA Cup drubbing at Grimsby - ever City's most bitter rivals - hurried him toward the sack.

Now blood began to seep from that self-inflicted wound. At the club's annual meeting, it became clear how overstretched finances had become. City were more than £300 in debt. First team wages for the year soared to £729 while gate receipts generated just £611. The committee moaned that more had been expected of players paid so well.

They were quick to weed out those they didn't rate. The side which opened City's second Football League season with a 1-1 draw at Rotherham included six debutants. Only three of the side - two Scots, right-back Quentin Neill and forward John Irving, and Lincoln-born half-back Ned Mettam - had figured in that first ever League fixture at Bramall Lane a year earlier.

City's second match of the campaign was the inaugural League fixture at Anfield. There was a big Scottish influence in the Lincoln team but an even greater one in Liverpool's. Their whole 11 was Scottish, eight of whom were Macs. A 4-0 defeat at Anfield was to prove no disgrace. En route to the Second Division championship, MacLiverpool won all 14 home games, conceding just six goals.

Early October brought the most memorable match yet to John O'Gaunts. Newcastle United, just relegated from Division One, had recently thrashed Arsenal 6-0 and were desperate to reclaim their place among the elite first time round. In a magnificent game a late goal by Albert Flewett, a summer recruit from Mansfield Greenhalghs, clinched a 2-1 win for Lincoln. Flewitt and Donald Lees, a Scot with an accent so broad the club brought in supporter Sylvanus Lovatt (who had a Scottish mother) to translate, had each made their debuts on the opening day at Rotherham and were settling into a profitable strike partnership.

City's growing credibility brought them a mid-season invitation - with a very welcome "substantial inducement" - to visit Millwall Athletic. Only Arsenal, from the south, had so far gained entry to the League but Millwall were eager to build bridges with League clubs. They were already fully professional and, in front of 3,000 people, outplayed City to win 4-0. The London fans were disappointed with Lincoln's display and it was a salutary lesson to Lincoln not to rest on any laurels.

Back in the League, heavy defeats - 6-0 at Small Heath and 5-1 at Newcastle – set one or two alarm bells ringing. But successive victories over Northwich Victoria, Arsenal and Burton Swifts in January lifted City into comfortable mid-table. When Liverpool arrived, already crowned champions and still unbeaten, in March, Lincoln almost meted out that first defeat. Flewett's goal in a 1-1 draw thrilled the 4,000 crowd.

City finished a more promising season eighth out of 15 and in positive mood. Famous opposition had visited John O'Gaunts. Liverpool. Newcastle

United. Woolwich Arsenal. And then there was Darlington who arrived for a friendly on a foul, freezing, windswept, sleet-carrying November afternoon. Now there was a match to remember. "Taken as an exposition of football," the Gazette reported of City's 1-0 win," the game was altogether a failure but nevertheless considerable amusement was obtained out of it. The pitiable aspect of the players, standing shivering with their backs to the storm waiting for the ball which was probably mixed up with two or three of the men rolling in the mud on the other side of the ground could not help but draw forth a smile."

John O'Gaunts had staged its first night game, a 1-0 friendly win over Sheffield United illuminated, near the touch-lines at least, by Wells Patent Light, a series of paraffin flares on poles. The team had advanced. In Irving, Flewitt and Lees, City possessed a strong forward line while Neill, awarded a benefit by the club, Mettam and Herbert Wilshire were reliable defenders. Revelry was high in May at the football club's first charity fixture: a City XI v the Blue Beard Pantomime Company. Strawson, influential in team selection after Roberts' departure, had every right to hitch up his trousers, tilt his bowler hat to a jaunty angle and feel satisfied. Optimism abounded. But that future, so intriguing and exciting, was about to unleash its first crisis.

With the new season fast approaching, the club's annual meeting at the Black Goats Hotel concluded with the customary vote of thanks to Robert Dawber. His health was widely drank. Ten days later, at 8.30am on August 30, aged 59, he died.

Dawber had increasingly suffered bouts of poor health but nothing which appeared life-threatening. His death, on the eve of a new season, was a shocking blow. It brought his benefaction, so vital to the creation of Lincoln City, into sharp focus. Even in recent years when he had become a virtual recluse, he remained generous towards the football club. His disappearance into Canwick Road cemetery was a grievous loss which threatened to sound the football club's own death knell.

Dawber died the day before City opened the season at home to Arsenal. The crowd, arriving at John O'Gaunts, was stunned as the news spread. Even a 5-2 win for Lincoln, both sides wearing black armbands, was hard to celebrate. With the grief came uncertainty. Dawber had no family to inherit his commitment to Lincoln City. Would the executors of his will look favourably on the football club and let them stay at John O'Gaunts ? The club could only wait and hope.

City's fortunes on the field proved erratic. Their first away match took them to Darwen where they were hammered 6-0 by a brutal home side. Goalkeeper John Broadment, in his second game for Lincoln, suffered a broken shoulder which ended his professional career. Young local 'keeper Tom Hart was drafted in for the next game at Rotherham and looked as nervous as a long-tailed cat in a room full of rocking chairs. The south Yorkshire side won 5-2 and Hart, like Broadbent, never played for Lincoln again.

City's first 11 Second Division games yielded 62 goals. At John O'Gaunts, Port Vale were thrashed 6-1 but Grimsby won 5-1. City lost 5-2 at Arsenal and 3-0 at Notts County in the first match at the new Trent Bridge ground. Two stalwarts departed. Neil, having put on weight, slowed up and, after a 3-1 Boxing Day home defeat by Bury, retired. He emigrated to South Africa. Irving, unhappy to languish in the reserves, left for the less exotic climes of Newark Town.

New Year brought the news the football club had dreaded. Lots at an auction in the Central Sale Rooms, on Bank Street, included "freehold building estate situate in the parish of St Peter at Gowts in the City of Lincoln and usually known as the John O'Gaunts football field." This bland description referred to the home and heart of Lincoln City.

The area of 18,884 square yards, enthused the agent, "can be laid out so as to be most conveniently intersected by a new main street. A rapid demand for houses which may be erected thereon may be confidently expected." The football club was told to vacate at the end of the season.

As a frantic search for another ground commenced, anxiety permeated through to the team. They were thrashed 7-1 at Port Vale and 11-3 at Manchester City, still the club's biggest ever defeat. Evan Roberts, a 24-year-old signed from Kettering to replace Broadbent, kept goal in the Maine Road debacle then never again for Lincoln. This was a tough season for City 'keepers.

Victories from their last two matches - Crewe, the last League visitors to John O'Gaunts, were beaten 5-2 - lifted Lincoln to the top of the bottom four. They survived another application for re-election but that was irrelevant unless another ground could be found. Talk of dissolving the club prompted several key players to jump ship. These included Flewett, 30 goals in 56 games for City, who joined Everton and Lees who moved to Barnsley St Peter.

But the committee wasn't going anywhere. Football gurus they were not but, faced with an off-field crisis, they rose to the occasion. Their contacts around Lincoln were plentiful and with one, Colonel Swan, agreement was reached to use a site, already containing a football pitch, just over the Drain from John O'Gaunts. City moved to the Bank and drew back from the brink.

With the reprieve came a new financial burden. John O'Gaunts had cost almost nothing with Dawber quick to waive the rent in difficult times. Sincil Bank required serious rent. This, along with the cost of equipping the new ground, persuaded members that the football club should be put on a more businesslike footing. Two weeks before the new season, at a meeting chaired by city MP, CH Seely, the club became a limited company. The committee became a board of directors.

Sincil Bank was a better arena than John O'Gaunts. The pitch was excellent while spectators enjoyed an unimpaired view from gentle slopes rising along both touch-lines. After the grandstand was brought across from the former site the ground met, just, the minimum capacity allowed for League clubs. The only drawback was poor access. There was an unhealthy crush after the first game - a goalless friendly with Gainsborough - and a bigger one followed the first League fixture, a 1-1 draw with Arsenal.

The second League tussle at Sincil Bank was a hair-raising affair against Grimsby. The visitors won 5-2 but didn't stick around to celebrate. At the final whistle City fans, furious at Grimsby's aggressive tactics, particularly toward rookie Scottish goalkeeper John Mann, chased Town's players off the pitch. Were those two clubs never going to get on ?

City had a thin time in the League but respite came in the FA Cup with a 13-0 first qualifying round win at Peterborough and then a 3-0 victory at Worksop. Grimsby were drawn to visit Sincil Bank in the third qualifying round - good news for the treasurer but bad news for Mann. Still fragile from his earlier ordeal, he was again "sorted out" by Grimsby and dropped several rickets in a 4-2 defeat. Exit Mann from City's first team forever. Richardson Shaw took the number one jersey for the next match, a 2-1 home defeat to Burton Wanderers: his last game for Lincoln. Just what was it with goalkeepers and Lincoln in those days ?

With crowds below the break-even figure, more ground improvements needed and the team bottom of the table, pressure was mounting on several fronts. Full-back Archie MacFarlane attributed his poor form to toothache. With exhibitionist panache he had the offending molar removed in public "by electricity" in Lincoln Cattle Market. It didn't help. Defeats at Newcastle (5-0) and Liverpool (6-1) manacled Lincoln to another re-election struggle.

Supporters were grumpy again and urged the club look closer to home for talent rather than bringing in "obscure and useless castaways." Exempt from criticism was new goalkeeper Leon Boullemier. Less exotic than he sounded - born in Stoke-on-Trent, signed from Stockport County - "Bully" soon became a firm favourite with some fine displays behind a vapid defence. Only his resistance limited City to conceding 13 during a New Year double-header in the north-east, beaten 8-3 at Middlesbrough and 5-0 at Newcastle.

In January 1896, the club, bottom of Division Two and deep in debt, got radical. They advertised for their first paid manager. Of 60 applicants, sports journalist Alf Martin got the job. Martin arrived with a decent pedigree as a journalist but few football credentials. He was a qualified referee and a long-time committee member of Midland League side Grantham Rovers, his home-town club. His football credentials ended there and his appointment angered Strawson who refused to work with the hack and stepped back from the club he loved.

Martin's first act was a skilful one. City's first manager, like every one since, had to think finance first, football second, and somehow he convinced the players to accept a five shillings per week pay cut. A writer in the Lincolnshire Gazette asserted: "Football of a professional character seems to have reached the same state as the commercial world - the supremacy of the capitalist over the small man. The moneybags are too powerful with the result that the number of points in the league table are in direct ratio to the average gate." And this was 1896 !

Martin managed to lift City off the bottom. Scottish brothers William and Matthew Gillespie began to locate the net regularly and for the second successive season victories from their last two games lifted City to 13th. This time they were spared a re-election ordeal - only the bottom three had to apply. But the manager had neither cash - the Gillespie brothers were sold to Newton Heath and Manchester City to discharge debts - nor contacts to recruit quality players. Also, he did not have a free hand, with his every move debated by the executive.

The new stadium at least opened up some money-spinning avenues. A cycle-meeting at Sincil Bank attracted 250 of the country's top cyclists and a crowd of 4,000. As well as serious racing there was a novelty event in which the last three competitors across the line took prizes: a system from which City would have profited in the Second Division.

Had that system been adopted for the 1896/7 season, Lincoln would have taken the title. It was a wretched campaign. Two wins from the first three games offered an illusion quickly shattered by 12 successive defeats, then after a 1-0 win over Darwen, six more defeats. Numerous panic signings came and went, making scarcely a ripple on the first team. Wiped out 8-0 at Notts County and 7-0 at Gainsborough, City were shapeless and demoralised.

Not just on the pitch. Off it, with the brown stuff entering the fan, several directors suddenly distanced themselves from club affairs. This heaped pressure on the hapless Martin and it told in his book-keeping. An audit in March revealed a deficit of £400 when Martin's accounts suggested the club was in profit. He was promptly dispatched back to journalism.

City's gamble had failed spectacularly. Martin had steered the football club to the brink of extinction. The supporters labelled their side "Martin's Comedians" but placed most blame on those who hired Martin. "It was a long time before the Lincoln public forgave the management for the fiasco of a team in the season 1896/7," recalled season-ticket holder Ernest Pullein in 1915.

After Martin's hurried departure, Lincoln returned to one of their own. James West had been a founder member of the football club but never held office, preferring instead to work closely alongside the officers. A qualified referee, he had officiated in Second Division matches and had many contacts in football particularly in the north-west. He was the nearest to a 'football man' City could get if they appointed from within. Importantly, he took the job in an honorary capacity, saving a wage.

The season was beyond redemption. City won only five of 30 games to finish with 12 points, eight adrift at the bottom. Again, they survived the re-election vote but this time by a narrower margin from an ever larger, more ambitious pack wanting in.

Martin had left one off-field legacy at Sincil Bank which was to prove of immeasurable value for many years. He identified the goodwill and energy among the workers of Lincoln: poorer supporters who could not afford the higher ticket prices needed to buy eligibility for the board. Martin convinced the directorate that these men could contribute in practical terms to the club and a working men's committee was established.

Under West, the summer months brought plenty of player traffic. Boullemier joined Reading but the Scotland link remained active. On the opening day of the 1897/98 campaign City fielded five debutants in a 5-0 defeat at Newton Heath. For two of them, Scottish imports Burns and Dailly, the match represented the beginning and end of their Lincoln careers.

It was another desperate season. The team was disjointed and resources slender. City faced a difficult start of three away games on FA orders after crowd trouble at the previous season's visit of Newton Heath to Sincil Bank. The referee, that day, had fled from the field in a hail of stones and bricks after two dodgy penalty decisions.

A League victory didn't arrive until November when West fielded three debutants - goalkeeper William Wilkinson and wingers Fred Howard and Williams Ross - at home to Newton Heath and they helped Lincoln to a shock 1-0 win. Barnsley-born Howard then joined the catalogue of one-show-only City careers. A thousand loyal Lincoln fans travelled to the Northolme only to see their side's FA Cup hopes emphatically squashed 5-0 by Gainsborough. City visited Luton Town for the first time and Wilkinson was busier than he liked. Luton won 9-3.

Form was particularly dire away from Sincil Bank, with no victories from 15 games. In four seasons, City had registered only five Second Division away wins in 60 attempts. This time round there was not even a late-season rally with only one win from the last nine games. The 1897/98 season closed with a feeling among supporters of "It can't get any worse." Strawson, who had returned as soon as Martin left, again pleaded for City's re-election at the annual meeting. This time, with four successive bottom-four finishes behind them, it was no foregone conclusion but he was successful. Had he not been, many felt the club would have been dissolved.

Could it get worse ? Well, it got quite a lot better. West again shuffled his pack during the summer and this time made some shrewd signings. He persuaded players of experience and proven quality to join Lincoln. In came former Nottingham Forest wing-half Tich Smith and William McMillan, from Lanark. Right-winger David Pugh arrived from Wrexham. The biggest coup was the signature of mountainous left-back Will Gibson who had played at the highest level in two countries with Sunderland and Glasgow Rangers. In the unflappable Gibson, a member of Sunderland's "Team of all Talents" earlier in the decade, and the wiry McMillan, City enlisted two wise rocks of full-backs.

Now, for the first time, they fielded a settled side with seven men playing at least 30 of the 34 League games. City harvested 31 points. Not great but relatively successful, lifting them to 12th out of 18. There was a curious occurrence when Long Eaton visited Sincil Bank in April. The 3,000 crowd saw the match stopped while Professor Williams, from Cincinnati, parachuted onto the pitch from a hot-air balloon. He "rather spoilt the dignity of his descent, however, by taking the opportunity to scatter from the balloon pamphlets advertising Newark beer."

This time City could sit back in May, nice and relaxed, hitch up their trousers, and do some vote-casting as Loughborough and Blackpool (Darwen dissolved) begged for another year in the League. Blackpool, seeking re-election for the first time, were voted out. Harsh that, considering a certain other club had survived four applications in six years.

A new century approacheth. During the summer of 1899, the zeal of the working men's committee bore fruit with improvements to Sincil Bank. A covered stand, seating 400, was built on its western side and wooden railings were erected round the dressing rooms to increase players' privacy.

West was also busy - and persuasive. In came two experienced strikers. From Tottenham Hotspur came Dumbarton-born Jimmy Hartley, a small, rugged livewire with First Division experience at Burnley. Tommy McCairns, all pace and dribbling ability, previously with Grimsby for five years, joined from Notts County.

From Mansfield came goalkeeper Alf Webb. Two wing-halves were recruited: John Cowley, from Hinckley and former Celtic star Peter O'Rourke, a tough tackler who, said West, was also "likely to raise the social standard of the team." Left-winger Robert Ritchie arrived from Aberdeen and right-winger Archie Mowatt from Newcastle United. West signed the first black player to play for Lincoln, John Walker, a left-winger from Heart of Midlothian. Walker was unable to settle though and soon returned to Scotland where, sadly, he died less than a year later.

West was ambitious. He, more than anyone, wanted First Division football and persuaded the board to field a reserve team in the Midland League to help bring on younger players. Extra costs incurred by this could be met because West's first full season had ended with the club making a profit. They banked £100 after all wages and expenses had been paid.

Word spread about the interesting signings and 3,000 people turned up to watch the first practice match in mid-August. Something else new was City's kit. Green shirts and black shorts, donated by Bainbridge, replaced the traditional red and white stripes.

It seemed a case of green for stop when City won only two of the first 10 games. But they rallied and, for only the second time, finished in the top half of Division Two, ninth out of 18. Their home form was excellent with only Sheffield Wednesday, on their way to the title, winning out of 17 visitors to the Bank.

West, having weeded out Martin's errors, had built a promising side. McMillan, Gibson and O'Rourke missed only eight games between them. Hartley and McCairns contributed 25 goals. Pugh's pace and crossing from the right made him a feared opponent. John Cowley, spotted by chance by a City director, formed a muscular central defensive partnership with Derbyshire-born Charles Bannister. A true stopper, aware of his limitations, Bannister admitted: "I may not be able to play football myself but I can stop those who can."

In two-and-a-half years in charge, West had transformed Lincoln from a re-elected rabble on the brink of closure to a well-knit team expecting to finish in the top half of Division Two. This achievement had been noted around the country not least by Newton Heath, over whom City completed a double. Right at the start of the 1900/01 season the Manchester club came in for West. An ambitious man, with many friends in the north-west, the offer - a well-paid position at a club of much larger potential - was irresistible to him.

City were desperately sorry to see him go. For the first time since joining the League, they had achieved forward momentum. West had set them galloping in the right direction but switched horses at the most awkward time - the very start of a season. At short notice, a ticklish decision landed in the directorate's lap. Who now ?

3.
New heights, a canny Scotsman and an ill-treated bullock

THROUGHOUT the 1890s, as Lincoln City wrestled with early traumas, close by at Notts County, quietly, effectively plying his trade at centre-half was a taciturn but highly-respected Scot called David Calderhead.

A formidable defender, Calderhead was a much-revered captain of County. He was strong and decisive, read the game astutely and distributed the ball well. He was always calm. "If an earthquake split the ground between his legs," County fans used to set down their glasses of mild and say, "he wouldn't panic. Oh no. He'd jump, but only after sizing up the best way to jump."

Calderhead was inspiring in a solid, Uncle David, sort of way. Not for him, extravagance. No way, grand gestures. Why use two words when one would do ? But his integrity and reliability made him a County hero.

Ayrshire-born, the young Calderhead had played three seasons for Queen of the South before moving south. He was soon appointed County skipper and became their defensive heart. He played in the 1894 FA Cup winning side against Bolton Wanderers and would have collected many more than one full international cap had Scotland's selectors not leaned against men who worked outside their native borders.

By the end of the 1899/1900 season Calderhead had played more than 300 senior games for County but was unlikely to add more. After a 4-3 defeat at Preston in early November 1899 he was dropped by the selection committee. Many supporters felt this was premature but Calderhead was confined to the sidelines for the rest of the season with no hint of a recall.

During the summer months, the 35-year-old pondered his future. Lincoln Council debated whether to invest in a set of trams. Martin Keyworth, a butcher's assistant, from Grantham Street, was fined 16 shillings for ill-treating a bullock, dock-workers in Grimsby rioted and still Calderhead pondered. Summer began to turn, in traditional style, into autumn, when James West resigned from Lincoln City. This opened an unexpected door for Calderhead. Come and manage us, said the City board. So he did.

As, for the first time, Calderhead parked his cheeks on the manager's chair at Sincil Bank, he could reflect on one advantage denied to his predecessors. He inherited a team with confidence and cohesion. West had, in Webb,

McMillan, Gibson, Bannister, Cowley, Smith, McCairns and Hartley, assembled good Second Division players. Calderhead saw no reason to tinker too much. During his first season he brought in only three men. All were Scots. Centre-half John Crawford was recruited from Renton, Dumbartonshire. Maverick striker Peter Proudfoot, skilful if fragile, joined from Lanarkshire club Wishaw Athletic. Most exciting to City fans was the arrival of vastly experienced winger Tom McInnes from Nottingham Forest. Given a full Scottish cap as a teenager, McInnes had failed to add to it but played more than 100 games for Forest and, like Calderhead, possessed an FA Cup winner's medal.

Despite losing nine of his first 15 matches, Calderhead did not panic. There were no changes. One defeat in 13 games between January and April vindicated the manager's confidence in his squad. They were a streetwise and robust bunch as illustrated by a visit to Stockport in March which brought a 1-0 defeat then post-match hostilities.

Right-back McMillan recalled: "Bill Gibson, Tom McInnes, Jack Cowley and myself were coming off the field, the dressing rooms then being in a hotel adjoining the ground, when a spectator threw some mud at Gibson and Gibson hit him. Gibson slipped and fell as he struck the blow and when I stood over him a man in the crowd kicked me. We got into the hotel and one of the players who was annoyed over our treatment turned round and threw a chair at spectators. They retaliated by smashing the windows. The rest of the team left the hotel by the usual way but we went out by a back way and were two fields away before the crowd saw us. We were chased for four miles over the fields before we finally got away."

If some away territories were hostile, City offered little on-field hospitality to most visitors to Sincil Bank. They were mean and efficient at home, conceding 11 goals in 17 games. It was the defence, with the trustworthy Webb behind, on which consolidation was built, particularly in the second half of the season with nine clean sheets out of 15. That ensured another top-half final position - eighth out of 18. Suddenly, City weren't having to justify themselves to the League's annual meeting every May. Their credentials were further enhanced when Pugh, selected for Wales, became the first City player to gain full international honours. At last, Lincoln felt they truly deserved senior status and it propelled them excitedly toward their tenth season in the Football League. The 1901/2 season was to prove the best yet. Almost a century later, it remains by far the best yet.

Supporters, now back in red-and-white - the green experiment had been brief and unpopular - arrived at Sincil Bank in force for City's opener against Burnley. They were comforted to see plenty of names they knew and liked on the teamsheet but there were three new men. George Fraser - yes, a Scot - had joined from Sunderland and lined up at right-half. Calderhead gave chances to two local youngsters, striker John Dixon and left-half Percy Blow. Having played the last game of the previous season Blow had done enough during the summer to relegate the ageing Bannister to the reserves.

Burnley, burning to reclaim their place in the First Division, was a tough opener but City ground out a 1-0 win. Smith scored early on and the defence, superbly marshalled by Webb, absorbed heavy pressure to keep the sheet clean. Another debutant, the newly-installed scoreboard, had good news to impart on its first outing.

After victories at Port Vale (2-1) and at home to Chesterfield (4-0), with Dixon on target in each, City had, for the first time since joining the League, won their first three games. A 2-2 draw at Gainsborough saw the first point dropped but significant things happened elsewhere that afternoon. City reserves' 3-1 Midland League win over Walsall featured an exceptional performance from 21-year-old striker Denis O'Donnell.

O'Donnell had been discovered scoring goals for fun in the north-east for his home-town club Willington Athletic. Calderhead had felt he was one for the future but now heard that O'Donnell had hit the bar, had a goal disallowed and generally waltzed round the Walsall defenders like they were wardrobes. The manager ruminated. He looked at the fixture list. Next up at Sincil Bank were Middlesbrough, one of only two sides - West Brom were the other - above Lincoln after four games. What a deep-end debut it would be. Could the youngster cope ? Calderhead hitched up his trousers and decided: "There's only one way to find out!"

It was a big game with a big atmosphere. Middlesbrough arrived with 600 travelling fans. Sincil Bank was full of noise. Out trotted O'Donnell, plucked from a suburb of Newcastle, for his debut against Newcastle's bitter rivals. Would he be fazed ? Hey, he looked the calmest man in the ground. After 20 minutes, McInnes delivered a cross from the left and O'Donnell reacted quicker than the defence. 1-0. Middlesbrough equalised after a rare lapse from Webb but 10 minutes after half-time the fairy-tale was completed. McInnes' corner bobbled free from a melee and O'Donnell lashed it instinctively into the net. The nerveless O'Donnell made James Bond look like Worzel Gummidge.

Another difficult match followed - Lincoln's first ever visit to Bristol City. Another highly creditable result - a 1-1 draw. The city was agog. Much more of this and Lincoln City would spot the glorious silhouette of Division One shimmering on the horizon. A dose of reality followed with another two draws and the first defeat. The defeat arrived, disappointingly, 2-1 to Stockport. The lowly Lancashire club was still struggling to replace manager MJ Earp who had quit to go and fight the Boers in South Africa (ex-City right-back Quentin Neill was in the conflict too). Still, City had stayed unbeaten longer than anyone else in the League.

O'Donnell supplied Lincoln with a spark of individual brilliance among the team nous. He scored at Stockport, in City's 4-0 FA Cup victory at Worksop Town's New Cricket Ground and again in the next round, in a 1-0 home win over Doncaster Rovers.

The season was ticking over nicely, though Calderhead was too experienced to take anything for granted. He saw every match as a potential banana skin. If it wasn't a potential banana skin it was a stumbling block-in-waiting and if it was neither of those it was most certainly a possible hiccup. He was a great believer in taking each game as it came, even then a tired old cliche, but it meant his players were always motivated. They next accounted for Barnsley, after a replay, in the cup. Back in the League, Burton United were thrashed 6-0 in Derbyshire. Nine of City's 11 in that game - on November 23 - had started every game so far that season. To complete a decent day's work, City reserves overwhelmed their Burton counterparts 14-2. In early December, Neill was killed as a result of an "accidental explosion" in South Africa and City sat fifth in Division Two with games in hand of the quartet - Middlesbrough, West Brom, Arsenal and Preston - above them.

A 4-1 defeat at West Brom dented the promotion momentum but maybe minds were on the match five days ahead: an FA Cup visit to James West's Newton Heath. At stake, a place in the lucrative first round proper. City, furnished with revenue from big crowds at Sincil Bank, spared no expense. The team travelled to Manchester on Friday, arriving at the Boar's Head in time for tea. Then, off to the Palace Theatre. A tour of the city followed on Saturday morning before the players arrived at the ground at lunchtime to find the pitch in superb condition for the middle of December.

Plenty of City fans had travelled and were in good voice. Loudly did they howl when, in the fifth minute, O'Donnell was felled by an appalling lunge from home right-back Harry Stafford. O'Donnell was left in a heap and had to be carried off. Until half-time - no substitutes then of course - City soldiered on with 10 men. Yet by the interval, galvanised by a sense of injustice, Lincoln had dug deep and led 2-0, Hartley twice converting crosses by Smith. The home side rallied after half-time and pulled a goal back but Gibson, McMillan, Crawford and Blow were magnificent. Lincoln went through 2-1.

After the match, Calderhead, who normally avoided journalists, could not contain his anger at the challenge on O'Donnell. "Our ambition is to have a team who play football," he said. "But we also want that team protecting from men like Stafford. I know a few on the ground who would have been prepared to swear it was manslaughter if anything had happened to O'Donnell - and two inches would have done it." When, 12 days later, Newton Heath visited Lincoln for a Boxing Day League game, Stafford was not present. Neither was West as his team went down 2-0.

City's reward in the FA Cup was a thin one. They were drawn to visit Oxford City, a Southern League side which had existed for only eight years. Before the cup tie Lincoln had four league games from which points had to be plucked if that dream of promotion to Division One was to remain.

First up was a visit to Preston North End, no longer labelled "the best team in the world" but, stung by relegation from the top flight, still a daunting outfit at Deepdale. City's only previous competitive visit to Deepdale had brought a 4-0 defeat in a quagmire on a foul, god-forsaken day of howling gale, ice and rain. This time there was no 4-0 defeat. It was 8-0. And the weather was worse.

It was truly a drubbing out of nowhere - City had lost only two of 19 league and cup games. As the goals flew in and the storm deepened, there were remarkable scenes of capitulation from Lincoln. After the seventh goal, Hartley "gave in and left the field, completely done up." After the eighth, Smith and Gibson "came off in a collapsed condition."

When City's players reached their dressing room, according to the Lincolnshire Echo, "it was impossible to get their boots off in the ordinary way. They had to be cut off the feet of all 11 players and when their stockings had been pulled off, they [author's note: the players, not the stockings] had to be led to the bath where some of them sat for five or 10 minutes before they could feel their arms at all." A bit parky, then.

City took time to get that debacle out of the system. They collected just one point from the next two games to slip to fifth, still in the promotion race but without games in hand. They returned to winning ways at Chesterfield where Smith scored the only goal and O'Donnell, now almost fully fit again after the Newton Heath mugging was the star.

So, on to Oxford City, a true minnow and unknown quantity which blocked City's path to the last 16 of the cup. Still in its infancy as a club, Oxford had far exceeded expectations by battling through this far. To be drawn at home to a League club had really got the City of Dreaming Spires dreaming.

The White House Ground, and every vantage point surrounding it, was packed. The crowd of 5,463 was easily a club record while every overlooking tree and building contained people craning for a view. The Mayor of Oxford, no less, was present to see if the part-time team, including two school-teachers, a blanket-maker and a bookbinder, could turn over "mighty" Lincoln.

Oxford fought hard and, though Lincoln were clearly the better side, the match entered its last 15 minutes still goalless. Then Smith's cross was flapped at by home goalkeeper Benson and Hartley headed home from two yards. The home fans were silenced, then roared with relief as Hartley was signalled offside. It finished 0-0. Back to Lincoln on Wednesday.

City had the job three-quarters done. By the Wednesday replay they knew if they could complete it, they would be at home to a First Division giant – Blackburn Rovers or Derby County - in the last 16. Lincoln duly won the replay with comfort. McInnes and O'Donnell lifted them to an early 2-0 lead and McInnes added a killer third goal seconds after half-time on the way to a 4-0 victory. Gate receipts of £65 left the club happy enough that Hartley had been flagged offside four days earlier.

When, three days later Derby beat Blackburn 2-0, anticipation in Lincoln went into overdrive. Derby had been tipped for the cup this year by no less an authority than CB Fry who had played against them for Corinthians in an early round. Now these top men were coming to Sincil Bank.

Derby offered £450 to switch the tie to the Baseball Ground but were swiftly rebuffed. Ticket demand far outstripped supply. Specifically for this game, a new 1,050 capacity stand was built on Sincil Bank's northern side. The bridge over Sincil Drain was doubled in width to accommodate the crowd. The cup-tie captivated the county and beyond with special rail excursions laid on from Grimsby, Louth, Grantham, Spalding, Boston, Peterborough, Horncastle, Doncaster, Chesterfield and Derby. Sincil Bank could have been filled twice over. It was for this was the sort of occasion that Mortimer, Bainbridge and Strawson had addressed the throng in the Monson Arms years earlier.

As the pre-match hubbub intensified, Calderhead decided his players should lie low. Five days before the match, to Sutton-on-Sea they headed and booked into the Bacchus Hotel. Remote from the excitement and attention of Lincoln they walked along near-deserted beaches for 10 miles each morning. Ball work followed between 2.30pm and 5pm, then back to the hotel for table-tennis, cards or billiards. Supper at 8pm, bed at 11pm. It was a taste of luxury for City's best squad yet. The players were used to each other, liked each other and spirits were high. Could this happy bunch, orchestrated by the stern-faced Scotsman, fleece the Rams ?

City returned to Lincoln, through light snow, on Saturday morning. They lunched at Strawson's restaurant, where young Jack had served as a boy even before the FA Cup existed. When they reached the ground, packed with people long before kick-off, they learned that Derby were at full-strength. So were Lincoln.

Snow started to fall heavily as the match kicked off. Lincoln were inches from a perfect start. In the second minute, Gibson drifted in a free-kick and Hartley's header brushed the foot of a post. Four minutes later, that new stand was almost lifted off its stanchions as Derby's defence got in a tangle and McInnes stole possession close to goal and lashed home.

The Rams regrouped and soon began to dominate. City suffered a heavy blow when Crawford was carried off injured after 25 minutes. Even without the influential centre-half, they stayed firm and protected their lead until half-time. Little old Lincoln were 45 minutes from a place in the FA Cup quarter-final. Derby attacked furiously straight from the restart. They switched to six forwards to stretch City's weakened defence and three minutes into the second half Warren pounced for the equaliser. Immediately, Crawford hobbled back on to the pitch but was clearly unable to contribute. Suddenly, Warren burst through again and his shot wriggled beneath the flailing Webb. When, 15 minutes from time, the Rams striker completed his hat-trick, City's great cup run was over. But Lincoln, even reduced to 10 men, had severely tested a top-flight side. Out of the FA Cup they went with the warmest ovations at the final whistle from a record crowd of 16,435 which had paid record receipts of £428 10s 7d.

A hangover followed. A week later City, deprived by injury and illness of Crawford, O'Donnell and Hartley, lost 3-0 at Blackpool. Local boy John Asnip made his debut in Hartley's place at Bloomfield Road but never played again, another tiny, evanescent twinkle in the cosmos of City's history.

If the promotion dream was to survive, Lincoln had to shrug off the cup defeat quickly. A 5-0 win over Stockport augured well but then goals started to dry up. O'Donnell, invariably singled out for rough treatment, was hospitalised with a leg injury and six matches in March brought City only four goals. Only two conceded meant none of those games were lost but a spate of draws sent City slipping out of the promotion race.

March ended with the visit to Sincil Bank of runaway leaders West Brom. Another big match at the Bank - and a big performance by Calderhead's team. Watched by a near full-house, Hartley's 52nd minute goal sentenced the Throstles to only their third defeat of the season. But City were still 16 points behind West Brom and nine behind Middlesbrough. There was no time to make up that sort of ground.

The season ended brightly with three wins - including a 3-0 triumph that doomed neighbours Gainsborough to finish bottom - from the last four games. A tremendous season ended with one more high - revenge for that Preston humiliation. Resigned to finishing third, well behind the promoted pair, Preston arrived at the Bank on the last day of the season. They took the lead just after half-time but Proudfoot equalised and, five minutes from time, from a goalmouth melee, the ball fell to Hartley who hooked in the winner.

City finished fifth. One more point would have lifted them above Preston and Arsenal into third. All season, only Derby, in that titanic cup tie, had beaten

Lincoln at Sincil Bank. In 17 home league games, they conceded four goals. Three players - Webb, McMillan and Proudfoot - were ever present while another four - Crawford, Blow, Smith and McInnes - missed three games or less. It was a happy team supervised by a calm, intelligent manager. There had been times during this super season when even the stony-faced Calderhead, whose bowler hat rarely strayed from his immaculately groomed hair - even in the bath - must have felt like hurling said hat skyward and whooping maniacally.

Attendances had been high. There was money in the club. The city was proud. Time now, surely, for the big push for that promised land of Division One.

4.
High hopes, loose screws

FOR ANYONE connected with Lincoln City, the summer of 1902 was a groovy time. Salad days. The paint was hardly dry on a fresh, brand new century, full of hope, confidence and joy and the 20th century, no doubt about it, was going to be Lincoln City's.

The club was at its highest ever point in the League with its strongest squad and its soundest financial base. A solid foundation was in place and Calderhead and Co had already started to build. Now it was a question of stacking up the storeys. Division One. The FA Cup. A long-term niche among the elite. Glory and wealth. Respect. 'Ere we go.

It didn't quite work out that way. On a graph of Lincoln City's League placings, 1892 to 2000, the highest point remains, to this day, 1902. The wheels did not fall off immediately but there was a steady and then steep decline which saw Lincoln twice dip out of the League before all was swallowed by the maelstrom of the First World War.

Expectations for the 1902/3 season were higher than you could shake a stick at and City started well. Four wins from the first five games included a satisfying 1-0 triumph, secured by O'Donnell's goal, at Preston. In October, after a 1-0 win over Gainsborough, City topped Division Two for the first time. Now this really did look like it. The business.

Euphoria was quickly punctured. Overwhelmed by their glimpse of the peak, City failed to win any of their next five games. Manchester United (formerly Newton Heath) became the first away side in two years to win a League match at Sincil Bank. West Ham, from the Southern League, visited for the first time and were beaten 2-0 in the FA Cup but the cup trail ended in the next round at Barnsley. After four successive defeats in January, Lincoln were in mid-table, all thoughts of promotion abandoned for this season.

They were forced to look to the County Cup for any glint of silverware. Grimsby, as usual, were in the final and won it 3-2 after a replay. Lincoln's players fuelled old grudges with a hasty post-match exit. They lingered briefly while Grimsby skipper Dave Gardner collected the cup but had left to catch a train by the time Gardner asked the small crowd to give the beaten finalists three cheers.

City finished 10th in Division Two. Respectable, but a step sideways. Calderhead's decision to switch O'Donnell to the right-wing had misfired with the youngster scoring only once in 24 games after October. Cracks appeared in the compact team of the previous year. Crawford was sold to Nottingham Forest while the ageing McMillan, Gibson and McInnes lost their places after Christmas.

In the summer, Hartley and Proudfoot returned to Scotland. The departure of Hartley, the first Lincoln player to score 50 League goals, was much regretted but feelings were mixed about the mercurial Proudfoot. Undoubtedly highly-skilled, he was hard to spot in more physical contests and became the butt of some Sincil Bank fans who taunted him as "Old Mother Proudfoot." When the barracking started, his inclination to get involved shrivelled further and he became the first, but certainly not the last, player to leave Lincoln feeling 'got at' by supporters.

Calderhead had some head-scratching to do. Off came the bowler hat, though, of course, only in the privacy of his office. After two seasons of serene upward mobility, this was his first taste of adversity. A five-match unbeaten start to the 1903/4 programme was promising enough but a fade followed. When City visited Glossop, who had gathered a single point from their first six games, and were thrashed 5-0, there were whispers in the works and the pubs.

City were beaten 4-0 at both Arsenal and Stockport and Webb carried the can. Almost ever-present for the last four seasons, he was dropped in favour of young Yorkshireman Ernest Boast. With the defence suffering, McMillan, discarded the previous summer, was hastily re-signed, slotted straight back in at centre-half and rewarded for his shoddy treatment with a well-attended benefit match against Grimsby.

Calderhead failed to halt the downward curve. A 2-1 defeat at bottom-placed Blackpool in mid-January triggered a sequence of eight defeats in nine games which exhumed the almost-forgotten spectre of a re-election struggle. That spectre was banished by successive single-goal victories over Port Vale, Bradford City, Chesterfield and Bolton, with three of the winning goals coming from O'Donnell. But if the previous season brought little movement forward, this saw a step back. City finished 12th, three points above the re-election line.

Hard though he tried, diligently though he scouted, doggedly though he wore his bowler hat, Calderhead never took Lincoln forward again. The next two seasons saw the complete break-up of the famous 1901/2 side. City finished ninth out of 18 then 13th out of 20. Budget-juggling was the constant priority and though players were bought, better ones were sold. The supporters were saddened when Crawford, a quality defender and firm favourite, was cashed-in. Now highly-promising right-back Albert Groves, picked up for next to nothing from Middlesbrough junior football, was sold on to Sheffield United after just 27 games for Lincoln. It was a transfer policy rooted in necessity. The club was under financial pressure with attendances hit, not just by poor results, but - something few managers consider in their summer planning - a typhoid epidemic.

As typhoid swept through Lincoln in the mid-winter of 1904/5, claiming more than 1,000 lives, Sincil Bank offered little to cheer the stricken. Only an FA Cup run lifted the gloom. Lincoln overcame Watford and Burnley to earn a visit from First Division title-chasers Manchester City. The epidemic kept the crowd down to 8,000 but on a memorable afternoon at Sincil Bank the stars in light blue were pushed to the limit before winning 2-1. Lincoln's supporters went home with a moment of genius from Manchester City's Welsh international striker Billy Meredith to cherish. With his side leading 1-0, Meredith stepped up to take a penalty. Goalkeepers, then, were allowed to move six yards off the goalline and that's what Lincoln 'keeper George Buist did to make Meredith's target smaller. The Welshman ran up several paces, shaped to shoot hard but then lifted the ball gently and precisely over Buist into the top of the net.

The cup run contrasted with a low-key, sparsely-attended league programme and again the financial lobsters began to nip. At City's 1905 annual meeting in the Blue Anchor, Strawson reported that the financial year had been "one of the most trying and distressing."

Only transfer fees, he said, were keeping the club going. Gate receipts, £2,222 in 1904/5, nowhere near met the expenses of running a football club. The board hit the players with a demotivating wage-cut while the reserve team's Midland League expenses were slashed. For Calderhead, however, there was only thanks and praise. The Scot's "economical methods" and "judgment of football" were lauded by Strawson. So was his loyalty. Calderhead had consistently "refused the blandishments of other clubs."

Now came the news that City fans had feared most. Denis O'Donnell was sold. With 31 goals in 118 games behind him, the 25-year-old joined First Division side Sunderland for a then record fee of £370. Lincoln had truly reverted to the unhappy cycle of the previous decade. Sell to survive. Aim to stay up.

Calderhead's sixth season in charge brought a further acceleration to the club's decline. Five points from the first three games proved illusory. City's attack was punchless and a 4-0 home defeat by Wolves in October drew a succinct verdict from the Lincolnshire Echo: "The front line that appeared against Wolverhampton ought never to appear again." The only striker to net with any frequency was William McLeod, a summer signing from Tyneside club Hebburn Argyle. He scored eight goals in 13 matches and then, to the fans' dismay, was sold to Leeds City in November for £350 plus proceeds from a friendly. Crowds dwindled further.

In January came an FA Cup tie which was to alter the shape of Lincoln City's history. Chelsea, just relegated from Division One and hot favourites to go straight back up, were drawn to visit Sincil Bank. Lincoln fought back valiantly from 2-0 down late on to earn a 2-2 draw. They travelled to London for the replay as rank outsiders and were reduced to 10 men by an injury to right-back Ted Dixon in the opening minutes. But the ten men agitated the huge Stamford Bridge crowd by taking the match, at 0-0, into extra time. At the 90 minute-point came a bitter fruit controversy. Delicious, refreshing lemons were handed out to Chelsea's players but none to Lincoln's. Only Chelsea goalkeeper Jack Whiting attempted to right the injustice when he gave City left-back Walter Simpson half his lemon and said: "You've deserved that." The exhausted half-a-lemon was passed round City's team and heroically galvanised them. Lincoln held firm and grabbed a spectacular winning goal, a scissor-kick by ex-Kilmarnock left-winger Norrie Fairgray.

It was a memorable but isolated triumph. Derby County terminated the cup run and Lincoln struggled on in the League. Failure to win any of their last six matches left only Burton United below them in the final reckoning. For the first time in nine seasons, it was re-election time again. Burton went for a Burton, polling 23 votes, five behind both Lincoln, who survived and Fulham who joined the League.

Whispers in the works and pubs grew louder. "Should Calderhead go ?" they asked in the Blue Anchor and the Reindeer. "Has he achieved all he can at Lincoln ?" they debated in the Golden Cross and the Manvers Arms. The City directorate appeared perfectly satisfied with their man but a decision was made for them. Lincoln's shock FA Cup win at Chelsea had impressed the west London club's board. They noted Calderhead's achievements on a shoestring at Sincil Bank and said: "Yo, Caldy, come to Chelsea !" That was one blandishment too many. He went.

His reign had run out of steam before its conclusion but Calderhead had proved the value of a manager with experience within the game. So what next for City ? Another shrewd, streetwise operator ? Another football man who had "been there and done it ?" No. With a close eye on mounting debts, City chose to save a salary. Team matters passed to Jack Strawson.

The 49-year-old took over a poor squad containing one star, the speedy Fairgray. He played in the opening match of the 1907/08 season then followed Calderhead to Chelsea. By Christmas, City were in the bottom three and on the crest of a slump: seven successive defeats. Strawson reacted, as in the bad old days, by wholesale shuffling of the team. FA Cup humiliation followed, a 5-0 defeat at Stoke City. To rub salt in the wounds Stoke met Gainsborough at home in the next round, a draw which would have brought City a desperately needed payday.

When Oldham visited Sincil Bank for the first time, they were quickly reduced to nine men by injury but still eased to a 2-0 win. Lincoln, accused the Echo, were "feeble." Several City directors responded to the crisis with brio, confidently predicting that Lincoln would escape the three re-election slots. The corpse twitched vigorously with home wins over Chesterfield (4-0) and Leeds City (5-0) but even the morale-boosting victory over Leeds had an unwelcome twist. The match was interrupted when a 30-yard section of grandstand buckled in a gale. No-one was hurt but it caused repair-bills the club could ill-afford.

As February turned, as age-old tradition demands, into March, the board called a crisis meeting. The club's position was "desperate" in playing and business terms. Strawson, fearing the worst, wrote to all other League clubs to get City's re- election plea in early. Aware that Tottenham were the most attractive of the clubs wanting in, he hung his hat on the "Keep out the southerners" peg, a calculated risk with still only four London clubs - Arsenal, Chelsea, Clapton Orient and Fulham - among the League's 40 members.

Only sensational form could save City from the bottom three. They responded with a 1-0 home defeat to everyone else's whipping-boys, Glossop. Another 1-0 defeat, at Leicester Fosse, condemned them to seek re-election with a month of the season still left. The worst was widely feared. It was the sixth time in 16 seasons that City had to go cap in hand and it had been their most insipid performance as a League side. Lincoln finished bottom, two points behind Chesterfield and nine behind Grimsby. This annual meeting would provide the most taxing test yet for Strawson's charm and eloquence.

Seeking entry to the League were Tottenham and Bradford Park Avenue while Burton sought re-entry. Spurs appeared to pose the biggest threat. In 1902 they had made history by winning the FA Cup as a Southern League club, the only side from outside the Football League ever to lift the trophy. It was a feat which still carried great glory and mystique six years later. For weeks before the annual meeting the north London club had been brashly predicting they would be voted into the League - and had even resigned from the Southern League in readiness.

Proactive and hugely ambitious, Spurs lobbied extensively, particularly the League's committee members. Strawson, rather desperately, reminded clubs of Lincoln's "convenient railway links." City hoped that Spurs' recent record – an unspectacular fifth, sixth and seventh in the Southern League - would be considered more relevant than their bravado.

On May 29, D-day brought a shock for both Lincoln and Spurs. Bradford ghosted in at the far post. Grimsby polled 32 and Chesterfield 23 to retain their status but Bradford, with 20, pipped Lincoln, 18. Spurs took 14 votes and Burton 1. So City fell out of the League. And Spurs stayed out.

Or did they ? Three weeks later, Stoke resigned from the Football League on financial grounds. A vacancy reappeared. "That'll do nicely," thought Lincoln who felt, surely, as they polled more votes than Spurs at the annual meeting, they were reprieved. Not so. A special general meeting of the League was organised at the Midland Hotel, Manchester.

Officers of each involved club addressed the meeting. With their loyal vote-base in the provinces, Lincoln polled equal with Spurs on the first vote, 17-17. Stoke, having re-applied after a boardroom U-turn, received six votes. After Stoke were struck out a second vote was taken: Lincoln 20 Spurs 20. A third poll, again 20-20. "How are we going to sort this one out ?" wondered the League's management committee. They decided that another vote would be taken, this time just by the management committee themselves. Very cosy. Spurs got the nod 5-3 and Lincoln, feeling devastated, indignant and diddled, tumbled out of the League.

No-one could dispute that Spurs were a bigger club of more economic value to the League but the manner of City's demise won considerable sympathy. Commiserations poured in, mainly from clubs in the north and Midlands. But commiserations would not settle City's large debts - debts which a drab fixture list back in the Midland League would only increase. At City's annual meeting the board, now chaired by Cornelius Taylor, took flak. Former player John Irving, who had served briefly as a director and was now a licensee in the city, led the dissent. He was cheered when he suggested: "We have men on the directorate who do not know a football from a balloon. I don't believe in putting men on the directorate who merely have money. Put on men who know football." Taylor's retort - "If we have good men who understand finance and routine, that is enough." - was hardly convincing.

Irving's point was taken, at least partially, on board. A "football man" was not employed but Strawson resigned as a director to concentrate on team affairs. A tatty season followed with City involved in two competitions, doing well in both and enjoying neither. The Midland League pitted them mainly against reserve sides and they won it by 13 points. They also joined the northern division of the United League whose fixtures were squeezed untidily between clubs' main commitments. City finished runners-up but few people watched.

Neither competition interested fans used to Football League fare and attendances plummeted. Even a reduction in ground admission, from 6d to 4d, did little to extract supporters from the Saturday afternoon pub. There was one reminder of the big time - an FA Cup first round visit to First Division side Liverpool. But this time there was no preparatory week at the seaside. It was an economy day out. Straight to Merseyside, thrashed 5-1 and back again.

All that mattered was that Lincoln got back in the League and Strawson had a cunning idea. To make the target bigger, why not form a Third Division ? He chaired a meeting of like-minded clubs and though it came to nothing, the volume of interest suggested the notion was worth pursuing. From City's perspective it could wait anyway because their emphatic Midland League triumph dispatched them to the Football League's annual meeting confident of reclaiming their place in Division Two. They duly did so, polling three votes more than Chesterfield who tasted the bitter fall from grace.

League status regained, supporters who had turned their backs returned in droves. Five thousand attended the first pre-season practice match on August 18 and, not for the first time, a new season was hailed as the start of a new era. By now, the durable George Fraser was the sole remnant of the 1901/2 glory season. City brought in James Kirk from Newark Town, Edward Scanlon from North Shields, Ronald Mackenzie from Chelsea (he never played a first-team match for the London club) and Andrew Greig from Inverness Clachnacluddin. Supporters monitored the arrivals with intrigue. Were they jewels, cleverly spotted and uncovered by the wise Strawson ? Or more of yer "obscure and useless castaways ?" Between them the quartet were destined to total just 64 games for Lincoln.

City's return to the big time sent them first to Leeds City and a chastening 5-0 defeat. By the second away game, 10 days later at Manchester City, Strawson had pressed the panic button. Five of the team that played at Leeds were dropped. Manchester City won 6-2. Greig shuffled off Maine Road and out of Lincoln's first team forever. If he had bought a return ticket from Inverness, the return half was still valid. In both matches, only excellent displays by another summer signing, 23-year-old goalkeeper Tommy Fern, from Worksop Town, kept the scores down.

A familiar pattern of struggle was set as City languished in the bottom two. Defeat to Birmingham League opposition, 2-1 at Crewe Alexandra, was a depressing way to squander FA Cup hope. The arrival of skilful left-winger Tommy Yule - yet another Lanarkshire lad - supplied a much-needed crowd favourite. His popularity soared with both goals as City won 2-1 at Grimsby to leave their rivals in a big pickle near the foot of the table. Four successive victories in March helped lift City to 15th out of 20 and spared what would have certainly been a tricky re-election ordeal. Instead, neighbours Grimsby suffered the ultimate blow, voted out of the League to be replaced by Huddersfield Town. An unfamiliar name from the north-east, Hartlepools United, applied for League status - but polled only one vote!

Next season it was Lincoln's turn to suffer again. During the 1910/11 campaign the first team were rarely out of the bottom two and, in the Midland League, the reserves rarely out of the bottom one. Despite the heroic Fern, heavy defeats stacked up: 5-0 at Derby, 5-1 at home to Wolves. At high-flying Chelsea, still managed by Calderhead, City trailed just 1-0 at the interval. The half-time score was relayed back to Sincil Bank where 2,000 people watching the reserves raised a collective eyebrow in approval. Final score: 7-0. More grief followed: 5-1 at Blackpool, 4-1 at home to Hull. 4-0 at Stoke City in the FA Cup. And that was just before Christmas! Happy New Year opened with a 6-0 defeat at Bradford Park Avenue. Strawson, so eloquent in committees and boardrooms, was finding team-talks tougher.

"Very strong things are being uttered in the works," warned the Lincolnshire Echo. "It's time the directorate woke up to the gravity of the situation." The directorate's plaintive response that there were just no better players around to be signed was received with cynicism. The Echo raged: "It is not enough to say there is a screw loose somewhere. There are several screws loose - and very loose."

The screws stayed loose. In each of their last 12 matches Lincoln scored one or nil. In 38 League games, they managed 28 goals. Scoring was the problem. And defending. Only Stockport in Division Two and Forest, bottom of Division One, conceded more goals. Supporters' anger manifested itself in ugly scenes at the last home match of the season against West Brom. Two borderline penalty decisions went against Lincoln and at the final whistle the referee bore the brunt of a season of Sincil Bank frustration. He was chased into the dressing room by angry supporters and required a police escort out of the city. Lincoln finished four points adrift of Barnsley at the bottom. Re-election time already. Now this could be tricky.

Strawson agitated on the wisest approach. He opted for humility, nay, grovelling. To every League club he wrote, nay simpered: "The railway arrangements to Lincoln are simple and convenient [author's note: those were the days!]........our ground is acknowledged to be perfect in every respect........the sole reason for our having to seek re-election is the remarkable number of players we have lost during the season to serious accidents........two lying at death's door for several weeks........we acknowledge with sincere gratitude the sympathy and practical help from several League clubs........ knowing full well your tolerance for misfortune caused solely by accidents we ask with confidence for a continuance of your kindness in reinstating us in our old position as members of the League."

Chairmen up and down the country read the unctuous missive - and quite a few kicked it into touch. City lost their senior status by the narrowest margin, 18 to 17. Agonising not just because it was by a single vote but the club that pipped them was Grimsby. The Mariners were back in at Lincoln's expense. Hartlepools tried again - and again polled just the one vote!

Ousted again, City were quick to resume pressure on the League to set up a Third Division. The League's management committee was unenthusiastic but, under duress, advertised for clubs to register as potential members of a Division Three. Lincoln, Chesterfield, Hartlepools, Darlington and Rochdale were keenest and Strawson presided over a meeting at the Kings Arms Hotel, Sheffield, to drum up further interest. There was plenty, and not just from the north. Sixteen clubs which pledged to join the new tier included Portsmouth, Cardiff and Croydon Common.

An entrance fee to Division Three was set at 10 guineas but the potential members were far more enthusiastic than the League they wanted to join and the plan was shelved. Instead, City joined the Central League. This was a new 17-strong structure which contained 10 reserve sides of Lancashire-based League clubs, plus the first teams of Bury, Crewe, Glossop, Port Vale, Southport, Stockport and, out on a geographical limb, Lincoln.

During the summer, one worry lifted when the club reached a new tenancy agreement for Sincil Bank with Colonel Swan. For the first 14 days of the new season however, following that crowd trouble at the West Brom match, the ground stayed shut on FA instructions. After a slow start - just one win in five, City adjusted well. They quickly grew accustomed to the level of football and the railway timetable for trains to Lancashire. Built on the goals of a Scot, a Yorkshireman and a Geordie - Sandy McCubbin, Billy Batty and Walter Miller - City took the title by six points. In 32 matches, they scored 81 goals with McCubbin, Batty and Miller contributing 53.

The Central League captured supporters' interest much more than the Midland League - even Everton and Bolton Wanderers reserves had more kudos than Newark and Denaby United - and attendances revived. When the FA Cup brought Grimsby to Sincil Bank, more than 10,000 saw City win 3-2 to exact some revenge for losing their League spot to the Mariners. The victory sparked an interesting cup run. Next, Lincoln travelled north-east to beat Crook Town, also 3-2, before Stockport were beaten 2-0 at the Bank. That earned Lincoln a visit to Wolves where they stretched the Second Division side and went down only 2-1 to a winning goal allegedly poked into the net through the side-netting.

The title won with ease, another "Can we come back in ?" letter, signed by Strawson and chairman Pearce Milner, was circulated. Author, journalist, and prospective Unionist MP John Foster-Fraser had now joined the board and also lobbied. While the US Senate reported that the Titanic had "virtually ignored ice-warnings," Lincoln City, unlike the Titanic, came back up. It was another Lincolnshire swap with City replacing Gainsborough Trinity by an emphatic 27-9 margin at London's Imperial Hotel. Gainsborough accused Foster-Fraser of "pulling levers" to get Lincoln re-elected. He admitted he was at the Imperial

Hotel, talking to delegates on the eve of the annual meeting, but claimed he was just being friendly.

A week after gaining re-election, City attended the first annual meeting of the Central League, collected the championship trophy and resigned. Not without a few regrets. The venture had proved so popular that the working men's committee even held a ballot to check that supporters wanted to go back into the Football League. A large majority did.

Season tickets sold well for yet another re-entry. Most fans were realistic enough to expect another gruelling ordeal ending with a drop into some dungeon or other. But the 1912/3 campaign proved by far the pinnacle of Strawson's hegemony. For the opening match at Wolves, the team was given a rapturous send-off by crowds at Lincoln Midland Station. Despite a fine display by the redoubtable Fern, Wolves won 2-0 but City hit straight back with a 4-2 win at Stockport. This, despite the Lincoln party having trouble with a truculent railway guard as their Lincoln to Manchester train passed through Stockport. The guard refused to stop the train and the players had to travel into Manchester and back out again.

The season rolled happily along. For only the second time, City hit the top of Division Two - and actually spent three weeks there. Fern was brilliant. He had stuck by City in some lean times and his attitude and loyalty, as well as goalkeeping skills, were hugely respected throughout English football. Clem Jackson, unearthed from Nottinghamshire football, and Wattie Wilson, were two stout full-backs. When injury forced Wilson to miss Bradford Park Avenue's visit to Sincil Bank on Christmas Day 1912 it broke a sequence of 204 consecutive games for Lincoln by the Scot.

Then there was Tosh Barrel. Lincoln-born, versatile and tough as a diamond, he was a cult-hero, even back in days when a cult was only something a Scotsman wore. Adept in almost any position, his "they-don't-like-it-up-'em" style endeared him to supporters who also appreciated his loyalty to Lincoln when First Division clubs were reportedly chasing him. Another county-born player, John "Cracker" Manning, from Boston, tormented defences from the left-wing while cult-wearer McCubbin and "Wor" Wally Miller, were still firing up front.

Goals from Manning and McCubbin earned City a memorable 2-1 win in a monsoon at Nottingham Forest. Barrell scored twice in a 3-0 home victory over Leicester Fosse and bagged another as Bristol City were beaten 2-0 in front of 11,000. The FA Cup brought a shock 1-0 defeat at North-Eastern League side South Shields but, while they were never in the hunt for promotion, City maintained a steady upper mid-table position. Increased cash flow allowed upgrading of the South Park Stand to take place although a Christmas Eve gale ripped off part of the new work and deposited it in the opposite goalmouth.

Free from anxiety over re-election, City completed a prized double over Forest, Barrell again on target in another 2-1 win. Tosh ended leading scorer with 13 goals including one in the penultimate match, a 3-1 defeat at Fulham in which John Inskip, from Ayrshire, played his only ever game for Lincoln City. McCubbin's double in a bristling 2-0 home win over fourth-placed Barnsley rounded off a buoyant season. Rustons Silver Band had played before every Sincil Bank fixture only three of which, out of 19, Lincoln lost. Attendances averaged 10,000. The sun shone, birds sang and Strawson's red and white army finished eighth out of 20.

The progress was not maintained. After seven matches of the following term Lincoln, having won just one, had only Nottingham Forest below them. In mid-season they went five weeks without scoring a league goal. McCubbin got injured and Miller, having been twice suspended for breaches of club discipline, was offloaded to Merthyr Tydfil. Those ever-present creeping debts forced the sale, in December, of Tommy Fern. Having missed only two games in four and a half seasons at Lincoln, he joined Everton for £1,500. The Merseyside club had been chasing Fern since New Year's Day the previous year when the goalkeeper saved two penalties in City reserves' 1-0 win at Goodison Park.

Strawson struggled to hold things together but it was clear by Christmas that it would be a duel between Lincoln and Forest to avoid bottom spot. In February, injuries bit deep and left-half Tom Strong was thrown in for his debut in a 2-1 home defeat to Blackpool. A tough, wiry, 23-year-old Geordie, Strong joined City on the recommendation of Denis O'Donnell who returned to his north-east roots after retiring. Tenacious and hard-tackling, Strong had shown plenty of promise for the reserves. Helped by the experienced Andrew Gardner he did well against Blackpool before making way next game for the fit-again Thomas Wield. Strong was an excellent prospect. Give him three or four years and he would be a fine player. But within that timespan, instead of enjoying a nicely-developing football career, he was dead. Killed in action.

City and Forest duly finished as the bottom two and, despite a vigorous campaign by Stoke City, were both re-elected. By the start of the following season the First World War was underway. When Lincoln travelled to Leicester for the first match, their players had to pick their way through crowds waiting to meet soldiers wounded and on leave. The League continued but football results looked foolish and irrelevant alongside growing casualty lists in newspapers. Crowds were halved as hundreds of thousands of men joined the forces. City' 3-2 home defeat to Bury on April 24, 1915, which left them 16th out of 20 in the final table, was their last Football League fixture for almost five years. City limped into limbo having lost a crippling £1,574 during the 1914/5 season.

5.
Cheated out of the League

APPALLING savagery. Murderous mayhem. Callous, futile waste. Call it what you like, the First World War certainly took a bit of shrugging off. Set alongside millions of shredded human lives, Lincoln City's problem - to get themselves a squad together for the resumption of the Football League - seemed pretty trivial.

But what Lincoln and every village, town and city in the country wanted in 1918 was to restore, as far as possible, normality after years of nightmare. To reinstate the familiar bits and pieces that composed good, old, prosaic and peaceful English everyday life. In the first decade of the century, the nation had taken football right to its heart so the resumption of the League, in August 1919, was warmly embraced. The return of a favourite pal.

During the conflict, City competed in the Midland Section of the War League. A few Lincoln players went off to fight but most went into foundries to help the war effort locally. They still played for Lincoln - for expenses only, professionalism having been suspended. The football club ticked over but matches drew small crowds. Players were committed to long factory hours so often the composition of teams was known only just before kick-off. It was ad hoc and untidy. Almost unreal, football going quietly, stubbornly through the motions while the big issue resolved itself across the Channel.

By Autumn 1918, hopes were rising that the end of the conflict was near. On September 7, City opened their War League programme with a visit to Oakwell and the following Monday's Lincolnshire Echo carried some apocalyptic headlines. "Somme Crossed In Face Of Vigorous Resistance.....Lenin Assassinated.....Lincoln City Win 6-2 At Barnsley."

When, two months later the Armistice arrived, clubs were told to see out the War League season. The remaining games were preparation for a return to the Football League nine months later.

There was plenty to do. For three years, understandably, with no end to the war in sight, not much thought had been given to life at Sincil Bank beyond the conflict. The football club, as a business, effectively hibernated. Several directors drifted away. The faithful Strawson organised the team and did what administration was necessary. In 1918 most pre-war players were still around but how many - four years on, would still be fit ?

A massive tide of post-war enthusiasm for football put City's directors under pressure to send the Imps, as they had become known, fast out of the blocks. So much to do, so little time. In May, 1919, a frantic summer of preparation ahead, Strawson, now 60, decided he didn't need the hassle any longer. He quit to go and run the Red Lion in Spalding. After 35 years, broken only by Alf Martin's brief stewardship of the team, Jack's gentle humour and tall, stooping frame no longer occupied an office at Sincil Bank. He left a void.

Cornelius Taylor and Billy Pogson, two directors whose cash had kept City afloat during the war, took charge. They could handle the paperwork but, even assisted by veteran right-back Clem Jackson, training and recruiting duties were beyond them. It was a loose, amateurish arrangement which consumed vital weeks when specific team-planning was required. Local journalist Herbert Green was offered the manager's job and when he said no, City turned to George Fraser.

A native of the Scottish Highlands, Fraser had arrived at Sincil Bank from Sunderland in 1901, one of David Calderhead's many recruits from north-east football. He grew to know every nook of Sincil Bank during 267 League games at right-half. After his playing career Fraser, a quiet and popular man, became Jack Strawson's brother-in-law and ran pubs in Lincoln. Soon after war was declared he joined the Lincolnshire Yeomanry Regiment only to be badly injured in a car crash. A long period in hospital followed but now he was recovered, resettled in Lincoln and enthusiastic for a challenge. Good job too, because awaiting him was a challenge of the tough variety. Appointed in July, his mission was to get City ready for Division Two - in August.

He soon discovered that squad-development had not advanced far. For their first Football League game after the war, the Imps sent out five players - Fred Ward, Clem Jackson, Billy Egerton, Billy Chesser and Alf Ball - who had played in their last match pre-war. They achieved a creditable 1-1 draw on the club's first visit to West Ham but ageing legs and a scrappy summer's preparation soon proved costly. The first two home matches brought defeats, 3-0 to Blackpool and 4-1 to West Ham. City were hammered 6-0 at Blackpool and Bristol City. The Imps had plenty of spare time to dwell on the drubbing at Bristol. Due to dodgy rail connections, they arrived back in Lincoln at 11.43am on Sunday - six hours later than from their visit to Ashton Gate in 1901. The railways weren't what they used to be! Next came a 6-1 thrashing at Tottenham. City lost 4-0 and 5-3 to Barnsley and 5-2 at Hull. Confronted with unprecedented interest in football, Lincoln produced the most wretched run in their history.

At the club's annual meeting in December supporters questioned the players' fitness but Pearce Milner maintained they were the best-trained men since he became chairman, in 1908. The board also came under fire for not being suf-

ficiently "interested and involved" though Milner slickly deflected flak by play-
ing a clever patriotic trump card. He asked for applause for director Samuel
Tonge who had just collected the Military Cross for his gallantry during the war.
Who could barrack a board with a war hero on it ?

Fraser badly needed some quality players. He had a nice, new telephone
in his office but couldn't use it to set up transfer deals because the club was
£1,600 overdrawn. A home draw against First Division Middlesbrough in the FA
Cup was helpful. The directors switched the tie to Ayresome Park for a guarantee
of just under £1,000. The move angered supporters, one of whom turned, anony-
mously, to verse.

"What will you do with your thousand pounds
O Lincoln City FC?
Will you try to renovate your grounds
Or spend it on the spree?
Have you decided to get new players
Your own League place to raise?
To go up football's 'golden stairs'
And win support and praise?
Or shall you just stay where you are
And leave the team depleted?
From every chance your own team bar
And by others all defeated?"

Even the Middlesbrough switch had a hitch. City travelled up to Teesside
on the Saturday only for the match to be snowed off and rearranged for
Wednesday. Instead of travelling back and then north again, Milner took the
squad to a hotel in Redcar where the bill for four days accommodation ate into
that guarantee. Finally, 'Boro won 4-1.

A grisly March brought successive defeats at Birmingham (7-0 in front of
30,000) then home and away to Leicester (3-0 and 4-0). The slump pitched City
into a re-election scramble and, said the Lincolnshire Echo "once more brought
to life the bogey of the last two in the league table - that ogre which every supporter of the club is heartily sick and tired of." Grimsby were doomed to finish
bottom. Lincoln or Coventry City would fill the other re-election slot. Lincoln
approached their last three games in dreadful form with no wins and three goals
in seven games. But two of those final three matches were against Coventry.

At times like this what a football club does not need is injustice. But that's
what torpedoed Lincoln. Injustice - as in a corruption of justice. Not a cruel
deflection or an untimely injury or a referee's decision which went the wrong

way. Those are bad luck. Here, in their time of greatest need, Lincoln City were hit by injustice.

With their pre-war record in mind the last thing the Imps wanted was an immediate re-application for re-election. Without Strawson's influence, it would be extremely difficult to survive. Equally desperate to stay above the bottom two were Coventry. This was the Sky Blues' first season in the Football League and owner David Cooke had spent heavily on players. But they hadn't made a good fist of it and, like Lincoln, knew they would struggle to be re-elected. So when the clubs met twice in a week they were huge games.

Saturday April 17: first round at Sincil Bank. In front of more than 10,000, Lincoln got lucky. Injuries deprived Coventry of their goalkeeper early on and their centre-half just after half-time. Against nine men, City eased to a 4-1 win. Now they were three points ahead of the Sky Blues, though Coventry had a game in hand. That followed three days later when they drew at Bury. So on April 24, the penultimate Saturday of the season, the Imps travelled to Coventry knowing that victory would make them safe. They lost 2-0.

All down to the last day then with Coventry and Lincoln level on points. Coventry faced the return fixture at fifth-placed Bury. Lincoln had to visit a powerful Huddersfield team, already promoted and waiting to meet Aston Villa in the FA Cup final. Fraser's men fought valiantly. They held the Terriers 0-0 at halftime and, during the interval, were buoyed by news from Gigg Lane that Coventry were 1-0 down. Huddersfield then moved into overdrive in the second half and won 4-2. Lincoln's players hurried back to the dressing room to receive the shattering news that Coventry had fought back to win 2-1. In the most heartbreaking fashion it was Lincoln sentenced to seek re-election. Predictably, three weeks later the votes went against them. They polled only seven, the lowest in 11 ballots they had faced since 1893. Out, along with Grimsby, went Lincoln, to be replaced by Leeds United and Cardiff City.

In Lincoln, head-shaking and depression. In Coventry, hand-shaking and jubilation but also, in one or two privileged quarters, another emotion. Guilt. Because certain Coventry directors and players knew, as their supporters mopped their brows and hitched up their trousers in misguided pride, that Bury had thrown that vital match at Gigg Lane. Collusion had taken place. Lincoln had been stitched up.

Rumours about Coventry's "stirring" comeback at Bury were soon circulating. The home side's performance, even for a game from which they had little to gain, had been extraordinarily lifeless. The Football Association set up a commission to investigate. Its wheels turned slowly. The commission met four times - always behind closed doors - in three years before announcing, on May 29,

1923, that they were satisfied that "an arrangement was made between Bury and Coventry City allowing the latter to win."

Eleven officials and players from Bury and Coventry were punished. Cooke, fellow Coventry director Jack Marshall and Sky Blues' skipper George Chaplin were among those who received life-bans from football. Later - some 20 years later - Chaplin lifted the lid, spilled the beans and sang like a canary.

"We decided that something must be done," he confessed. "I went to Bury with £200 in my pocket and when I left I had the feeling that City's prospects of gaining three points from the two games were not such a remote possibility. Things began to go wrong when Bury were leading 1-0 at half-time and I was in despair when one of the Bury players came into the dressing room and told me City were so poor Bury couldn't lose no matter how badly they played. But they came right in the second half with Mercer's two goals.

"While the City supporters were celebrating the club's escape that night I kept an appointment in the cloakroom of the King's Head Hotel where I handed over the final instalment of the sum without a word being spoken."

For the perpetrators, eventually, there was heavy punishment but for the victims, Lincoln City, nothing beyond hollow confirmation that they had been cheated of Football League status. By the time the facts emerged, Lincoln had suffered three seasons in which they moved closer than ever to extinction, a state to which they were almost resigned in the very week the commission delivered its verdict.

6.
"We must consider the advisability of closing the club down."

WHEN Lincoln City have a wound, someone is usually on hand with salt. As City were digesting their relegation from the Second Division in the summer of 1920, the Football League announced that a Third Division was, at last, to be formed. Grimsby were accepted into it because they had polled more re-election votes than Lincoln. The fact that City finished above their rivals in the Second Division was irrelevant. For the Imps, it was back to the Midland League.

A clearout of players followed with almost all the senior men departing. William Ashurst, Frank Chipperfield and Fred Linfoot, snapped up by Lincoln when Leeds City disbanded in 1919, were sold on to Notts County, Middlesbrough and Chelsea respectively for a combined profit of more than £1,500. Supporters were irritated to learn that, despite relegation, admission prices to Sincil Bank would remain the same but at least the Midland League supplied its customary title. City finished four points ahead of Notts County Reserves. They were also the last non-league side knocked out of the FA Cup. After beating Bromley 5-0 at home and Millwall 3-0 away, they were drawn at home to Fulham in the last 32. Prices were hiked up - the cheapest adult admission was two shillings and the most expensive seat 10s 6d - and a crowd of 12,500 paid record receipts of £1,637 to see City hold Fulham to a goalless draw before losing the replay 1-0 at Craven Cottage.

In April, with the Midland League title all but secure, Fraser moved on to Grimsby Town. Already waiting to move into the manager's office was a famous name at Sincil Bank: David Calderhead. This was the junior version (his old man was now in his 11th season in charge at Chelsea) keen for a first crack at management. Calderhead junior had played for Lincoln Boys in 1906 but failed to emulate his father as a player. Only the position - centre-half - was the same as Calderhead the Younger played for Chelsea, Motherwell and Clapton Orient without pulling up any trees. But he was warmly welcomed, his arrival stirring happy memories stored by his father's Lincoln team. No happy memories were to be added to the stockpile in the immediate future. Financial ferrets of the most aggressive, scrambling variety were about to be lowered down City's trousers.

A new manager and a new competition. The Third Division, after one season, expanded and split to form southern and northern sections. Lincoln were invited into the latter. It carried the kudos of Football League membership and brought new opposition - Wrexham, Wigan and Southport - into the fixture list. Calderhead, like his father a man of few words, pronounced himself "quietly confident" of doing well. Despite a summer drought the pitch was in excellent condition. The dressing rooms had been renovated. Tons of cinders were laid on the Sincil Drain side of the ground to make viewing more comfortable. The good ship Lincoln City was about to set sail into another new sea. Don the lifejackets. Mind the iceberg.

The Third Division North at first intrigued City supporters - 6,580, including Lord Monson, turned up for the opening home game against Walsall. But, when it soon became clear that this wasn't to be a Midland League-type charge to the title, supporters' interest waned. Times were hard and the price of admission hard to find. The euphoria of winning the war was steadily being usurped by grim hardships caused by having to pay for it. Unemployment was high. The cost of living was soaring (MPs had just voted themselves a pay-rise though) and housing conditions in Lincoln had never been worse. In some areas, squalid two-roomed tenements were shared by 16 people. There were 128 households to the acre where there should have been 16. Vagrancy was high. Whether to squander hard-earned pennies on Lincoln City v Halifax Town or Accrington Stanley was a decision to be carefully weighed, especially as Calderhead's early results were poor. City won only four league games before Christmas and were "giant-killed" at home in the FA Cup by Northampton Town who scored twice in the last five minutes to earn a 2-1 win. More than ever, City had needed a money-spinning cup run.

In December, Pearce Milner, chairman for just over 14 years, studied the books one more time. They reminded him that City's break-even figure was £350 per home game. The largest gate-revenue so far that season had been £230. "The directors have made up their minds," he announced," not to guarantee any more money. If Lincoln people want football they must help to pay." A week later Milner quit as chairman.

The venerable Cornelius Taylor took over but stressed it would be only for a year. He felt young blood was needed. Now Taylor studied the books and they made nasty reading. He decided to make the bleak details public. Only by selling players has the club survived, he reminded supporters, and unless income (crowds) improved the directors would have to "consider the advisability of closing the club down." The board had an idea. They sent a letter to 13 eminent local persons begging for financial help. A tad short on community spirit none of the 13 - including the egregious Lord Monson - bothered to reply.

Troubles crowded in. Thieves raided Sincil Bank and stole tools and playing equipment. Another fund-raising initiative - a shilling fund - flopped.

Timekeeping slackened. For the visit to Durham City on January 2, goalkeeper Robert Bainbridge arrived at Lincoln station only to see the team's train pull out. He caught a train to Retford but there was no connection to Durham so he returned to Lincoln. His plight came to the attention of newsagent George Doughty who loaded the player into his motor-cycle side-car and set off north at 11.15am. A tremendous effort but they didn't make it in time for kick-off and mid-fielder John Bryan had to go in goal. He did okay too, but City lost 2-0.

Crowds were poor, dipping to 3,107 for a visit from Accrington. Home matches were played in a desolate atmosphere and City finished 14th out of 20. Increased travelling costs contributed to a loss of almost £1,500 for the season. Almost two decades earlier, Calderhead senior had needed a season to assess his squad, then move forward. And he did it on limited budgets. But Calderhead junior was working on limited budgets with mostly poor players. In the summer, wage commitments had to be further slashed. Out went the two main men, left-half George Richardson, for £1,225, to Sheffield United and striker Robert Chambers, for £650, to League champions Burnley. As the 1922/23 season approached Lincoln City were being propped up by the savings of directors whose patience was wearing thin. Taylor again went to the people of Lincoln with a "Support us through the turnstiles" plea. "Don't you know there's a depression on?" they chorused in reply. You could see both sides.

It was a torrid introduction to management for Calderhead. He foraged for bargains. Goalkeeper Will Kendall stepped up from North Lindsey League side Broughton Rangers. Stylish Glaswegian dribbler Archie Kean moved north from Clapton Orient and forward Harry Pringle arrived from junior football in the north-east. Valuable experience was injected into the squad when former Blackburn Rovers left-half Levy Thorpe agreed to join. Thorpe had played high-level football since 1911 with Blackpool, Burnley and Blackburn and, appointed captain, had an immediate settling influence on the side.

Without threatening to finish top of the Third Division North - which was necessary to gain promotion - City's newcomers started to bed in and held a mid-table position. It was more efficient than exhilarating though, with few goals at either end, and as winter deepened, attendances slumped further.

At the club's annual meeting in October three directors, including former chairman Milner, declined to be re-elected. Those ferrets began to scramble and struggle and the players had to focus on winning matches while wondering if they would be paid. On December 30, 1922, City drew 1-1 at home to Barrow. Next came away games at Hartlepools United, Barrow and Darlington, each involving Friday night hotel stops. After a home match against Nelson, City were on their travels again to Nelson and Tranmere. The expense of five long away trips in six weeks, separated by just one poorly-attended home game, dried up

Lincoln's cash-flow. The bank overdraft stood at £1,750. The club was £3,000 in debt. On February 5 the players turned up to be paid as usual on Monday morning only to be told there was no dosh. "There's nae dosh," an exasperated Calderhead, leaning wearily against the elephant's foot hat-stand, might have told his team.

At a crisis meeting two days later, the players were asked to take a 50 per cent pay cut. Seven chose free transfers instead with £10 in lieu of two weeks money. That eased the overall burden and revised offers were made to the rest who, with admirable loyalty, stayed. The club was kept afloat until Saturday when Tranmere visited Sincil Bank for a game that had looked unlikely to take place. City were given the warmest of receptions by a 4,000 crowd and won 2-0.

Only the immediate threat had been lifted. The board laid it on the line. Taylor explained: "The directors have made so many personal sacrifices in order to keep the club going that, at long last, they have been compelled to recognise that the line of limitation, in this respect, has been reached. We do not feel that, as directors, we can be expected to carry on the club by continual remittances from our own private resources."

In the circumstances, bids would be accepted for any players and three first-team regulars were sold. Veteran left-back Fred Ward and promising right-half James McGrahan went to Wigan Borough and centre-half Bob Fenwick to Notts County. It left only 15 professionals, including untried youngsters and City were forced to field local amateurs. They were beaten 7-1 by bottom-of-the-table Durham and then 9-1 by a Wigan side including Ward and McGrahan. The Wigan debacle owed much to a first-half injury to Kendall which forced full-back George Greaves into goal.

When they visited Sincil Bank a week later, Wigan director Mr Welsh, having observed the Imps' penury, bought 100 ten-shilling shares in the Imps, a magnificent gesture. The club's plight started to strike a chord outside Lincolnshire. Two senior members of the Football League's management committee - John Lewis and Charles Sutcliffe - travelled up from London. It was their address to a public meeting, attended by more than 1,000 people in the Drill Hall, which galvanised the community around its football club. Lewis and Sutcliffe reminded the audience of the prestige a League club brought to a city. Only support through the turnstiles, they warned, could preserve the club. The receipts of every home match had to pay three weeks wages.

Message received. Supporters dug deep. Crowds edged back up to the 5,000 mark, below the break-even figure but enough to keep the club going. Thinking caps were put on. A whist drive at the Victory Cafe ('dancing 'til 2am') raised £5. Lincoln City Football Supporters Club was created to find 1,000 subscribers to put in £1 each. James Irving, son of former City player John, launched a separate scheme - more realistic in a recession - to raise £1,000 by selling one-shilling shares.

The board had a bright idea. They purchased a motor car - a Vulcan 4-5 seater 16hp - and started raffling it at 1s a ticket. When the FA heard about it and ordered City to abandon the scheme, Lincoln Mayor Coun J Hague urged supporters who had bought raffle tickets to let the club keep the money. Only eight claimed back their shilling. At a charity night the ball used in the FA Cup tie with Fulham was auctioned. Three times it was sold but donated straight back by well-wishers and £33 13s was raised. An autographed portrait of Prime Minister Lloyd George fetched a fiver. It was during this frenzy of supportive activity that the FA commission delivered its verdict on the Bury v Coventry scandal.

On April 28, 1923, the first Wembley FA Cup final, between Bolton Wanderers and West Ham United, attracted 125,000 people. King George VI was among them, preferring to attend that spectacle than Lincoln City's Third Division North fixture with Accrington at Sincil Bank the same day. Shrewd move. In front of 4,000, the Imps' game was an "exceedingly tame" goalless draw but thanks to the players' loyalty and some serious rallying round by the community, somehow City had made it to summer. They had stared down the barrel and, thanks to great collective energy and affection for the football club, survived. They had teetered on the ledge of extinction but clung on.

It was stressful on that ledge, but not lonely. The Third Division North's impact, in travelling costs, had been severe. Halifax, Tranmere and Durham all struggled badly to survive. Hartlepool were losing £50 per week and all of Rochdale's players were available for transfer. Stalybridge Celtic, despite finishing 11th, headed for the sanctuary of the Cheshire League. Times were also hard below the Football League. Scunthorpe ended the year £4,000 in debt.

Rallying round continued through the summer. Boxing and cycling events at Sincil Bank were well-attended. So was an August Bank Holiday Gala which enjoyed a stroke of luck when the Harmston Agricultural and Horticultural Show, with which it was due to clash, was cancelled due to an outbreak of Foot and Mouth. A balloon, released at the gala, came to rest three weeks later in a garden in Hanover, Germany winning its owner a cash prize.

But Calderhead had to get City up the Third Division North table. Attracting bums on to seats is the best way to stay solvent and a winning team is the best supplier of bums to seats. The manager brought in Archie Roe, who had been scoring plenty for Arsenal reserves, and centre-half Alf Jewett, also from Highbury. Both quickly became popular, and Kendall was brilliant, but too many other players were poor and another season of treading water followed. Only 10 wins from 42 games left many seats at Sincil Bank unwarmed by bums as City limped to 19th out of 22.

With the wolf, fangs poised, again snarling at the door, the fans were mortified when county-born hero Kendall joined Everton for £1,250. Kean was sold to Blackburn. The tide of energy, that had so recently supported City at the club's lowest point, ebbed. Only ten per cent of shareholders turned up to the 1924 AGM and, out of more than 600 Supporters Club members, only 40 attended their annual meeting. Eroded by the constantly uphill battle, Calderhead quit. Football management was not his bag so he followed Strawson into the licensing trade, taking over the Newmarket Hotel in Lincoln.

Taylor had called for new blood at the boardroom helm and he got it. Sam Tonge became chairman and the feisty James Irving vice-chairman. Tonge, Derby-born but resident in Lincoln since 1891, was a successful businessman, devout Catholic and member of the Unionist Association. His First World War service had been notable. In action with the 7th Lincolns, Tonge had already earned several mentions in dispatches when he found himself in a tight spot at Maresches on November 1, 1918. Encountering eight enemy soldiers in a house he shot three, convincing the other five to surrender. He then entered the cellar of a neighbouring house, accompanied only by a sergeant, and brought out 46 enemy soldiers and three machine-guns. For this noble deed, Tonge was awarded the Military Cross which he collected from the King at Buckingham Palace in May 1919.

After helping clean up Europe, he returned to the laundry business which he had set up in Lincoln's Clasketgate in 1908. He was quite a big fish in laundry - honorary secretary of the National Launderers' Federation and a governor representative on the Launderers Trade Board. Without a doubt he could offer sound advice on how to get the Imps' kit sparkling clean but could he get the club into profit and up the table ? The new hierarchy reduced season-ticket prices from 50s (St Andrews Stand) and 25s (ordinary admission) to 45s and 22s and appointed Horace Henshall as manager.

A Black Countryman, Henshall arrived from Chesterfield where, aged 34, he was finding searing bursts of pace increasingly hard to summon out on the right-wing. He brought copious experience from a playing career which, interrupted by the war, spanned 18 years and included spells at Aston Villa, Notts County, Sheffield Wednesday and Chesterfield.

Henshall's first match in charge - the opening fixture of the 1924/25 season - was City's 903rd game in the Football League. A 1-0 home win over Wigan Borough, it was unique in that David Bolan scored for Lincoln. Bolan had been signed to fill Kean's inside-left role, a daunting task for a lad recruited from Durham junior football. His debut winner proved the high spot of his Imps career. He was immediately dropped and subsequently played only two more games, in October. Bolan remains on a short list of men to have played in three or more Lincoln games, all of which City won.

With only the top club going up, the 22-strong Third Division North was a horribly difficult dungeon to escape. Henshall steered City to eighth, a rise of 11 places but still some way from promotion. At least the new boss got them moving in the right direction although his first campaign brought FA Cup embarrassment with exit to Alfreton of the Central Alliance. Lincoln had claimed the Derbyshire club's ground wasn't suitable for a cup tie so Alfreton, watched by 3,592 packed into their tiny stadium, celebrated their 1-0 triumph long and loud. The 50 City fans that had been allocated stand tickets made a brisk and sheepish exit.

Some old "friends" fetched up in opening fixture of the 1925/6 season: Coventry City, still in a state of national disgrace after the Bury fiddle. Lincoln had a chance to chew over old times on a boiling August afternoon and Coventry again had the last laugh with a 3-2 win in front of 15,257.

Making their debuts for Lincoln that day were Henry Havelock and Walter Webster, both shrewdly picked up by Henshall in the summer. Henry Havelock, built like the proverbial brick outhouse, joined from Hull City. He held the ball well, was strong in the air and capped his debut by scoring City's second goal. While City had a tradition of excellent centre-halves they had not been over-endowed with buccaneering centre-forwards so the crowd quickly took to Havelock. He scored twice at Wigan Borough and twice more in successive home wins, 4-1 over Grimsby (in front of a Third Division North record crowd of 13,078) and 5-1 over Walsall (in front of 2,460 !) After scoring 17 goals in 27 games for City he was on his way. Sold to Portsmouth.

The hugely-promising Webster passed even more fleetingly through Lincoln. Henshall had heard on his Staffordshire grapevine that Walsall's right-back was worth a close look and tempted him to Sincil Bank. An accomplished defender, Webster was appointed captain straight away, and quickly became rated among the most promising players in the Third Division North. A rock, per-haps, round which to build City's defence. Nope. After 12 games he was cashed in. Off to Sheffield United for £1,650. In October, left-half Richard Rushton, who had missed only five games through injury since joining City 15 months earlier, was sold to Sheffield Wednesday.

Henshall found talent haemorrhaging out of the club but returned from a mid-season scouting trip to Ireland with a ruddy-faced left-back called Paddy McConville. The Irishman beefed up a defence which conceded 19 goals in five games in January. At the other end, Lincoln-born striker Harry Andrews, given his chance late in the season, scored 12 goals in the last nine games as City fin-ished strongly. They sat 15th in the final table, one point ahead of Coventry but

22 behind champions Grimsby who rose into Division Two, the land, long-forgotten at Sincil Bank, of Preston, Manchester City and Chelsea.

That promised land of Division Two remained the idyll (Division One was a different planet) but Henshall needed to recruit. Several years of frantic fund-raising, allied to consistent selling of better players, meant that, for the first time since the war, during the summer of 1926 Lincoln could invest. Henshall enlisted one of the Football League's legends. Albert Iremonger, at 6ft 5in, had kept goal in 564 League matches during 22 season at Notts County. At 42 he was a one of English football's true celebrities who proved his fitness two weeks before reporting for City training by wielding a cricket ball for 8 for 27 for Notts Harrington against his old Notts County colleagues. In too came outside-right Charles Bosbury from Preston North End and flying left-winger Frank Pegg from Sunderland. To complete a set of impressive-looking recruits, big, bustling Billy Dinsdale was lured from Aston Villa, for whose reserves he scored 30 goals in 35 Central League games the previous season.

The ground, as well as the team, was upgraded. Dressing rooms were extended and, for the first time, players' lockers and wash-basins installed. The pitch was surrounded by a green painted fence replacing the hitherto ever-present rope. Henshall also acquired a back-room team of trainer Ted Wynter (formerly with South Shields and Hartlepool) and his assistant Dan Ludkin, who played 14 games for the Imps in the early twenties.

Tonge and Irving had gambled that investment in the team would bring good results which would bring good crowds which would bring increased revenue, etc. It was a bold move but the Depression, with massive unemployment, meant money was tight around the county. Despite decent form - Andrews notched hat-tricks in successive matches against Accrington and Crewe - attendances hovered around 4,000, dipping below for the visits of Accrington, Walsall, Ashington, Rotherham, Stockport and Crewe. City entered 1927 owing £2,150 and chairman Tonge, a more aggressive character than his predecessors, issued an ultimatum: "Support us or we will resign from the League."

"What we are faced with," he said, "is do we want League football ? The attendances up to date say no. If that is the true answer then we must resign from the Football League and be content with Midland League football." A lecture followed. "The club is run entirely for the public. It is your club and if you want it to continue in existence then you must attend the matches. You cannot expect anyone else to pay for your sport and entertainment. The directors have already advanced well over £2,000 this season to keep the club going."

He challenged the fans to register their loyalty by turning up in droves for the next home game. "There will be a first-team match here on Saturday next against Halifax. I appeal to you all to roll up in your thousands at this match to convince the board that you do want them to continue League football. It should not be necessary for anyone to appeal to you to support your own club. I am ashamed to do it and only do so to give the Lincoln public a last chance before we take the drastic action of placing all our players on the transfer list and dropping out of League football altogether."

So on February 19, while the nation's attention was fixed on the FA Cup fifth round (Arsenal v Liverpool, Reading v Brentford and South Shields v Swansea the pick of the ties), City's board waited to see if droves would turn up. The response was lukewarm - maybe the fans didn't enjoy being preached at. At 4,016, the attendance was 1,500 up on the previous home game but that figure included visiting fans and 417 boys allowed in free at half-time.

A much tinier gathering - 839 spectators - was present to witness strange scenes at Wrexham where, on a bitterly cold and wet night, the Imps finished the match with eight men. City arrived at the Racecourse Ground with only one set of kit in which the players, after 45 minutes battering by the storm, had to sit, drenched and covered in freezing mud, through half-time. Early in the second half, as Wrexham moseyed around in fresh, warm clothes, three Imps players - Alf Bassnett, Tom Maidment and Joe Robson - collapsed, unable to continue. Iremonger and Pegg were only sustained by helpings of whisky on the pitch. To great relief from the remaining players, the referee abandoned the game just past the hour.

Recovered from that ordeal, Lincoln blazed through March and April with seven successive wins, including 23 goals. Wingers Bosbury and Pegg were the architects of scoring chances enjoyed, in particular, by Dinsdale. In the last 11 games he scored 15 goals including four in a 5-0 home win over Durham watched by an encouraging 7,321. Crowds did perk up and City ended the season on fire with nine wins out of 12 to finish 11th. A total of 90 goals from 42 league games included 21 from 25 games for Dinsdale and 19 from 34 for Andrews. That strike-rate, as well as being highly entertaining, suggested that City had a chance of muscling in on the upper reaches of the table - maybe even having a pop at promotion - next season. McConville was considered a potential full international. Tonge did not waste the opportunity to canvas for cash again with the plea: "Look what we've achieved over the last two months. Now help us keep the players."

Never mind the players. In June, the manager left. Henshall had clearly been moving City in the right direction but, like West and Calderhead senior before him, was tempted away by a club with greater resources. Henshall was enticed a division higher to Notts County. Lincoln also spun the East Midlands managerial merry-go-round and tempted Harry Parkes from Chesterfield.

7.
Heroes all over the pitch

ON MONDAY June 13, 1927, a bright, fresh summer's day with luscious breezes tossing the branches of larch, oak and chestnut in Lincoln's many attractive parklands and chaffinches flitting and gambolling across the smooth expanse of Ted Wynter's lovingly manicured pitch, Harry Parkes, aged 38 and three quarters, parked his shoes for the first time under the manager's desk at Sincil Bank.

For five seasons Parkes had managed City's Third Division North rivals Chesterfield and, on resources little better than Lincoln's, steered them to a top-seven finish every season. Impressive credentials, and Tonge was delighted to have tempted Parkes away from Saltergate. Staffordshire-born, like his predecessor, Parkes had been a highly talented youngster, captain of both cricket and football first teams at Halesowen Grammar School. He played cricket in the competitive Birmingham League and was offered a contract by Worcestershire but chose to pursue full-time football instead. He joined West Bromwich Albion and played in an FA Cup semi-final before he was 18. Except for a brief spell at Coventry, Parkes spent all his playing career on West Brom's right flank, stepping up to become assistant manager during the war. He then managed Newport County and Chesterfield.

Parkes was well-acquainted with City's squad, having plotted their downfall twice a season for the last five years. He knew that Henshall had set down a good foundation and Parkes' first priority was to persuade the board not to sell anybody. A record loss of £2,583 was incurred during the previous season and the only immediate way of correcting that would be to sell players but the board courageously agreed to give Parkes time. All the key players were kept while the wage-burden was eased slightly by Iremonger's retirement. Cash was even found for a signing or two. Right-back Albert Worthy followed Parkes from Chesterfield. Iremonger's replacement was Len Hill, a Londoner unique to Lincoln City in two ways. He became the first Imp with 108 successive league games for Queens Park Rangers on his CV and the first to be cricket coach at Watford Grammar School.

Parkes started well with just two defeats in 14 games. Billy Dinsdale failed to score in the opening-day 3-0 defeat at Doncaster but did so in the next 10 games in which Bosbury and Pegg also notched 10 goals between them. Despite one or two spectacular lapses - a 5-1 home defeat to Hartlepools and a 9-2 thrashing at Darlington (who also missed a penalty) - City settled in the top six. The fans responded with attendances averaging 7,000 and touching 9,000. That meant increased traffic and City directors met members of the Lincoln Watch Committee to discuss congestion on match-days. The first parking spaces - 1d per bike, 2d per motor bike - were set aside behind the Sincil Bank Stand.

A 3-1 win over Ashington on January 28 left City fourth, but eight points behind Bradford Park Avenue. A 3-1 defeat at Bradford ended hopes of bridging the gap but another flying finish - 13 matches unbeaten - lifted Lincoln to second in the final table, eight points behind the champions. When Bradford, their title already secure, visited Sincil Bank in late April, they were soundly beaten 2-0. It was an uplifting run-in which reinforced belief that promotion was now achievable again. Dinsdale had bustled, scrapped and elbowed his way to 29 goals in 43 League and Cup games. The crowd loved his 110-per-cent-at-all-times style.

It was much City's best season in the Third Division North. They passed 50 points for the first time and vindicated the board's decisions to appoint Parkes and hold on to their star players. The board's next task was to quash unsettling rumours triggered by an unexpected source: the demise of trams. The last tram was soon to circulate Lincoln and, as train traffic intensified, another railway station was needed in the city. Among speculated sites was Sincil Bank. Tonge was quick to point out that, as long-term tenants, City had first option to buy the land, but the station speculation concentrated minds on the club's dependence on a landlord. Negotiations towards a purchase of the ground began with the redoubtable Colonel Swan. A net profit of almost £2,000 on the financial year gave the board some room for manoeuvre.

The summer of 1928 found expectations at Sincil Bank higher than for many years. The players returned from training a week early and supporters bought a record number of season-tickets. Harold Andrews joined Notts County, leaving City one down on the Harry front until Kitching of that ilk arrived from Worksop to fill Andrews' attacking role. Parkes bought Henry Roberts, an elegant young striker who played under him at Chesterfield. Harry Pringle got married, Dinsdale was his best man and the working men's committee, busy as ever, built new lavatories including the first 'Ladies', in the South Park Stand.

Expectations were high but form was erratic. Three defeats in the opening seven games included a 7-3 beating at Stockport. In only two of 10 games did City score less than three goals which meant that points were regularly banked but the consistency required of potential champions was absent. Three Christmas games illustrated the problem. On Christmas Day, Lincoln lost 3-2 at Hartlepools. On Boxing Day, at Sincil Bank, they crushed the same opposition 7-1 (Dinsdale and Pegg hat-tricks) then on December 29, unchanged, they lost 4-0 at Wigan Borough.

It was always entertaining though. "Give it to Dinny" was the crowd's favourite chant as again he progressed at just under a goal per game. He scored twice to help City negotiate an awkward FA Cup visit to the Giant Axe home of Lancaster Town of the Lancashire Combination. They won 3-1 and then, cheered on by 40 hardy visiting fans, beat Carlisle 1-0, Roberts the scorer, on their first visit to Brunton Park.

That set up a lucrative third round home tie with First Division title-chasers Leicester City. Eighty police officers - double the usual number - with RAC back-up, were on duty to control a bumper crowd of 16,849. All minor matches in Lincoln were cancelled as the city's football fraternity got behind their team on the big day. The players let nobody down. Leicester were full of confidence and class but the Imps tore into them. Hill saved a first-half penalty to keep the score goalless at half-time. City poured forward after the break and Dinsdale had a goal disallowed for offside before the Foxes snatched a heartbreaking 86th-minute winner. It was a great effort from Lincoln but there was a tragic post-script. Bosbury had taken his place on the wing despite feeling a chill. Straight after the game he was confined to bed and soon became gravely ill as tuberculosis developed.

Leicester's visit was another good earner but when Bradford Park Avenue came in with a bid for Dinsdale, the City board could not resist it. Every player had his price. Dinsdale's was £1,500. The fans were devastated but the number nine shirt retained its scoring power. It passed to Kitching, who had played six games early-season, when Dinsdale was injured, and scored just once. Now, given a chance to stake his claim on a permanent basis, the Grimsby-born striker scored the only goal of the game on his return to earn Parkes a satisfying win over Chesterfield. Quick over the grass, quicker of thought, Kitching scored 13 goals in the next eight games to inspire the following ditty from local wag Benny Dix:

> *"He's kanny, he's kute and klevver is Harry.*
> *He dussent mind a bit of fetch and tarry.*
> *He's up to all the tricks*
> *And when he's neer the sticks*
> *You kan bet he won't wonder or tarry."* (Sic)

City were also buoyed late in the season by the return of Will Kendall who, partly due to injuries, had not settled at Everton or in a brief spell at Preston. Lincoln finished sixth, 15 points adrift of the title which again went to Bradford, this time City emulating their Park Avenue rivals of a year before.

On July 14, Bosbury died after first receiving - literally on his deathbed - a free transfer. Tonge, having sold his laundry business, stepped down after six years as chairman and moved to Bournemouth. Ted Simpson took over as chairman. Another respectable season followed, Lincoln finishing fifth, but most drama occurred off the pitch. In September, after a home match with Port Vale, fire completely gutted the South Park Stand. No-one was hurt, the blaze having broke out at night, but £3,000 damage was caused.

Simpson peered across the smouldering ruins and pledged: "This will act as an incentive to us to build a non-flammable stand and I believe nothing short of concrete will suffice." The insurance company paid up quickly. Helped by public donations, within six weeks a new, 1,500-seat, roofed stand was open. It was twice as big as its shabby predecessor, with terracing in front. And it was concrete.

Colonel Swan had set a purchase price of £4,874 for the ground and supporters' donations were also invited towards that. The club wrote to a selection of wealthy residents who, with the club on a relative high, responded much more positively than those asked when City were desperately in need of help in 1923. With the club able to contribute some cash of its own, a mortgage was obtained. On November 16, 1929, Carlisle United visited for the first match played at Sincil Bank with the stadium under the football club's ownership. City celebrated with a 4-1 win. An official ceremony to celebrate the purchase followed, performed by that well known terrace-dweller, Master of the Burton Hounds, Sir Julien Cahn.

From the new stand, supporters watched City again win more than they lose but without threatening the top three. In the opening game, Kitching collected an injury which ruled him out until February but again that number nine shirt carried luck. Henry Roberts climbed into it and scored 23 goals in 21 games including two batches of four, in a 4-2 win at Carlisle and an 8-0 home demolition of Tranmere.

During the season Parkes tinkered with the side. Scouts in the county turned up two local nuggets. Outside left Walter Lax was spotted playing for Albion Works in the Gainsborough League. Ted Savage a box-to-box right-half was recruited from Louth Grammar School. Aged just 17, Savage was pitched in for his League debut at Carlisle and thrived. Alf Young, a tireless, composed centre-half, arrived from Workington and settled into the number five shirt. Kendall moved on again, to Sheffield United, with reserve 'keeper Billy Meeson stepping up for the last 11 games.

Parkes had acquired a reputation as a shrewd businessman. The summer sale of winger Evan Jenkins, promising but still to prove himself over time, to Burnley for £1,500, appeared good business. Conversely, Henry Roberts' transfer to Port Vale for a paltry £150 was mystifying. Roberts had initially been freed by City a year earlier only to be recalled after a boardroom change of heart. When his chance in the team arrived he could hardly have seized it more spectacularly yet he left for £150. Within a year of joining Vale he moved on to Millwall and played for England in a full international against Belgium.

The fans' bewilderment at that strange piece of business was assuaged by the return of one W. Dinsdale. Hugely popular as a person, as well as a player, his return, after only 14 months at Bradford, was a masterstroke by Parkes. To replace Kendall, in from Newport County came Jim Maidment, brother of former Imp Tom. Walter Buckley joined from Bradford to partner Young at the back. From Hull City came Philip Cartwright to fill the outside-right berth tragically vacated by Bosbury.

The reinstated legend scored in his first three games back and City, after losing their opener 2-1 at New Brighton, won the next 10 to sprint top of the division. Crowds averaged a healthy 7,000 and 10,840 were inside Sincil Bank on October 25 for the visit of Chesterfield, the Imps' likeliest challengers for the title. A 1-1 draw suggested there was little between the sides and it looked likely that Parkes' present and former charges would be hard to dislodge from the top two. But which would occupy the only slot that mattered ? You got nothing for coming second in the Third Division North.

In Savage and Lax, City had unearthed two jewels. Savage, still a teenager, oozed quality, and read the game like a veteran. Lax, given his debut on his 18th birthday the previous season, was the sort of skilful winger crowds love to see. Always eager to take on defenders he loved to cut inside and shoot, as evidenced by six goals in eight games in October and November.

An 8-3 crushing of Barrow in the FA Cup (Dinsdale 3, Lax 2, T Maidment, Cartwright, Kitching) stirred hopes of an FA Cup run alongside the promotion charge. City were drawn away to non-league Scarborough and seemed well in control, 4-2 up at half-time. They lost 6-4. Still, League progress continued smoothly. Just two defeats in 15 games kept their noses in front of Chesterfield, Tranmere and Stockport. They visited Stockport on January 3 and as the Imps team departed for the north-west, the day was dawning dark and freezing. The trough at the foot of Lindum Hill was frozen solid so the first milkman to pass had to smash the ice to enable his horse to have a drink before starting its rounds. At that very moment, milkmen throughout Stockport were facing similar problems and thick, freezing fog still hung thickly on Edgeley Park as Lincoln lost a pulsating game 4-2. The Mayor of Lincoln, Coun CH Doughty, travelled to the match. His expert assessment: "They certainly deserved to gain at least one point and in my humble judgement were entitled to two."

City hit back with a brilliant 6-3 win at Carlisle with Pringle and Savage outstanding and Dinsdale grabbing a hat-trick. When Lax got injured, Frank Pegg replaced him and rolled back the years to score five goals in three games, including a hat-trick in a 5-0 win over Rochdale. When Lax was fit again, Pegg was summarily dropped. Easter brought two home games - a happy circumstance both for the bank manager and a team used to winning at home. Two victories - 4-1 over Halifax, 5-1 over Carlisle - were each watched by almost 20,000 people who went away thinking this could be the time - the first time - that Lincoln earn promotion through points not votes.

Still, as at any football club, cynics lurked among the supporters. A 2-0 defeat at struggling Crewe and a 3-1 home defeat to Rotherham prompted a few suggestions that City didn't really want promotion. That was a difficult argument to sustain in the light of their tremendous season and especially matches like the one at Tranmere where City went 3-0 down but scrapped back to draw 3-3. Looming up on April 22 was a Wednesday-night visit to Saltergate that would certainly sort out who "wanted it." City had 55 points, Chesterfield 54. And Lincoln had a game in hand.

The Imps' fans headed for Saltergate in force. Three trains-full had travelled on February 28, only to see the match snowed off with the ground packed. Now the hordes set off again. For Parkes, what a visit to the stadium he controlled for five years !

In front of 20,092 people, the match began at 6.15pm. By 6.35pm, City were 2-0 down. Then the red and white sea went wild as Dinsdale pulled a goal back on 36 minutes and, three minutes after the break, Lax cut in and shot low. Chesterfield goalkeeper Dolman reached the ball but couldn't keep it out. 2-2. Ten minutes later Pynegar restored the home side's lead. 3-2. City piled forward. In the closing minutes Dolman felled Lincoln's inside-right Bob Whalley in the box. Penalty. This was the season's defining moment. Saltergate held its breath. Even the leaning spire craned over a little further to get a better view. Kitching stepped up to the spot - but struck the ball straight at Dolman. Seconds later the final whistle sounded. Three sides of the ground erupted with joy, the other side silently hitched up their trousers, cast one last look at City's disconsolate players and headed for the station.

It was a night of pivotal, all-consuming passion and both sides carried the after-effects into the following Saturday. A hungover Lincoln lost 5-3 at Accrington. Chesterfield demolished Gateshead 8-1 to move three points clear with one game left. The Spireites were champions. In Lincoln, the "They don't want promotion" brigade crowed. Chairman Simpson raged: "Supporters who say we deliberately lost the League championship are simpletons."

City soon cashed in their two teenage stars. Savage joined Liverpool for £2,500 and Lax went to Blackpool for £1,500. The sales allowed more than £1,000 to be paid off City's mortgage (the FA also advanced a low-interest loan) but aggrieved the supporters. Dinsdale, after 25 goals in 36 games in his comeback season, also left to return to his native Darlington with a final tally of 89 goals in 126 appearances for City. "Is that it then ?" asked the fans in the Portland Arms and the John Bull. "No bleedin' ambition !" they lamented in the Golden Eagle and the Shakespeare. But Parkes had plans.

Cash was allocated to him for players and he bought heavily. Left-back Jim Smith joined from Doncaster. Harold Riley, an inside-right, and George Whyte, a versatile left-sided player arrived from Accrington (they were in the Accrington side which extinguished City's promotion dream in May.) Right-half Charles Pringle brought experience from more than 300 appearances for St Mirren and Manchester City. Goalkeeper Dan McPhail arrived from Portsmouth in a straight swap for Jim Maidment.

Another swap deal saw Frank Pegg join Bradford City in return for 23-year-old striker Allan Hall who had scored 50 goals for the Bantams' reserves the previous season. Early in his career, Hall had been the subject of a big-money move from Doncaster to Middlesbrough. Full of promise, as yet only partially fulfilled, to him would fall the onerous challenge of replacing Dinsdale. Helpful to Hall was the arrival of inside-right, Frank Keetley, also from Bradford where the pair had worked profitably together. These were interesting new faces but the team that had come so close last season had been broken up. Had City dismantled too soon and blown it ?

It appeared not when Darlington and Hartlepool visited Sincil Bank for the first two games of the season. Darlington were beaten 2-0 with Hall and Whyte scoring on their debuts. Hartlepool were trounced 6-0 (Hall and Whyte on target again.) Faced with the challenge of replacing the legendary Dinsdale, Hall found a solution. He set about becoming a legend himself. City's new men knitted together straight away. On September 19, a 3-2 victory at leaders Gateshead, with McPhail starring, moved them top. The ice-cool Hall, with Riley and Keetley quick and busy round him, formed a frightening attacking thrust. That trio shared the goals as second-place Southport were hammered 7-0 at home in mid-November.

Ill-fortune intervened in October when Wigan Borough, financially embarrassed, resigned from the League. They were not replaced and their record expunged so City, having already beaten them twice, lost four points and, briefly, leadership of the division. The FA Cup first round delivered a trip to Manchester Central, an ambitious outfit who had been trying to break into the League for several years. They again tried unsuccessfully when Wigan resigned (Manchesters United and City both opposed Central's claim) so they relished an immediate chance to roll over a League club. City visited their Belle Vue home and in the middle of the speedway track registered a thoroughly professional 3-0 win.

Worthy, McConville, Young and Buckley formed a resolute back-four in front of the reliable McPhail. City had conceded five goals in 10 games when, at full strength, they visited Crewe Alexandra on December 5. So how they came to lose 8-1 remains one of the great mysteries in the history of world football. FA Cup exit followed. After drawing 2-2 with Luton Town of the Third Division South, City lost 4-1 at Kenilworth Road.

League progress, though, remained serene. Hall scored twice in a 3-1 win at third-placed Wrexham. Chester, having replaced Nelson, paid their first League visit to the Bank on Boxing Day and Hall hit a hat-trick in a 6-0 victory. At Darlington, Hall hit three again in another 6-0 win. When Halifax visited Sincil Bank in mid-January, City had a score to settle. At the Shay Ground, in early September, the west-Yorkshire side registered a 3-0 win - the only match all season in which Lincoln failed to score. Revenge was sweet. Riley and Hall made it 2-0 at half-time. Then, as Halifax watched Hall like hawks, Keetley added six in the second half and Riley another to crown a 9-1 scoreline.

A volatile visit to Walsall followed. During City's 3-0 win, left-back Jim Smith, seriously fell out with the natives. In the second half, Walsall winger Wheeler trapped the ball between his legs and Smith kicked at it but struck his opponent. Wheeler keeled over and was carried off, apparently unconscious, though he was fit to resume five minutes later. Smith was booed and barracked by the home fans for the rest of the game then chased off the field at the end. Even the dressing room corridor offered no sanctuary. There he was confronted by a woman who clobbered him with her handbag. A police escort was summoned to keep Smith away from a 100-strong mob and he was sneaked away in a private car.

City still led the table. Next came the big one. To the Bank came Gateshead, one point behind. More than 14,000 people watched one of the scrappiest games of the season settled by a scrappy second half goal - but it went to Hall. A great result, despite a poor display, but an even poorer performance followed when City travelled to meet New Brighton, who had won two games out of 26. Complacency crept in and New Brighton won 2-1.

If a promotion-winning side needs luck, City had their share now. Gateshead missed their chance to gain ground by losing at home to Chester. Then, as the City party waited at Manchester railway station after the New Brighton game, they bumped into an old pal. Burnley striker George Beel was waiting for the same train after a Turf Moor game. Beel, Lincoln-born, still lived in his native city, commuting across to play for the Clarets. He had spent nine months with City just after the war and, chatting as the train hurtled east, came over all nostalgic. Parkes promptly signed him and seven days later Beel was in the Imps line-up - and scored - in a 3-1 home win over Barrow. In the next nine games he scored six invaluable goals.

City, though not in great form, continued to grit out points. Carlisle and Rotherham were beaten 3-1 at Sincil Bank. An excellent 1-0 win at Stockport was clinched by Beel's strike on a day when challengers Gateshead, Crewe and Southport all dropped points. Then came a mid-March jitter. A 1-0 defeat at Tranmere and a 1-1 home draw with York, in which Pringle scored an own goal and Whyte put a last-minute penalty against the post, got the conspiracy theorists talking again.

Those cynics were subdued after a 5-1 Easter Saturday win over Accrington Stanley left City three points clear at the top with much the best goal average. Would they draw strength from the experience of the previous season? Would they hold their nerve? Did they want to go up?

Maybe not. Out of nowhere came only the second home defeat of the season, 2-1 to lowly Doncaster. City squandered their third penalty in four games, Worthy, this time, the culprit. Comparisons were drawn with the home defeat to Rotherham which triggered the fatal slump at the same stage of last season. Lincoln had taken four points from five games and looked jaded.

In an emergency, head for Skeggy. Sensing the tension in his players and the pressure around the city, Parkes took his men to Skegness for a week before the next fixture, at Rochdale. This was a real chance for City to stamp their authority on the promotion issue. Rochdale were miles adrift at the bottom, having collected one point from the last 23 games. Gateshead faced a much tougher trip to Accrington. At Spotland, a desolate atmosphere from a crowd of 1,938 offered a stark reminder that the Third Division North was still, for some, a barren arena. 'Dale were down and City kicked them, 5-3. Back on track.

City arrived back in Lincoln well into Sunday morning and by noon they were on the way back to Skegness to prepare for the visit of Crewe a week later. While the German population pondered whether to vote Hitler or Hindenburg, the Imps luxuriated by the seaside. They enjoyed fresh air and space round their ear 'oles instead of having to deal with the constant, if well-meaning, "Are we going to do it then lads?" platitudes. City had a big score - literally, 8-1 - to settle with Crewe whose promotion challenge had fizzled out. Hall scored twice in the first half, Riley headed two after the break before Hall completed his hat-trick. A 5-1 win boost Lincoln's goal average to 2.32. Gateshead's, after beating Stockport only 1-0, was 1.97.

Three games to go. On April 23, Hitler's National Socialist Party made massive gains and so did Lincoln City. Goals from Hall, Cartwright and Whyte earned them a 3-0 victory at Carlisle and cheers raised the visitors' dressing room ceiling when news was telephoned through by Ted Simpson at Millmoor that Gateshead had lost 2-1 at Rotherham. A Rabelaisian journey back from Brunton Park, cheering and singing and eating pork-pies all the way, ended as dawn was breaking on Sunday. With two games left - Wrexham at home, then Hartlepools away - City required just one more point.

Considering their away form - six defeats so far - City were desperate to tie it up against Wrexham. Back they went to Skegness until noon on Saturday. A crowd of 14,938 chewed their nails up to their elbows as the match entered its closing minutes still goalless. Minutes, seconds, from promotion. But still one telling thrust from Wrexham could ruin everything. At last came the final whistle. City were back in Division Two and the stadium dissolved into raptures. These were all captured on film by cameramen from the city's "Enterprise Kinema" at which a full screening, attended by the Imps' players and management, followed on Tuesday night. The movie-house was packed with supporters who watched the rather poor match then heard players address them through the "talkie apparatus." The loudest acclaim went to Hall who finished with 42 goals in 40 League games. "The fact that I am top goal scorer in the northern section is due to the other fellows. We have had a team of triers," he said, modestly.

Congratulations telegrams arrived from Doncaster Rovers, Rochdale, Leicester, Tranmere, Newport, Sheffield Wednesday, Huddersfield, Luton, Hartlepools, Millwall and Hull but there was still the visit to Hartlepools to discharge. City lost 4-3 so finished ahead of Gateshead only on goal average. They scored 106 goals and conceded 47 to Gateshead's 94 and 48. Lincoln had collected 34 out of a possible 40 points at home where only three matches drew crowds of less than 7,000. A season of rare joy had been knitted into Lincoln City's troubled history.

Hall struck two goals at Hartlepool to finish with 50 from 46 League and cup games. His had been the starring role but there were heroes all over the pitch. The experienced McPhail, never extravagant, had been consistency itself, often making saves look simple due to positional sense. Worthy was a worthy right-back and Smith sound at left-back. Young and Buckley clicked in central defence and when Buckley broke a leg in January, Pringle, whose rugged presence had fully replaced the livewire talents of Savage at right-half, dropped back comfortably. The loss of Lax was amply compensated by Whyte's guile and dead-ball expertise on the left. Cartwright sparkled on the opposite wing. Then there was Riley, Keetley and Hall, the latter one of three ever-presents along with McPhail and Whyte.

Four hundred people attended a Victory Ball at the County Assembly Rooms, decked out in red and white. The city, lifted by football like almost nothing else, had a spring in its step again. Lincoln were leaving the Third Division North behind. They had burst the chains. Bye-bye Barrow, Rochdale and Accrington. Or would it be just au revoir?

8.
"Eschew violent criticism of the management"

AFTER serving a 12-year sentence in the clammy confines of the Third Division North, Lincoln City were back in the airy, sunlit expanse of Division Two. But had they escaped the wilderness for good or were the catchers, nets in hand, on the way?

The Second Division of 1932 comprised a very different gang of clubs than when Lincoln had last been there in 1920. Only eight - Bury, Fulham, Grimsby, Nottingham Forest, Port Vale, Stoke, Tottenham and West Ham - bridged the gap. In the intervening years, the League empire had expanded and the new season would send Lincoln to Wales and Devon for the first time to meet Swansea and Plymouth. Other intriguingly unfamiliar opposition included Southampton, Millwall and Charlton. Fixtures with Spurs and Preston promised glamour while local derbies against Grimsby and the two Nottingham clubs guaranteed big crowds.

This was Lincoln City's big chance for self-improvement. Season-ticket sales hit record levels with more than £1,200 banked during the summer. The promotion campaign had yielded a fat profit of £1,376 8s 3d. In the midst of a recession, few clubs had made a profit, so many were forced to consider selling players. The City board found themselves with cash to spend in a buyer's market and spend they did.

Almost before the fag-ends had been swept up after the Assembly Rooms ball, virtually the whole squad had been re-signed. Only George Beel, who served a brief purpose very usefully, departed. To the title-winning squad, Parkes added more than £1,500 worth of new players. Most - £600 - went on tricky winger Jackie Wilkinson, an early Harry Redknapp, who agreed to step down from Newcastle United in the First Division.

Parkes imported plenty of experience into his squad. From Preston came the versatile Alf Horne. Formerly with Alvechurch, West Brom, Stafford Rangers, Hull City, Southend and Manchester City, before spending three years at Deepdale, Horne was happiest at right-half but could fill most positions on the pitch. Thirty-two-year-old striker Joe Cooper, after eight seasons at Grimsby, was recruited from Blundell Park. Right-back Jack Buckley joined after eight seasons with Doncaster Rovers. Tipperary-born centre-half Cornelius (Con) Moulson, a centre-half full of promise, was signed from Bristol City. Inside-right Chick Reed arrived for £125 from Sheffield United. Parkes recruited from far and wide - William Powell and Iorwerth Williams moved east from Southern League side Merthyr Town - while City were also deluged by letters from local men. Hundreds of requests for trials arrived from aspiring pro's aged from 14 to 40.

Sincil Bank was also improved. The St Andrew's Stand was demolished and a new 2,250-seat structure erected. Terracing was laid in front of the stands along both sides of the pitch. Trainers Ted Wynter and Dan Ludkin always spent the summer months manicuring the pitch, which was acknowledged as among the best in the country. Again they got busy. A weeding party was held. This was not a "Bring-a-bottle-listen-to-some-tunes-pull-up-a-few-weeds" type of weeding party. Under the supervision of Wynter the pitch was separated by string into narrow lanes. Along each lane a young lady, specially recruited for the task, crawled, pail in hand, inspecting every inch of the turf for weeds.

With interest rejuvenated, a heavy footfall was expected round Sincil Bank and Lincoln's licensees spotted an opportunity. The Licensed Victuallers' Association asked for an extension of pub opening hours to 6pm instead of 4pm on Saturdays between August 27 and May 6. LVA secretary GR Sills applied on the grounds that football matches were "special occasions." Not special enough, felt city justices who rejected the application despite no objection from the police.

With a redeveloped ground and a manager and team in which the supporters had confidence, there was a vivid sense of anticipation around the city as the first fixture - a short, mouth-watering trip to Horace Henshall's Notts County - approached. Still, some fans are only happy when they are moaning. One took a look round the improved Sincil Bank, returned home, truculently hitched up his trousers and wrote straight to the paper that the ground was "a golden cage with no bird." True, there were tough obstacles and much better opposition ahead and the Imps' auditor JW Hurst called on supporters to "be British" and "eschew violent criticism of the management." The stark fear of immediate recapture by the TDN stayed largely unspoken.

A more enticing first fixture was hard to imagine. Notts County had just regained their Division Two status having topped the Third Division South two season earlier - but as recently as 1925 they finished in the top half of Division One. England's oldest professional club, County's local rivalry with Lincoln was one of the deepest-rooted in world football. Now City had a chance to show Henshall that the foundation he set down at Lincoln seven years earlier had been fully developed.

August 27 brought a great exodus from Lincoln on the short journey south. Sixteen weeks earlier, fewer than 4,000 people watched City's title-winning season conclude at Hartlepool. Now 20,987 squeezed into Meadow Lane. Despite the flurry of new signings, Parkes stayed loyal and fielded the same 11 who had com-

pleted the championship campaign at Victoria Park. In goal, the calm McPhail:
Worthy and Smith, two resolute and popular full-backs; Pringle, part of the Sincil
Bank furniture at right-half; Young and Buckley, who knew eachother's game so
well at five and six; on the right wing, Cartwright, now with two Third Division
North championship medals - Bradford 1928, Lincoln 1932 - on his mantelpiece.
Or, who knows, in his drawer; inside-right Frank Keetley with an extra reason to
look forward to the first game - his brother Tom was a Notts County forward; on
the left, Riley and Whyte - Accrington's finest ever exports; then there was Hall, a
prize-fighter ready to seize his chance.

It was Keetley who re-opened City's Second Division account. The red-and-
white legions melted into paroxysms of joy when he stooped to head Cartwright's
corner into the net. Lincoln led 1-0 at half-time. Percy Mills netted a penalty to
bring County level and that's the way it stayed. A highly respectable away point
on the return to a higher level.

Two days later, at 6.15pm, Second Division football returned to Sincil
Bank. Swansea Town's first visit to Lincoln drew a Monday evening crowd of
12,534 and City, unchanged, unveiled a vibrant display of attacking football.
Another Keetley header opened the scoring after 10 minutes and Riley made it 2-
0 just after half-time. Swansea were well-contained. Three points from two games.
After-match pints in the Ripon Arms and the Tap and Spile tasted very sweet. Keep
this up and Division One lay ahead.

A dose of realism was supplied by three successive defeats: 1-0 at home to
Port Vale, 3-1 at Swansea and 2-0 at Millwall. City's first ever visit to Swansea's
Vetch Field was almost preceded by tragedy when a taxi, carrying five Imps players to the match, collided with a bus. The taxi driver was seriously injured but his
passengers got off relatively lightly. Buckley needed eight stitches to facial cuts
and missed three games but Keetley, McPhail, Worthy and Pringle, though shaken,
were able to play at the Vetch. Alf Horne came in and made a lively debut and
Lincoln acquitted themselves well before a last-minute Swans goal gave the scoreline an emphatic look.

Southampton's first visit to Sincil Bank followed and Joe Cooper, deputising for the injured Hall, found the net in City's 1-0 win. Hall was back for the visit
to Bury and scored twice in the second half to salvage a 2-2 draw from a 2-0 half-
time deficit. Two wins, two draws and three defeats were an acceptable harvest
from City's first seven games.

When the first two Saturdays of October brought Grimsby and West Ham
to Sincil Bank, the season exploded into life. Grimsby's first visit for seven years
drew a crowd of more than 14,000 and City responded with a 6-3 win. Horne, concussed in the opening minutes, carried on gamely and, reaching the dressing
room at the final whistle, asked: "Have we won ?" "Yes," his team-mates could

have replied, "with Keetley, Hall and Wilkinson scoring twice each." Seven days later came a result which raised eyebrows all over the Second Division. West Ham, just relegated from Division One, arrived with internationals Puddefoot, Barratt, Watson and Ruffell in their ranks but were trounced 6-0. Cooper scored three times - City's first Second Division hat-trick since Billy Egerton's against Barnsley in 1915 - Hall added two and Wilkinson the other.

Bang in form, City travelled next to Fulham for a match which had always extra edge - a meeting of the previous season's Northern and Southern Section champions. The Southern Section, especially, considered their domain much the stronger. This time, Fulham prevailed though only narrowly, 3-2, in front of 25,500. Dozens of southern-based club scouts took the opportunity to inspect Hall and he duly scored.

When City were beaten 5-2 at Oldham a week later a clear pattern was forming. Difficult to beat at home, the Imps had not won in six attempts away. Spurs arrived at Sincil Bank having hit 37 goals in 13 games but were held 2-2 (Hall scored twice). City's first visit to the Valley brought a 4-2 defeat at Charlton (Hall, for the fifth time in nine games, scored twice.)

Harold Larwood and Bill Voce were getting busy in the Antipodes. Larwood took 5 for 96 and Voce 4 for 110 to restrict Australia, without Bradman, to 360. This news filtered through to the Imps' squad during one of many connection breaks on their train trek down to Plymouth Argyle at the start of December. There, at the division's most far-flung outpost, City gave their travelling fans their only away victory of the season. After nine minutes Riley, canny as a fox, slipped through a pass which Hall pursued like a cheetah before supplying a rapacious finish. Sixty seconds later, Cartwright flitted down the wing like a butterfly and centred for Hall who struck like a cobra. 2-0. Just before half-time Cartwright flitted down the wing like another butterfly and Riley swooped like a long-eared bat to secure a 3-0 lead which was never threatened. The generous Argyle fans gave Lincoln a warm ovation from the field and City moved to within one point of Plymouth in eighth.

The pattern soon resumed though. Strong at home, fallible away. City lost 4-1 to Manchester United on their first visit to Old Trafford (earlier visits had been to the Claytons ground), 3-0 at Chesterfield and 3-2 at Port Vale. At Sincil Bank, Stoke won 3-2, Bradford drew 2-2 and Chesterfield were beaten 5-3 in a Boxing Day thriller. The FA Cup third round, to which City passed automatically as a Second Division club, brought glamorous Blackburn Rovers to the Bank. Up went admission prices and off to Skegness for six days went City's squad. The players practiced on the beach, sprinted round the cricket ground and warmed their toes at Skegness Sun Castle solarium. It didn't work. A crowd of 13,276, peering through thick fog, saw Rovers ease to a 5-1 win.

This season's menu was interesting. Instead of heading for Peel Park for the umpteenth time, at the end of January, City set out to locate, for the first time ever, the Dell. Southampton had won the Third Division South title at their first attempt in 1922 and existed solidly in Division Two ever since. The cramped, troglodyte Dell had a reputation as a cup graveyard for First Division clubs. There was almost no room between the touch-lines and supporters - a far cry from spacious Sincil Bank - and at one corner padding had been installed to prevent players crashing painfully into adjoining houses. The character of the ground and novelty of the opposition combined to make visiting the Saints one of the most evocative prospects of City's season but it transpired to be a thoroughly lustreless day. Freezing cold weather, with rain sweeping in off the Solent, kept the crowd below 8,000. Many home fans chose instead to use the "abundant opportunities for skating in the district" according to the Lincolnshire Echo. City found themselves on thin ice. Already without the injured Hall, Worthy, Smith, Buckley and Cartwright, they lost Pringle to an early knock. The ten men left were well-beaten 4-0 in what the Echo described as "one of the most uninteresting games in which Lincoln City have participated." There was a poignant post-script. Pringle never played for City again. Captain of the championship side eight months earlier, the tough-tackling Scot's Imps career ended on a freezing, grey afternoon in a half-empty ground nearer to France than Lincoln.

Lots of snow meant City played only twice in February. They returned to action with a 3-1 home defeat to Oldham on March 4, followed by a 5-0 defeat at Preston a week later. As the transfer deadline approached, the chilling possibility of relegation was still alive. City sat only four points ahead of bottom-placed Charlton, though it was highly congested down there with Chesterfield, West Ham, Grimsby, Oldham and Burnley in between.

On deadline day, Parkes swooped to purchase two half-backs. From Newcastle United, for £675, came George Mathison and, from Huddersfield, Bill Dodgin. Following the Preston drubbing, this duo went straight in the team for the visit of fellow strugglers Burnley to Sincil Bank. Parkes also gave a debut to Bernard Towler, a 20-year-old local boy who had been scoring freely for the reserves. Burnley arrived in poor form and could hardly believe their luck as they headed west again with a 4-1 victory. With two away games - at Spurs and West Ham - coming next, City needed to hit back hard.

It was not all bad news on the day of City's drubbing by Burnley. Allan Hall, on his way back from injury, scored a hat-trick in the reserves' 7-1 win at Newark. He returned to the first team for the daunting visit to White Hart Lane. A brand new half-back line was fielded with Dodgin and Mathison lining up either side of Con Moulson. Moulson had impressed consistently for the reserves but played just once for the first team, in a 3-2 defeat at Port Vale. Now the 26-year-old got his big chance. Parkes had made the big decision to trash City's title-winning half-back line. Pringle had already gone to Stockport. Buckley never re-established himself after the Swansea car-crash and would soon be at Rochdale. Young was tried in an unlikely forward role at Tottenham but, finding his left-half spot usurped by Mathison, drifted into coaching duties.

Spurs, locked in a duel with Stoke City for the Second Division title, were the division's highest scorers - 32 games having brought them 83 goals. Within 12 minutes they had added two more. Brain converted a sixth-minute chance then Mathison tripped Hunt in the box and Evans beat McPhail from the spot. Most of the huge crowd - 33,930 was the official figures but more than 40,000 were present - loved it but City hit back through Hall to make it 2-1 after 21 minutes. Seven minutes before half-time came controversy when Hunt appeared to punch the ball into the net but Walsall referee ER Westwood allowed the goal. Still, City battled. Hall was a constant threat and created the chance, eight minutes after the break, from which Horne reduced the deficit again. Spurs held on for a 3-2 win but it was a much more encouraging display and another followed, a point collected from a goalless draw at Upton Park. Into April it was desperately tight with half the division still not safe from the relegation spots.

Whereas Horace Henshall, like Calderhead and Strawson before him, favoured bowler hats, Parkes preferred a trilby. No doubt he felt like hurling it joyfully into the air when Fulham were beaten 3-0 at Lincoln. Three days later, Hall scored twice to earn City a surprise point from a 2-2 draw at Forest. The fixtures had fallen kindly, offering two home games at Easter. A goalless Good Friday draw with Bradford City, then 24 hours later a 2-0 win over Plymouth (Riley and Hall), extended City's unbeaten run to six games just when they needed it.

Another rearranged match - at Bradford City the following Wednesday - yielded another point, which put Lincoln virtually safe with three games to go. A visit to champions-elect Stoke provided the predictable beating, 5-2, so Lincoln approached their last home game - against Manchester United - still one point short of mathematical safety. A storming start, which brought goals in the first 18 minutes from Hall and Reed, settled nerves, though the match then turned into a real scrap. United were eventually subdued 3-2 in a match peppered with heavy challenges - one of which, on Mathison, triggered a 21-player brawl. City were safe.

For the final game, at Bradford Park Avenue, the injured Mathison was replaced by debutant Iorwerth Williams and City were stuffed 6-0. But not only had Lincoln finished above the bottom two - Charlton and Chesterfield occupying the death slots - but 18th out of 22, also above Burnley and West Ham. Optimistic studiers of the table observed that just six more points would have put City in the top eight. Jack Strawson, now aged 74, retired and living in London after quitting the Red Lion, could feel proud that the club that he helped to create had held its own among the relatively big boys. Now it was feet up for the summer break knowing that August would bring another attractive fixture list - enhanced by Bolton and Blackpool, relegated from Division One.

***

Summer of 1933. Late on June 16, a Friday night, licensees around Lincoln were about to close up. "Last orders please," they yelled in the Blue Anchor and the Struggler. "Ain't yer got no homes to go to ?" they bawled in the Lincoln Green and the Albion Tavern. "Time gentleman please," they hollered in the Portland Arms and the City Vaults. Out spilled Lincoln City fans, dwelling in small clusters on pavements to continue conversations fuelled by pints of cooking and stout.

"Parkes has got to buy," asserted one. "Smith's past his sell-by date. He's got to go," offered another, swinging a boot drunkenly at a passing cat. "Hall must stay," ventured a third. "Whatever else happens, Hall must stay." "Oh aye," his mates concurred with passion. Hall, the consensus insisted, must stay. What they could not know was that at that very moment, as a musty Friday night inched - just like every Friday night before it - towards Saturday morning, Hall was signing for Spurs.

Hall simply had to go, insisted the board. Promotion cost a packet. The rash of recruits during the previous summer set the club back more than £3,000 and sent them deep into overdraft. City had already been forced to borrow £1,000 from director Arthur Taylor and Spurs' payment of £2,350 for Hall was the only way of controlling the remaining debt. The supporters, of course, didn't see it that way. They just saw the departure of a man who, apart from being hugely popular off the field, had scored 65 goals in 72 league matches in the last two seasons. Goals without which City wouldn't have got up or stayed up. At a stroke, the sale of Hall stripped the fans of optimism. Now it would more than likely be a hell of a struggle to stay up.

The arrival of Tom Keetley from Notts County, despite a goal tally of 94 in 103 games for the Magpies, could not placate those fans. Inside-left Tom Feeny, also from Notts County, joined in exchange for Harold Riley. Left-back Jack Reddish joined from Spurs, where in six years he had played only six first-team games. Outside-left Douglas Rowe arrived from Luton but the loss of Hall was all-consuming for the supporters and it was with unease that almost 10,000 turned up for the first match of the season at home to Millwall.

Unease was well-founded. Millwall won 1-0 and City started badly with just two wins and six goals in 10 games. On October 7, Germany withdrew from the League of Nations, Gordon Richards rode Golden King to victory (his 247th winner of the season, breaking Fred Archer's record) and Con Moulson got injured in a 2-0 defeat at Blackpool which sent City into the bottom three. Moulson's calm authority had brought Ireland's international scouts sniffing round, and was expected to form a main plank of City's resistance in the ordeal ahead. Now he was ruled out for several months. Wilkinson also got injured and was replaced by Doug Rowe who not only deputised capably, scoring five goals in 11 games, but also had a brother who wrestled for Great Britain in the Olympics.

Parkes had the age-old Lincoln City problem with which to wrestle. He needed to recruit but had little dosh. In came inside-right Robert Iveson, another Spurs reserve. Trying to fill the void left by Hall, Parkes brought in Herbert Marklew, a miner, from Dinnington Main, near Sheffield. Marklew's two games in November only illustrated the gulf between colliery football and Division Two of the Football League. Another miner, Walter Hunt, got three games up front, scored no goals and was dispatched from the first team forever. Inside-right Vince Hodkinson, who had last played senior football for Blackpool six years earlier, was thrown in to the first team for a home game with Plymouth in October - and that was the beginning and end of his City career. Harry Pringle, now 33 and son-in-law of a director, was called upon for three more games. His best days were long-gone. It was messy, unsettled team-selection and left City in the relegation zone.

On December 1, the crisis deepening, City's board decided to gamble. They paid a club record £1,250 for 23-year-old striker Johnnie (Jock) Campbell from Leicester City. Ayrshire-born, Campbell had spent two and a half seasons with Leicester after moving down from Dalry Thistle. He had a goalscoring pedigree but he joined a struggling team. When Brentford paid their first visit to Sincil Bank, on December 16, and won 2-0, City were dumped on the bottom of the table.

A week later, Campbell's first goal for Lincoln helped pull off a shock 2-1 win at just-relegated Bolton. Hopes that a corner had been turned rose with a 1-0 Christmas Day victory over Port Vale but misfortune returned five days later when the steady McPhail dislocated an elbow in the 27th minute of a match at Millwall. Goalless at the time, the score ended 4-1 to the Lions as Feeny deputised in goal. McPhail missed the next 10 games, mostly due to the injury but partly to a 14-day ban for fighting at Port Vale.

City opened 1934 with a crunch game at Sincil Bank. Bottom of the table, their first visitors of the year were Manchester United, next to bottom, four points away. It was a match Lincoln could not afford to lose. United took the lead through Brown after two minutes but Chick Read levelled for City on the half-hour. Lincoln played their best football of the season after half-time with Whyte putting them ahead on the hour and Campbell, Wilkinson and Read adding further goals in the last 10 minutes. It was a tremendous boost and when City demolished Fulham 5-0 in their next home game (Whyte 2, Campbell, Horne, Read), perhaps the sequence of good results necessary to climb the table was underway. Not so. After the Fulham fireworks came the dampest of damp squibs with a run of six defeats in seven matches which kept the Imps shackled firmly to the bottom. With their away form awful, four away matches in five games looked ominous. So it proved. They lost them all - at Hull (2-0), Southampton (3-1), Bradford City (3-0) and Plymouth (3-0). Over in the north-west, former Imps defender Levy Thorpe, a stalwart of the 1920s, still aged only 43, was reported to be "dangerously ill" and in "straitened circumstances." It was a condition matched by City.

Nottingham Forest, themselves far from free of relegation worries, hammered City 6-2 on March 17 to leave Lincoln five points adrift. Next visitors to Sincil Bank were Grimsby, whose supporters arrived ready to gloat at length over the League table. Grimsby were eight points clear at the top and almost certain to be in Division One next season. City held their rivals 3-3 but it looked certain to be the clubs' last meeting for a long time. A crowd figure of just 8,723, many from Grimsby, suggested that City's fans were resigned to the drop.

On Easter Monday, Lincoln lost 1-0 at Swansea to a penalty converted in the fifth minute by left-back Wilf Milne. In the 501st game of his career it was Milne's first goal and he celebrated long and loud that night - callously, because his goal virtually sealed Lincoln's relegation. On the way to their next match, at Oldham, City's team bus passed two funeral corteges. A 3-0 defeat meant their reinterment in the Third Division North was a certainty. Lincoln's last act as a Second Division club was to draw 2-2 at home to Bolton, denying Wanderers the win that would have regained their Division One status.

The point took City's final tally to 26 from 42 games - seven points behind also-relegated Millwall and eight behind Manchester United on the safety line. A home record of won seven, drew seven and lost seven required serious reinforcement by points banked away from home. But City collected just five out of a possible 42 on their travels.

With the depression of relegation and the tightening of recession - City's annual report revealed a loss of £1,898 12s 5d - came recrimination. The AGM was stormy with the directors lambasted for not spending enough cash on players following promotion. That was harsh considering the gamble the board had taken in investing £3,000 in players to achieve promotion. The sale of Hall was bitterly criticised. He alone would surely have scored enough goals to rescue City. Ironically, Hall, too, had endured a wretched campaign. He played just twice for Spurs, made no impression at White Hart Lane and had already been offloaded to Blackpool.

Two seasons in Division Two culminated in rough treatment for the board. Great joy followed, a year later, by great blame. That's football. "We ventured and lost," said Simpson. "But I think I would sooner do that than not venture at all."

9.
Down among the dead men

ARSENAL lifted the Football League championship at the end of the 1933/4 season. It was their second successive title, their third in four seasons and their domination of English football, moulded by the legendary Herbert Chapman, was underway.

The Gunners - the Team of the Thirties - took the title by three points from Huddersfield who, under Chapman, had been the Team of the Twenties. Tottenham, attracting huge audiences, finished third. In the FA Cup final, Manchester City, including Frank Swift and Matt Busby, beat Portsmouth 2-1 in front of 100,000 people at Wembley. Manchester City's FA Cup quarter-final against Stoke City had been attended by 84,569 at Maine Road. In April, a packed national stadium could have been filled twice over for the England v Scotland clash. England won 3-0 with goals from Brook, Bastin and Bowers.

Football had become huge before the First World War and increased momentum still further after the 1915-1919 hiatus. This sport was no passing phase. It gripped the nation and influenced millions of daily lives. Every decade, it grew. With depression, unemployment and the General Strike ravaging the country, families urgently sought and needed a glimpse of glory, however reflected it may be. The 1930s inscribed true legends into football history. Cliff Bastin. Stanley Matthews. Alex James. Pongo Waring. Ted Drake. Stan Cullis. David Jack. Great figures who towered over a sport watched by legions of enthusiasts. Turnstiles clicked merrily. For the big clubs of English football, these were glory days and they feasted upon a banquet of popularity, fame, self-confidence and hard capital but Lincoln City were back down among the dead men.

As Ted Simpson acknowledged, Lincoln had gambled and lost. Two seasons in Division Two cost the board £4,500 and, a month after relegation, the football club's bank loan was increased to £6,000. No glory here. Just cost-cutting. Parkes got a vote of confidence from the board but his wages were reduced to £8 per week. The squad was pared down. After 12 years at Sincil Bank, Harry Pringle joined Grantham Town as player/manager. Mathison was sold to Gateshead for £100 and several fringe players were freed.

City's reduction to the Third Division North ranks was starkly illustrated by their opening-day fixture. Rochdale. But they started buoyantly and the 3-0 win was the first of four successive victories including a 4-3 triumph on City's first visit to Field Mill, Mansfield Town having now stepped up from the Midland League. The brisk start lifted Lincoln straight to the top but form was not maintained. With the Northern Section still offering only one promotion place, clubs didn't have to sink far down the table to be out of the running. City lodged some impressive displays - home wins over Gateshead (5-1), Walsall (5-1) and Barrow (6-0) - and Campbell, Wilkinson and Iveson troubled most defences. But big wins were interwoven with scrappy failures.

Shorn of promotion hope, the fans turned their backs. Attendances fell below 3,000 and the financial vultures began to circle low again. The new Third Division North Cup failed to excite. City went out in the first round to Walsall after a replay, the two games watched by a total of 2,588 people. Yet again, the board pleaded with the fans to direct their toes toward the Bank but hardly encouraged them by selling Wilkinson to First Division title-chasers Sunderland. That provoked groans which increased when, a month later, Iveson was flogged to Wolves for £2,500. On the day that the classy Iveson made his debut for Wolves he was replaced in the Imps' team at Chesterfield by Sydney Bates, a lumbering amateur with only two reserve games as a trialist behind him. Chesterfield won 3-1. Bates never scored for Lincoln.

City finished fourth after a strong finish brought 20 points from 12 games. The resurgence came far too late to form a championship challenge and Parkes missed several games to pursue scouting missions. Only the effervescent Campbell, top scorer with 17 goals, illuminated a grey season.

Parkes had to substantially rebuild but the club was skint. Eight players were freed and two - John Reddish and Joe McAteer - transfer-listed. Incomers consisted mostly of junior and local players but the City boss did pull one plum out of the rich, dark, figgy pudding that is the annual farrago of freed players. Tranmere Rovers surprisingly released Billy Meacock, a strong centre-half reportedly being watched by First Division clubs. Parkes nipped in to convince him to join Lincoln.

It was an isolated scoop. Elsewhere, City struggled to attract players and several they released early in the summer were re-engaged. Exciting possibilities arose when Allan Hall fetched up in Lincoln and said he would like to return to Sincil Bank. After struggling at Spurs, Hall had moved on to Blackpool but it was the Tangerines' demand of a lofty transfer fee that blocked the striker's return to Lincoln. Instead, still aged only 27, he dropped down into the Midland League and signed for Gainsborough from whom Blackpool accepted a much smaller fee.

The new season opened with City striking a rich vein of home form. A 6-0 opening-day thrashing of Accrington augured well. Campbell then notched a hat-trick as Crewe were dispatched 6-2. Next came a sweet day for skipper Alf Horne. His 119th League appearance for City brought his first hat-trick, all three from the penalty spot in a 3-0 win over Stockport. Briefly, City were top but again consistency proved elusive. Only one victory in seven matches between the end of October and Christmas left them, like the man who fell into the sewer, simply going through the motions.

In January came an exotic diversion; the Imps' first trip abroad. They accepted a guarantee of 1,800 Dutch guilders (£200) to play a Dutch National B side in Rotterdam. In front of 6,000 people, City lost 4-2. A more sombre occasion followed later that month. At 11.55pm on January 20, 1936, King George VI rolled a seven. Oldham were the next visitors to Sincil Bank and the teams, wearing black armbands, marched slowly onto the pitch in a double line while a band played the funeral march. The crowd sang a verse from the King's favourite hymn (Peace Perfect Peace) and as the last words faded, total silence descended for one minute. Every head was bowed. The first verse of the national anthem followed before, as a final tribute, Bernard Towler scored twice in a 2-1 win for City.

A similarly funereal air was to be found at City board meetings with the Imps losing around £90 per week. The club had already taken out a second mortgage for £2,000 and the directors trod the footsteps of several of their predecessors, warning of dire consequences unless more spectators watched matches. "Lincoln sportsmen must rally round, otherwise extinction of one of Second Division founder members" (SIC) boomed the front page headline in the Echo. "Gallant 4,000 cannot save Lincoln City by their own efforts," advised the sub-heading. But the denizens of Lincoln had heard it all before and attendances stayed low.

Again, City finished fourth but had been reconciled since Christmas to a further stretch in the Third North. Within days of the season's end, Mansfield Town slipped a three-year contract under Parkes' hooter and he liked what he read. He departed with a valedictory swipe at the stayaway Imps' fans. "One thing stands out," he said. "When we played Wrexham at Lincoln in October, we were at the top of the Northern Section and we had a gate of only 5,000 with takings of £298 on a fine day."

So the architect of City's great escape into Division Two departed....well, at least he ceased to be manager. Strangely, although he took over as Mansfield boss straightaway, Parkes continued to operate from his Lincoln office for another three weeks. He even set up his first signing for the Stags, winger John Roy from Norwich, on the Sincil Bank telephone.

Farce surrounded the appointment of Parkes' successor. A short-list of four was drawn up and interviewed by the board. On June 17, City announced that former England, Newcastle United and Manchester United defender Charlie Spencer, current manager of Wigan Athletic, was the new man. He would start at Sincil Bank on Monday June 22. But wait ! The Imps had jumped the gun. On June

19, Wigan announced they were refusing to release Spencer from the five-year contract he had recently signed. Sheepishly, the City board reconsidered the three other candidates and plumped for Joe McClelland.

McClelland, 52, was a big man with a gruff, honest manner and much experience of working below football's poverty line. Halifax was where Joseph Bentley McClelland was born, had lived most of his life and gathered his football knowhow. A former secretary of Halifax and District Football Association, he was deeply involved in the formation of Halifax Town FC whom he managed from 1911 to 1930. He switched to Sheffield Wednesday, where he was assistant manager for four years until ill-health forced him to quit. Now, two years later, he felt fit enough to take over City and enthusiastic enough to accept wages of £6 per week - 25% less than Parkes. McClelland's business record - under him Halifax showed a £20,000 profit on players transactions - obviously appealed to the City board.

The club had recorded a year-on-year loss of £2,442 and that meant only one thing: selling players. They hung on to Moulson, capped during the summer for the Irish Free State against Hungary and Luxembourg, and star striker Campbell. But the influential Watson brothers, William and Arthur, were sold to Chesterfield. McClelland browsed through his bulging contacts-book and in came left-back Fred Corbett (from Manchester City), right-back Jack Hartsholme (Stoke City), inside-left Richard Deacon (Northampton), left-winger William Dowall (Bury), outside-right John Callender (Ashington), and striker Albert Taylor (Bristol Rovers).

There was good news for boozers. During the summer, the Lincoln Imp Social Club opened in the gymnasium beneath the South Park Stand so for the first time in many years alcohol could be sold on the ground. Most supporters were delighted but one shareholder railed against the development. He recalled days, early in the century, when there were licensed premises attached to Sincil Bank and, shockingly, "men used to spend the whole game in them." If they adopted that decadent approach from now on, at least they would be putting cash into the club's till.

A few celebratory post-match pints were justified as McClelland immediately shaped an ordinary squad into a team capable of challenging for promotion. Four debutants - Corbett, Deacon, Dowall and Callender - lined up for the opening match at Accrington and Callender scored twice in a 2-1 win. Moulson was soon cashed in. He joined Notts County for £2,000 just nine games into the season, but four wins in the first five games - and especially impressive home form - convinced the fans that McClelland's Imps could be worth watching. Wily, he was, but also revolutionary. Talking tactics in training, Mac unveiled a magnetic screen and discs to usurp the traditional chalk and blackboard. Space age.

Campbell scored hat-tricks in 4-1 home wins over Southport and Halifax then all five in a 5-3 win over Rochdale at Sincil Bank. Wrexham were beaten 6-2 with the veteran Horne chipping in with two goals. Meacock was a mountain in defence and Callender and Deacon soon became favourites. McPhail's star was waning though. The goalkeeper, now in his sixth season at the Bank, was slowing and had a bad day when City visited Chester who were five points clear at the top. Chester won 7-3.

City remained in the top three and eight successive victories, each including at least one Campbell goal, in the New Year thrust them to the forefront of the title-hunt. McClelland told supporters: "We want promotion. Do you ?" and urged them to get to matches and bring a friend. To inspire the players he pinned a notice to the dressing room wall pledging that "if you are successful in gaining promotion the whole of the first team players and as many others as possible will be retained."

These were significant times in British history. Edward VII abdicated and Hitler's increasing audacity was alarming more and better-informed people. Anti-aircraft searchlights were installed in Lincoln. City just kept on winning. A 4-3 win, including another Campbell hat-trick, over Darlington on February 6, left them third in the table, three points behind Chester and two behind Stockport. A month later, Chester visited Sincil Bank and the crowd figure at last climbed back into five figures. 11,478 saw City's 3-0 win with Campbell scoring one and Towler, now enjoying his best spell after several years on the periphery, the other two. The next home game, a 1-0 win over Port Vale, attracted more than 13,000.

Defeat at Sincil Bank sent Chester's promotion bid into nosedive, leaving a two-way sprint between Stockport and Lincoln. City kept their nerve in style with a 6-0 home win over Barrow. Next came a visit to Gateshead and the Imps cruised to a 5-0 victory, including yet another Campbell hat-trick.

With two matches left, City were top. The penultimate game sent them to Hartlepools whose home record was inferior only to Stockport and Lincoln. City were beaten 3-1 to slip to second going into the last match of the season. That last match ? Stockport v Lincoln at Edgeley Park. Victory would have sent the Imps back up but in front of a record crowd of 26,135 they were beaten 2-0 in controversial fashion. Both goals came in the space of five second-half minutes, the first when McPhail appeared to be bundled into the net, the second from a dodgy penalty. It was a cruel way to miss out but the runners-up spot exceeded expectations and McClelland's reward was a £25 bonus and a new three-year contract. He showed his commitment by moving to Lincoln from his Sheffield home of many years.

Again McClelland had little cash to spend but, in Halifax, they teach you a thing or two about making silk purses out of sows' ears. In search of players, "Supermac" travelled more than 1,000 miles in 10 days. In from Burnley came George Nevin, a left-back who, in an earlier spell with Newcastle United, had once been hit in the neck by an orange thrown by a West Ham supporter at Upton Park. Echoes of the club's earliest days returned with the recruit of two Scots - Jock Kerr from Clyde, as cover for Campbell, and inside forward James Wylie from Partick Thistle. Wylie instantly offended one or two patriots by describing English football as "kick and rush" compared to the superior Scottish game. He never made Lincoln's first team. Most interestingly, McClelland signed outside-left Joe Clare from Norwich City. Clare was a clever, imaginative winger with an eye for goal and a diverse career history which included spells at Manchester City, Wigan Borough, Accrington Stanley, Arsenal and Margate.

As a flying winger, Clare took a keen interest in the summer's main topic of football debate. FA president W Pickford called for sliding tackles to be abolished. Before Clare could get too excited, a wave of opposition from traditionalists swept the idea away. Former Imps left-back Fred Ward - a master of the sliding tackle genre - having moved on to run the Golden Eagle in Lincoln, described the notion as "piffle." One innovation would be in place for the new season though - arcs on the edge of each penalty area.

As McClelland's second season - the 1937/8 term - approached, the ever-present lobbying for support got more proactive. Ads were placed in newspapers. A sinister-looking figure pointed menacingly at readers and accused: "As a townsman it is your duty to support a town's institutions." Then, in capital letters, "GOING TO THE MATCH ?" Plenty got the message judging by healthy season-ticket sales at 50 shillings each. Unemployment in Lincoln had dropped below 3,000, a fall of 5,000 in four years, so there was a bit more money about. McClelland, positive and skilful with journalists, expressed confidence about building a challenge for promotion. He also had a dig at team-selection by committee. "The ideal selection committee," he confided gruffly, hitching his trousers up round his ample frame, "consists of two members, one of whom is unable to attend the meetings."

City started brightly. Clare was an instant hit, creating four of the goals (Campbell scored four) in a 7-1 win over Wrexham. In the next two home games Barrow were beaten 5-0 and New Brighton 4-1. While Clare and Campbell sparkled up front, Meacock motored around meatily and knowingly at the back alongside the veteran Whyte. A firm favourite too was Lincoln-born Billy Bean, now established at right-half after several seasons developing in the reserves.

In September, City travelled to Gateshead where, five months earlier they played in front of 1,224 people. This time, with the clubs first and second in the table, the gates were shut at half-time on a crowd of 20,792. Campbell scored City's goal in a 1-1 draw. The gentleman Scot scored twice in a handsome 4-1 win at Darlington when former Imps hero Billy Dinsdale, now back living in Darlington, popped into the away dressing room for a post-match chat.

City topped the division after a gritty 1-0 win at Rochdale at the start of November. In a match high on muscle and low on finesse, Callender's 15th minute goal was protected from a 'Dale onslaught by resolute defence led as always by Meacock, who ended the afternoon in Rochdale Infirmary with facial wounds. The resistance looked in vain when, in the 90th minute Hartshorne was penalised for handball in the box. Ex-Imp Walter Hunt struck the penalty well but McPhail saved brilliantly low to his left.

All seemed set fair for a sustained promotion drive but the wheels started to fall off on a hostile afternoon at York City in early December. In blizzard conditions and near darkness, City were beaten 3-1 and finished the match with eight players. Towler and Niven had already hobbled off by the 87th minute when Corbett got into a fight and was carried, semi-conscious, to the dressing room. Only there, after the match, did City learn that Corbett had been sent, as well as carried, off. A one-match suspension and £5 fine followed. More ill-fortune accompanied the FA Cup. In a second-round tie at Harry Parkes' Mansfield, City perished 2-1 to a cruel 87th-minute winner when McPhail's punch-out struck Stags player Crawshaw on the head and rebounded into the net. In January, City fitted in another flit to Holland, this time to play the full Dutch national side at the Sparta Club, Rotterdam. Lincoln were outclassed 5-0 and whether they needed the distraction in the middle of a promotion quest was disputable

Injuries struck key players. Clare played only three matches out of 12. Skipper Henry Raw played three games in three months. Hartshorne, an anchor at right-back, fractured his ankle at Rotherham on March 12 and was ruled out for the season. Most crucially, a series of niggling problems sidelined Campbell for all but three matches after January 1.

Still, by the end of March, Lincoln were one of seven clubs separated by two points at the top of the division. Four defeats in five games punctured the promotion bid and some lack-lustre displays prompted accusations from fans about some players' Friday night activities. First-teamers were allegedly spotted at dances on the eves of big games. The club publicly defended the players but several were disciplined. Out of the promotion picture, most attention on the last day of the season focused, not on Barrow where City lost 4-1, but Sincil Bank where Lincoln reserves beat Peterborough 4-1. In goal for Posh was Will Kendall. It was his last appearance as a professional, more than 15 years after his debut on the same ground for City against a Halifax side managed by none other than Joe McClelland. Small world.

The old allegations, that City did not really want promotion, were dusted down, polished up and brought out. Simpson described them as the "utterest rot" but a final placing of seventh was disappointing. It was of limited consolation for the football club to have a trawler named in its honour by Consolidated Fisheries of Grimsby.

Soon after the season Meacock was sold to Birmingham city for £3,000, a huge profit, and Callender, having scored 26 goals in two seasons, left for Port Vale. Now McClelland was less upbeat about prospects. "I'm not one of those super-optimists who think we are going to win the League, the Cup, Grand National, Derby and Ryder Cup," he boomed and was right on all five counts. Another influx of unknown Scottish imports prompted rumours that the Imp on City's badge was to be replaced by a thistle.

Just two points were collected from the first eight games of the 1938/9 season but there was an unreal, distracted atmosphere as Europe teetered on the brink of war. In September, a report of City's 0-0 draw with New Brighton shared a stop-press column with details of Hitler's key speech at Nuremburg. The season lengthened amid increasing fear that another war was inevitable. Trenches were dug in Lincoln's south and west commons

Still as long as the League operated, Ted Simpson expected his players to get stuck in and after a 6-0 walloping at Crewe, which dumped Lincoln bottom of the table in late September, he called a meeting of management and players and kicked ass. The board did their bit by finding a "substantial" sum to buy striker Walter Ponting from Chesterfield. He made his debut, replacing the fading Campbell, in an 8-3 win over Wrexham and followed that with a hat-trick in an 8-1 FA Cup drubbing of FA Amateur Cup holders Bromley. Having started the season with 17 goals in 14 games, City bagged 26 in five. But it was an oasis of excitement in a charmless season. The FA Cup trail ended 4-0 at First Division Portsmouth and for the first time in 13 years City fans had to inspect the bottom half of the Third Division North to find their team.

April 1, 1939, brought the briefest of cameos in a City shirt from goalkeeper Jack Thacker. McPhail had flu so Thacker - a youngster from Coventry - was pitched in for his Imps debut at Rochdale. Despite Lincoln's 4-0 defeat he did well and was selected for the next game at home to Rotherham. But he missed his train connection and never played for City again.

The Imps limped in 17th. A victim of the poor season was Campbell whose benefit, against Derby in May, drew only 3,486 people. A poor reward for a player who scored 104 goals in 184 games for Lincoln. He was released along with another two of the biggest names in City's inter-war history: George Whyte (299 games) and Dan McPhail (309 games). City's retain list was their shortest so far, just 11 players. Also on his way was Simpson who, citing business commitments, resigned as chairman after 10 years. He was replaced by former club treasurer George Wright, gas engineer and manager of Lincoln Corporation and a former Sheriff of Lincoln.

During the summer, 30 tons of topsoil were laid on Sincil Bank. City signed Ernest Hoyland, Rex Clayton and Sydney Broome from West Brom, Bristol City and Burnley respectively and Gracie Fields' decree nisi came through. At the start of the 1939/40 season City drew with Hull, lost to Darlington and beat Gateshead before, at 11am on Sunday September 3, war was declared. This time the Football League was suspended immediately, as was the Lincoln Billiards and Snooker League.

Into abeyance, again, went the Football League. For seven years City competed in makeshift regional competitions: The North Regional League, The Football League North Championship, the Football League War Cup North and the devastatingly appropriately-named War Cup.

Sincil Bank remained busy. As soon as war broke out, the South Park Stand and rooms below were requisitioned by the Air Raids Precaution service (ARP). The players' recreation room lost its snooker and table-tennis tables and became a "decontamination, clothing and reception room." Seats in the stand above were covered with 50 tons of sand to protect against incendiary bombs. The ARP later also took over the St Andrew's Stand in which Morrison Shelters were stored.

Again, professional contracts for players were scrapped and City's line-ups leaned heavily on guests. With several Royal Air Forces bases nearby, some of these guests - including George Robledo, Neil Franklin, Peter Doherty and Tommy Powell - offered high levels of fitness and ability and thrived in professional football after the war. While, on the field, the Imps again, like another man in another sewer, went through the motions, there was no loosening of the pressure on the club's ever-taut finances. At the outbreak of war, City were carrying substantial loans and the club was soon pursued hard by the bank to discharge those debts in the national interests. With the Imps' income almost non-existent there was as much chance of the loans being repaid as of Hermann Goering parachuting into Sincil Bank, peeling the swastikas off his uniform, yelling: "An mein head, son" and asking for a trial as a centre-forward, so in July 1941 the bank accepted payment of the interest only. With that burden lifted, and players employed only on a part-time basis, the football club managed to tick over. It even made a small profit in four of the seven seasons of Football League limbo.

The amorphous nature of English football during the war is illustrated by City's finishing positions. Still under the loyal McClelland, aided by assistant secretary George Knott, in the various competitions (sometimes two per season)

Lincoln finished 7th out of 11, 9th out of 36, 2nd out of 38, 19th out of 51, 11th out of 48, 36th out of 54, 15th out of 50, 53rd out of 56, 51st out of 54 and 46th out of 60. Crowds were small as local opposition - Grimsby six times in a season for example - became over-familiar and City's performances in the war's later years deteriorated because their quality guest players from the RAF were unavailable, bombing Germany.

Matches were sometimes abandoned when air-raid sirens sent players and spectators scurrying for cover. When the sirens often turned out to be false alarms Lincoln City, like many clubs, posted "spotters" on lofty perches who would signal 'play on' unless aircraft actually appeared on the horizon. Spotters were soon banned by the Ministry of Home Security.

In September 1945 a small quantity of South African oranges arrived in Lincoln's High Street shops. They were a portent of easing shortages and imminent peace. English football also took its first steps back to normality. With a view to restarting properly, with exactly the structure of 1939, in the autumn of 1946, single-season regional leagues were organised for 1945/6. City competed in the Division Three North (East) and finished ninth out of 10. The FA Cup resumed on an experimental two-leg basis and after accounting for Yorkshire Amateurs 5-2 on aggregate, Lincoln lost 4-2 (2-1 in each leg) to Rotherham. As peace resumed, there was a collective girding of loins throughout the nation as its population prepared to throw themselves back into much-cherished routines which had been stolen by the war. Football's boom-time lay ahead. There was a clamour to join the Football League with applications from Chelmsford City, Colchester, Gillingham, Hyde, Merthyr, North Shields, Scunthorpe & Lindsey, Shrewsbury, South Liverpool, Workington, Wellington Town, Wigan Athletic, Worcester City and Yeovil. But the League stuck by its pledge to resume with exactly the fixture list that had been aborted seven years earlier. The Imps got ready to start all over again at Hull. Compared to the austerity, uncertainty, pain and grief of war, even the Third Division North seemed like a groovy institution.

10.
Bill Anderson, the G-force
and a clandestine meeting
on Grantham railway station at midnight

JANUARY 12, 1913, a dark, wintry Sunday, passed unmemorably for Lincoln City supporters. The Imps' scheduled Division Two fixture at Leicester Fosse the previous day had been postponed due to snow. Nothing occurred. It was a blank weekend buried deep in the middle of a middle-of-the-table season. Not much reason then for City fans to dwell on January 12, 1913.

At least, that's what they thought at the time. But subsequent generations of Imps supporters were to look back on that date, smile nostalgically, pay homage and feel mellow deep inside. For on that day Bill Anderson was born.

Yes, there in the quiet village of High Westwood, tucked into the Durham countryside between Newcastle and Consett, William Anderson first peeped from the womb. Outside, England's north-eastern corner shivered as flurries of snow rampaged down from the Arctic Circle. Few people ventured out in the village. Those that did buried their fists deep into pockets in search of warmth. "It's reet parky mon," said passers-by. "It's a boy," Mrs Anderson was told.

As that boy grew, his talent at football was soon apparent. After representing his school, he moved on to Medomsley Juniors, a junior club of high repute based in the next village, two miles to the south. Young Anderson, a left-back, made impressive progress through youth and county football before turning professional with Nottingham Forest. He moved to Sheffield United then Barnsley before his playing career was cruelly truncated, aged just 22, by a fractured ankle sustained playing for Barnsley against Forest.

His agile brain was unimpaired though. Anderson returned to the north-east to work for shipbuilders Vickers-Armstrong and also became a fully qualified masseur and surgical chiropodist. He retained a close interest in football, scouting and spectating, and after the Second World War was ready to return full-time to the industry. Lincoln, looking for a trainer and assistant to the ageing McClelland, were alert enough to appoint Anderson in August 1945. An Imps behemoth was born.

To McClelland and Anderson fell the task of orchestrating City's return to the Football League. In 1939, players' contracts were frozen, not cancelled, so those still around six years later had the remainder of their deals honoured irrespective of fitness. The experimental 1945/6 season was unwieldy with City using more than 50 players, including seven goalkeepers. Clearly the management team had to look forward and only four pre-war players - Billy Bean, Jack Hardy, Geoff Marlow and Alec Thompson - were offered new contracts.

McClelland's most significant move was, on Anderson's advice, to tempt veteran centre-half Tom Johnson out of retirement. Johnson, a former team-mate of Anderson at Sheffield United, joined Lincoln only two months before his 35th birthday but brought enormous presence and self-belief to the side. For 17 seasons he had been the defensive lynch-pin at Bramall Lane and had captained the Blades in an FA Cup semi-final. Johnson's career history invited respect and his forceful personality demanded it.

Another former Blade recruited was left-half George Nelson, who owed his survival of wartime service to a football injury. Serving with the Navy, Nelson represented his submarine at football but got injured while stationed at Alexandria. When the submarine left port next day he was kept ashore for treatment. The craft was sunk with the loss of all hands. Fortune appeared to shine on City players in wartime activity. None were reported killed or seriously wounded.

Like most clubs in the Third Division North, City chose to keep their players part-time. Commitment to full-time wages represented a gamble with post-war hardships biting - supporters were even asked for spare clothing coupons to help kit out the team. The approaching season was an unknown quantity. Clubs could only guess at their rivals' strength after such a prolonged hiatus. Lincoln's team included a nucleus of familiar faces. Johnson, defender George Stillyards and midfielder Jimmy Grummett had guested during the war years, while Bean, Hardy, Marlow and Thompson were known from pre-war. But were these guys still good enough and fit enough?

As City's players took a ferry across the river Humber towards their opening fixture at Hull, thunder and lightning crackled above. An exuberant crowd of 25,586 was present for the first League match at the brand new Boothferry Park stadium. The souvenir programme (price 6d) contained a message of peace for spectators. "Be as vociferous and fully partisan as you like in encouraging your own team," fans were urged, "but if an opposing player does something with which you are not in entire agreement, do not beseech your own men to 'kick him in the teeth.'" No teeth were kicked during a drab 0-0 draw. The Imps' first home game - a 2-0 win over Darlington - was historic. It was the first Sincil Bank fixture since 1895 - that very first match against Gainsborough - that George Knott had not checked in the takings after the game.

Takings were high as City's crowds averaged around 9,000 despite erratic form. Supporters urged the board to spend and, in October, the squad was enhanced by centre-forward Jimmy Hutchinson who had impressed as a guest player in 1945. His £750 transfer from Bournemouth was sealed in almost total secrecy. Watched only by sleepy porters and hooting owls, Hutchinson and McClelland completed the deal during a midnight tryst on Grantham railway station.

Lincoln hovered around mid-table but enjoyed an interesting FA Cup run. They won 4-2 at Stockton, of the North Eastern League, to earn a home tie with Wrexham. After a 1-1 draw at Sincil Bank and a 3-3 draw at the Racecourse the clubs could not agree on a venue for the second replay - two days before Christmas. City wanted it in Sheffield. Wrexham preferred Villa Park. Lincoln director Charlie Applewhite pulled a fistful of change out of his pocket and Wrexham called heads, seven of which came down, to nine tails. Neither Sheffield United or Wednesday, however, would make their ground available at short notice. Neither would Leicester, Derby, Chesterfield or either Nottingham club before finally Manchester City agreed. This was a noble gesture because Maine Road was already hosting City and Manchester United's home games with Old Trafford still under repair from bomb damage. On a pitch of ankle-deep mud, the Imps battled to a 2-1 win with 17-year-old Grantham-born goalkeeper Don Footit making a heroic debut in goal. A lucrative third round visit from Nottingham Forest drew more than 17,000 to the Bank to see Forest win 1-0.

Anderson's influence was growing rapidly and a contact in the north-east unearthed Robert Owen. A left-half from Murton Colliery Welfare, Owen's constructive distribution from the back complemented Johnson's 'they-shall-not-pass' belligerence. With City still in mid-table, February sent the season into deep freeze. The Imps played one match in eight weeks as blizzards swept the country. Snow caused the roof of Grantham railway station, where Joe had so recently met Jimmy, to collapse. At Stamford Bridge, Chelsea's First Division match with Blackpool was halted when Blackpool winger Munro could not be located. He was found struggling in a six-feet-deep bank of snow behind a goal-line and it took two Chelsea players and a member of the St John's Ambulance Brigade to rescue him.

After the snow came floods. As Sincil Drain rose like the foaming Bosphorous, milk was delivered by boat to houses along Sincil Bank, one of whose residents, Mrs B Jackson aged 93, asserted with authority that these were the worst floods in Lincoln since 1877. When the weather finally relented, City entered May with nine matches still to play. They led 2-0 at Accrington but managed to lose 8-4. Seventeen-year-old striker Derek Dooley, having top-scored for the reserves, played two games and scored in both - against Wrexham and Barrow. After a 3-0 defeat at Bradford City on June 14, the Imps finally finished an uninspiring 12th.

In July, McClelland "moved upstairs." Genial Joe had held the club together during the war - the debt City owed him was immense - but was now 63. Observing the respect the new man had so quickly won from the players, McClelland was happy to cede power. Anderson became manager, his role encompassing team selection, tactics and transfer negotiations though chairman George Wright and his directors still had ultimate veto.

It was Wright and McClelland who had to deal with a dispute early in the summer when almost all City's players, advised by the Players' Union, returned their contracts unsigned. 'Don't accept the bare minimum,' was the union's advice and it bore fruit. Improved terms of £4 per week in the summer, £6 in the winter, were accepted. Dooley departed though. He switched to Sheffield Wednesday, citing barracking from supporters as the reason.

The squad clearly needed strengthening. Footit was lost to National Service so in came goalkeeper George Moulson from Grimsby. Younger brother of former City defender Cornelius, George had guested regularly for City during the war. In too came Yorkshire-born right-winger Jimmy McCormick from Fulham and inside-left Ken Walshaw who cost a four-figure fee from First Division side Sunderland. That was a sizeable sum for a part-time player but City were one of few clubs to remain part-time. Most clubs, furnished with fat receipts from record crowds during the first post-war season, took on full-time players. Lincoln resisted the trend despite recording a year-on-year profit of £2,755, comfortably their best ever from a Third Division North season.

Anderson's first season in full control started with a 3-2 home defeat to Hull, then got better and better. City lost only two of the next 18 games. Johnson and Owen formed a formidable central defence while George Stillyards excelled in a new right-back role, opposite the redoubtable Billy Bean at left-back. McCormick, Hutchinson and experienced Nottinghamshire-born pair Geoff Marlow and Harry Parr had more than enough ideas to trouble Third Division North defences but Anderson was still searching for the missing link; an out and out goalscorer. City fans were delighted to hear the boss, faced with speculation about players leaving, state: "We are not selling. We are in the market for players ourselves."

Attendances hit five-figures and a record 6,868 even turned up for a reserve game at Sincil Bank against Shrewsbury. There was an unfortunate blip in the FA Cup, a 2-0 home defeat to non-league Workington Town, but a 3-1 home victory over Rotherham took City top of the Third Division North at the start of December.

Next came the striker swoop. Anderson signed Benny Lester - the deal was struck on Sheffield railway station - from Hull. The move indicated a real ambition for promotion. Lester was hot property, having scored 18 goals in 27 League games for the Tigers. A settled Lincoln team, with Lester up front, Hutchinson surging into the box, McCormick and Marlow menacing from the flanks and Johnson and

Where it all started: the Monson Arms, on Lincoln's High Street, where Lincoln City's founding fathers gathered.

DAWBER & CO.'S
CELEBRATED ⬤ LINCOLN ALES.
THE OCTOBER BREWINGS OF THEIR
EAST INDIA PALE ALE
AND OTHER BEERS, ARE NOW BEING DELIVERED
IN SPLENDID CONDITION, FROM 1s. PER GAL.

These Ales now enjoy the highest Clerical, Professional, Hotel, and Public patronage, & are pronounced the purest & best extant.

The Brewery, Lincoln, 1861.

Cornering the Lincoln ale market: brewer Robert Dawber was City's most important early benefactor.

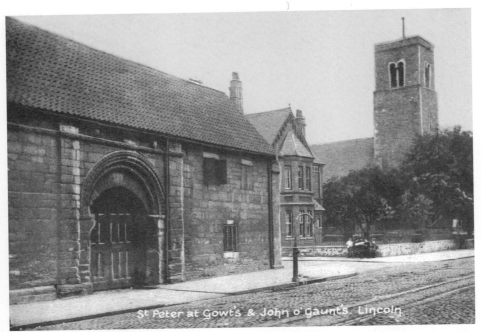

The archway still stands: through this historic entrance passed players and spectators to the early games at John O'Gaunts. The football field is long gone but the archway remains on the corner of High Street and Sibthorp Street.

Lincoln City's side lined up at the John O'Gaunts ground. Back row: Bailey (trainer), Buxton, Bennett, Neill, Mettam. Front row: Shaw, Smallman, Walker, Irving, Raby, Moore, Bates.

The City squad, 1904/05. Manager David Calderhead (second from left at back) had, three years earlier, steered Lincoln to their best ever season but was soon to depart for Chelsea.

February 22, 1908. The St Andrews Stand buckled in a gale during a visit from Leeds City. No-one was injured and, after a brief stoppage, the match resumed. Lincoln won 5-0.

Double winners: Lincoln City's 1911/12 squad with the Central League title trophy, which they won by six points, and the County Cup, which they secured by beating Grimsby 3-2 in the final.

Lincoln City's squad which finished 15th in the 1925/26 Third Division North.

Lincoln City F.C. Co. Ltd

—— Telephone No. 570 ——

Official Programme

No. 7   Saturday. October 4th, 1924   ONE PENNY

**THIS SPACE
TO LET**

Sign of the times: City's programme for the visit of Barrow on October 4, 1924, begs for advertisers...

...that's more like it: the programme cover for City's clash with Grimsby on October 24, 1925, is not so naked.

Lincoln City, 1927/28. Manager Harry Parkes is second from the right on the centre row. On the extreme left of that row is winger Charles Bosbury who, less than two years later, died from tuberculosis after falling ill following an FA Cup match against Leicester City.

The 1938/39 City squad. Manager Joe McClelland is in the middle of the centre row. Lincoln finished a mediocre 17th in the Third Division North, sustained by 16 goals from winger Joseph Clare (second from right, centre row).

Back in action: Hull City v Lincoln City christened Hull's new Boothferry Park stadium when the Football League resumed after the Second World War.

Bumper crowd: Lincoln City v Tottenham Hotspur, in Division Two on August 28, 1948, attracted 19,540 to Sincil Bank.

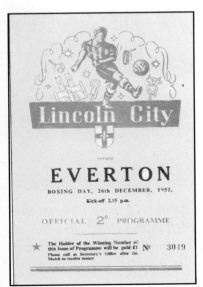

New to Sincil Bank: Everton paid their first visit for a Second Division fixture on Boxing Day, 1952.

One of the Imps' most enduring stars: Sandy the Labrador, who kept Bill Anderson (extreme right) company for many years, pictured with the City squad.

Those were the days: the famous old Sincil Bank terrace, now buried beneath the Simons Stand.

The Queen fetched up at Sincil Bank on a rainy day in June 1958. Note how full of joie de vivre Prince Philip appears. Note, too, that her Majesty is hogging the umbrella.

Do it this way: advice from Bill Anderson for John Milner, Alan Morton, Bud Houghton and Bert Linnecor.

Lincoln City line-up in their change strip of white shirts and black shorts and socks in the showers at Villa Park on their only ever league visit to that ground, March 1, 1960. Back row: Smith, Allen, Middleton, Heath, Gratton, Jackson. Front: McClelland, Harbertson, Hawksworth, Linnecor, Smilie.

The 1960/61 squad with manager Bill Anderson (back row, right). A few smiles are visible but they were hard to sustain through a season which saw Lincoln relegated to Division Three.

LINCOLN CITY FOOTBALL SUPPORTERS CLUB

WINNING CODES—Week ending October 6th, 1962

Total Subscriptions ...	278	6	0
To Committee Funds ...	111	6	4
Expenses, Printing, etc. ...	27	16	8
Prize money ...	139	3	0

PRIZE MONEY £139 - 3 - 0

TUESDAY, 2nd October, 1962   PRIZE £10 10 0
08-17-24   M. Reeve, 32 Ruckland Ave.   18   Mr. Lanes

WEDNESDAY, 3rd October, 1962   PRIZE £10 10 0
05-12-35   Mrs. Horne, Newton-on-Trent   18   Mr Lanes

THURSDAY, 4th October, 1962   PRIZE £10 10 0
13-26-35   Mr. E. Knight, Metheringham   83   E. Johnson

FRIDAY, 5th October, 1962   PRIZE £10 10 0
15-16-24   H. E. Close, 50 Mill Rd.   2   Mr. Childs

SATURDAY, 6th October, 1962
Highest Grand Aggregate of Three Matches (20 Goals)   £97 3 0
10-15-21   M. Harrison, Fledborough   Mr. Lanes
10-16-21   Mrs E. Crowe, 37 Gaunt St.   Mr. Withers
10-20-21   A. Graver, 14 Knight St.   Mr. Clapham
10-21-26   W. Sickler, 7 South Parade   Mr. Bradley
10-21-35   K. Osbourne, 223 Moorland Ave.   Mr. Rushby
Other combinations not forecast
5 Winners each receive £19 8s. 7d.

FOR WINNING CODES FOR TUES., WED., THUR., FRI., SEE PAGE TWO "LINCOLNSHIRE ECHO" Each Evening

WINNING MEMBERSHIP, 6th October, £1
04-28-33   Mr. Crane, Saxilby   Mr. Blanchard

MATCH DRAW, Winning Numbers, 6th October, 1962
1st No. 12824 £8 - 8 - 0   2nd No. 12306 £6 - 6 - 0
3rd No. 10315 £4 - 4 - 0   4th No. 12945 £2 - 2 - 0

BINGO

Every Monday Evening at DRILL HALL, BROADGATE, LINCOLN.
Doors open at 7 p.m., Bingo commences 8 p.m.   Admission 2/-, Bingo 5/-.
All money taken on Bingo is returned in Cash Prizes, which exceed **£150 every Monday.** Two "Golden Houses" of £25 each every Monday.

Worth entering: the supporters' club lottery in 1962. Without initiatives like these from the fans, Lincoln City might well have failed to survive the early 60's

Fruit juice or oxtail soup: that was the tricky choice of starter facing supporters' club members at their annual dinner in 1963.

The saviour: Frank Eccleshare (right) plots the course out of crisis with accountant Roy Chapman.

Meet the boss: Frank Eccleshare introduces City's players to new manager Con Moulson. Under Moulson, Lincoln lost every game but his "insistence on cleanliness and hygiene" was "exceptional."

Rare highlight: City beat Luton Town 8-1, with Billy Cobb scoring a debut hat-trick, on their way to finishing bottom of the Football League in 1967.

A great cup night: September 13, 1967, Lincoln City 2 Newcastle United 1.

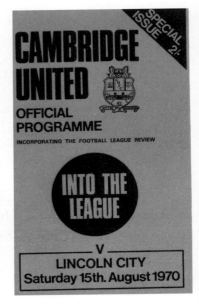

Double first: August 15, 1970. Bert Loxley's first match as Lincoln manager and Cambridge United's inaugural Football League fixture.

Owen governing behind, compiled six wins out of six in January. Lester scored just once in the six games but led the line cleverly and, heavily marked, freed Marlow and Hutchinson to score six each. The Imps' promotion credentials looked sound but still Anderson wasn't satisfied and recruited 5ft 4in left-winger Willie Windle from Rotherham. He scored on his debut, in a 3-1 win over Halifax and slotted in perfectly to the wide role vacated when Marlow was ruled out of the last 10 games by a muscle injury.

City approached Easter top of the table. On Good Friday, 17,657 were at the Bank to see a first-half hat-trick from "Wee Willy" Windle earn a 3-0 win over Gateshead. Next day, 1,400 travelling Imps fans were among the 18,863 at Mansfield which saw Hutchinson and Parr score in a 2-0 win which ended the Stags' promotion charge.

It was now a straight race between Lincoln and Rotherham for the championship and the penultimate match brought the two clubs head-to-head in south Yorkshire. Two games left: Lincoln 58 points, Rotherham 57. More than 20,000 people packed Rotherham's ramshackle Millmoor ground on a bright late-April afternoon. An hour before kick-off, a young Lincoln fan leapt over the perimeter fence, sprinted on to the pitch and planted a wooden Imp figurine on the centre-spot. Seconds later a Rotherham youngster raced on, plucked it out of the turf and threw it away in mock disgust. A burly policeman chased them off amid gales of good-natured laughter from serried ranks of supporters. These, of course, were the good old days.

Kick-off brought a great rush of noise as expectation gave way to raucous, bellowed encouragement. Lincoln started brilliantly. Hutchinson slipped a fifth-minute pass through to Wee Willy 12 yards out and he kept his head to score. Three minutes later another Hutchinson foray forced the ball free to McCormick who lashed the ball home. Two-nil up in eight minutes ! With Stillyards, Owen and Johnson outstanding, and Grummett and Parr relishing the battle, City defended doggedly and held on for the points. Windle and McCormick - two Rotherham-born players - had scored the goals at Millmoor to break the Millers' hearts. City were one small step - taking a point at home to Hartlepools a week later - from promotion. The step was taken for granted that night. Back in Lincoln the team was met by joyful crowds filling the High Street. Bill Anderson was dragged from the team bus and carried, shoulder-high, round town.

Seven days later, City lined up to face Hartlepools. Among the 20,024 crowd was a fresh-faced cherub called Peter Washbourn who, just before kick-off, watched a train pass beyond the Railway End. The steam-engine blew five times and little Peter turned to his Dad and said: "Dad, we're going to win 5-0 today." Incredibly, amazingly, spookily, City won 5-0. Hutchinson scored three, Lester added two and celebrations were long and loud. Rotherham, who finished one point behind, had the generosity of spirit to promptly dispatch a congratulation telegram. If anything could further improve Lincoln's day it was news that Grimsby had lost 8-0 to First Division champions Arsenal. The Mariners were relegated so would be back on the Imps' fixture-list next season. There is never a bad time to get promoted but this was the best time. Crowds were pouring into matches - 47,271,424 spectators watched Football League matches during the 1947/8 campaign, almost a million every Saturday - so entry to a higher division would maximise revenue from the tidal wave of interest. Anderson's reward was a £100 bonus and a new five-year contract worth £3,500. Now the board faced key decisions. Do they spend heavily on players? Do they make the players full-time?

Despite facing a big step-up in class, City retained most of their players part-time with just a handful - Johnson, Hutchinson, Grummett and Bean - turning full-time. The question of player-purchasing was taken partly out of their hands. Anderson was frustrated in all directions, making inquiries about 29 players and receiving 29 knock-backs. Aware that the club promoted from the Third Division North traditionally went straight back down, City fans lamented the absence of signings.

Lincoln were allocated a difficult first game of the 1948/49 season at promotion hopefuls West Ham. Upton Park presented a strange, grisly sight, still bearing heavy scars of war-time bombing. Under roofless stands and twisted girders 31,079 people watched the Imps earn an encouraging 2-2 draw. West Ham manager Charlie Paynter was impressed. "Whatever the Lincoln lads lack in finesse," he announced, "they are certainly a force to be reckoned with." The next two games - at home to Bury and Tottenham - were also drawn. The two matches attracted almost 40,000 people, many perched on new terracing built all along the Sincil Bank side during the summer.

The force, to which Paynter referred, stuttered. Not until their eighth attempt did Lincoln win - 2-0 at home to Leicester with Bean and Hutchinson the scorers. Anderson at last gleaned success in the transfer market, signing midfielder Fred Bett from Sunderland. On October 2, after a 2-2 draw with Sheffield Wednesday in front of more than 42,000 at Hillsborough, City languished 20th in Division Two. Then came the big - well - sensational, spectacular, Sinciltastic swoop.

Anderson, a glint in his eye, announced that, after months of pursuit, the Imps had signed Ephraim "Jock" Dodds from Everton. City followers - football fans everywhere - needed a double-take. Dodds was a superstar, scorer of 382 senior goals (161 peacetime, 221 wartime) and here he was joining Lincoln City. He cost a club record £6,000 - big bucks but good business considering Huddersfield and Oldham had both bid £8,000.

The Scottish striker was easily the biggest name ever to join Lincoln City. Bustling, powerful and bristling with self-confidence, he had a voracious appetite for goals. In four seasons he scored more than 100 for Sheffield United before moving to Blackpool for £10,000 in 1939. After playing eight wartime internationals for Scotland, Dodds - equally dangerous in the air or on the ground - spent a brief spell in Ireland with Shamrock Rovers before moving back to the English First Division with Everton. A quality player. So why Lincoln ? Old pals. Anderson, Johnson and Hutchinson were all former team-mates from Dodds' Bramall Lane days while his acquaintance with Anderson stretched way back to boyhood and their joint links with Medomsley Juniors.

Seven thousand City fans travelled to watch Dodds' debut at Grimsby and he didn't let them down, scoring twice as Lincoln salvaged a 2-2 draw from 2-0 down. Dodds scored too in his second game, but in a clash of two strugglers Lincoln were beaten 3-1 by Nottingham Forest.

The star's arrival could not compensate for a badly struggling defence. Johnson, now 37, was far too slow while Bean, 33, found Second Division wingers demanding. Four successive defeats, including a 7-1 thrashing at Blackburn, sent City bottom. To compound the defensive disarray the reliable Owen was injured in the Ewood Park massacre and ruled out for four months. In two home games, 10 goals were conceded to Luton (4-4) and Bradford (6-3). Moulson, capped for the Republic of Ireland against Spain and Portugal, only months earlier, took some criticism.

With City in the relegation zone, the board took stick. A gaggle of disgruntled shareholders led by Albert Bennett, son of the club treasurer from the 1890s, formed the 'Progressive Group' to lobby for change. Having copped increasing flak for not spending heavily enough on players - despite only weeks earlier investing a record sum in Dodds - chairman Wright and vice-chairman Ted Simpson decided enough was enough and, after a rancorous AGM, resigned. Chicken farmer Charles Applewhite took over as chairman and two new directors - 'Progressives' Godfrey Holmes and Harold Allman - were appointed.

At last, in December, more signings. Classy wing-half Doug Wright was bought from Newcastle for £600. Goalkeeper (and Nottinghamshire wicket-keeper) Arthur Jepson, aged 33, arrived from Stoke City and centre-half John Bickerstaffe was signed from Bury. All three made their debuts in a spectacular 4-3 home win against West Ham on December 18. Dodds' hat-trick - against three different goalkeepers after Ernie Gregory got injured, then two outfielders had a go - helped secure Lincoln's first win in three months. Wright looked thorough quality and was appointed captain for the next match. Jepson was competent. Bickerstaffe got concussed, looked rough and ready and conceded a penalty. He played in the next game before young Tony Emery at last got an extended run in the team.

Emery was a highly promising centre-half for whom City had already rejected a bid from Newcastle United. Lincoln-born, and still only 20, Emery had made his Imps debut in an FA Cup tie at Yorkshire Amateurs three years earlier but was then held back, playing just 15 games. Along with Wright he was to become part of the Imps team furniture during the most eventful and exciting decade in City's history.

Lincoln were bottom of the table going into 1949 but New Year's Day brought the first away win of the season - a shock 2-1 win at Tottenham with Dodds scoring both. He scored twice again in the next match, a 3-1 win over Brentford, but part-timers will always struggle to match the fitness of full-time opponents and just one win from nine matches left Lincoln adrift again. A 5-3 defeat at Leicester added to the worst defensive record in the League - 66 goals conceded in 27 games.

Just before the deadline, further cash was poured into recruiting. Veteran inside-forward George Eastham (a mate of Dodds) arrived from Rochdale. To replace the fading Stillyards and Bean, in came full-backs Dick Young, for £2,000 from Sheffield United, and Horace Green from Halifax. There was an extravagant twist to the signing of left-winger Roy Finch. After agreeing to a £3,000 move from West Brom, Finch was flown to Southampton, in a private plane chartered by one of City's directors, to sign on the eve of City's match at the Dell. Finch made his debut, but City lost 4-0.

Too late. The signings took the total spent on players during the season above £25,000 but it should have been spilled much earlier. The new men were asked to resuscitate a corpse. In Young's debut at home to Fulham, the Londoners went 3-0 up by half-time, prompting hundreds of spectators to leave during the interval. Dodds, reported the Echo: "retarded the progress of attacks when he got the ball and was never active enough."

A desperate Easter - two home games, a 0-0 draw with Barnsley and a 1-0 defeat to Queens Park Rangers - sentenced City to relegation. Of the 11 that played in the last match of the season, a 3-0 victory at Bradford Park Avenue, only two had played in the opener at Upton Park. Having won eight of 42 matches, Lincoln finished seven points adrift of Nottingham Forest. Perhaps as punishment, the players went on an immediate post-season tour to Iceland. In freezing conditions and on rock-hard pitches they beat Valur 2-0, KR Football Club 2-0 and Fram & Vikingur 1-0 before losing the showpiece match 4-1 to a combined Reykjavik XI. "In sport," predicted Anderson, "the Icelanders are a rising nation."

Back at the ranch, Applewhite hailed the 1948/9 effort a "bitter disappointment." The 1949 annual meeting, at which a record loss of £7,795 was reported, was volcanic. The Progressives nominated two men - Bennett and John Holmes - for elevation to the board against two sitting directors John Irving (a board member for 30 years) and Edmund Fasham. On a show of hands, Bennett and Holmes had a clear majority only to lose after the counting of proxy votes in a subsequent ballot.

There was uproar. "You rigged it," yelled the Progressives. "Twist." "Resign." Furore followed among the 126 shareholders present with the two sides - the Progressive followers well in the majority - hurling abuse at eachother. When the elderly Irving got up to speak he was loudly booed. "There would not be a football club in Lincoln but for Sam Tonge and my brother and I," he raged, adding immodestly, "I have more contacts than anyone in this room." Shortly afterwards, Godfrey Holmes and Allman - the Progressive voices on the board - resigned, citing immoral use of proxy votes as their reason. Allman - "seriously disturbed at the discord which prevails in the boardroom" - was a particular loss as the sixth biggest shareholder in the club.

With all this going on, hardly surprisingly, City made unspectacular progress back in the Third Division North although the crowds stayed remarkably high. Almost 15,000 watched the opening-day visit of Oldham. Again the season was underway before signings were made. Outside-right Harry Troops arrived from Barnsley at the end of August and impressed on his debut in a 2-1 win at York. In October, Anderson pulled off an exciting coup with the signing of former England international inside-right Jackie Robinson from Sunderland. The classy Robinson had played for England as a 19-year-old with Sheffield Wednesday and represented his country four times before the war. He scored six minutes into his Imps debut to set up a 2-0 home win over Darlington and was committed and impressive for his new club. But after scoring five goals in eight games a hammer blow awaited on Christmas Eve. Scoring his second goal in a 2-0 home win over Wrexham, he vaulted the goalkeeper and fell awkwardly, breaking his left leg. He never played professional football again and one of City's most expensive possessions was stolen away.

City, while usually in the top six, never threatened promotion and finished fourth behind Doncaster, Gateshead and Rochdale. Dodds scored 21 goals in 36 games but Wright and Emery took most playing honours. Wright's distribution, reading of the game and control of the ball shone vividly in the Third Division North while Emery's calm and forceful, but always fair, presence at centre-half comforted team-mates around him. In Wright and Emery, Roy Finch, Horace Green and Robert Owen, City had a nucleus of quality players but they needed more. Dodds departed in a blaze of national publicity. He was banned from the League for his involvement in recruiting English players for the Colombian side Millonarios of Bogota - a club not registered with FIFA. The charismatic Scot scored 38 goals in 60 games for City but it was hard to argue that another player now departing, George Eastham, had been a shrewd acquisition. The pace that underpinned his dribbling skills in the 1930s had long gone and he played just 27 games in 21 months with Lincoln.

Now Bill Anderson heard of a 17-year-old prodigy from the north-east, name of Bobby Robson. The Imps boss took a look at him, hitched up his trousers on the touchline, and thought: "He'll do." City director (and Billinghay farmer) Edgar Gilbert and trainer Alf Young separately had a look and supported the manager's opinion.

Robson's amateur terms with Middlesbrough were about to expire so Anderson visited the boy and his parents in Durham. By now, Fulham, Blackpool, Newcastle, Sunderland, Birmingham, Huddersfield and Southampton, as well as Middlesbrough, eager to keep their young star, had made contact but Robson wouldn't decide until he had seen Lincoln.

What a sensation it would be if this starlet, chased by some of the country's top clubs, could be convinced to drop down to the Third Division North. He travelled to Lincolnshire for the weekend, watched the Imps' 2-1 County Cup defeat at Grimsby, then returned north. Anderson, Young and Tony Emery immediately paid a visit to keep the pressure on but when they reached Robson's parents' house the boy had gone to evening classes. As they chatted to mum and dad, other managers started to roll up. While the gaggle of managers sipped tea, swapped cliches and nibbled custard creams the Lincoln contingent exchanged furtive glances then slipped out the back way. They fetched Robson out of his evening-class and took him to dinner but still he deferred and, when he returned home, announced that Fulham boss Bill Dodgin was the man with the favoured offer. His valediction to thwarted Bill: "I wish you had been a First Division club Mr Anderson."

The 1950/1 season opened in national gloom after England's poor showing in the World Cup in Sweden. The Imps' search for a striker ended in late September with the signing of 23-year-old Andy Graver from Newcastle. Graver agreed to move south after struggling to break through a Newcastle attack including Jackie Milburn, George Robledo, Andy Donaldson and Roy Bentley. He had started just one game for the Magpies, at Manchester City - and got injured early on in a collision with City goalkeeper Bert Trautmann. But the Newcastle fans' were dismayed when he left. His quicksilver presence in the opponents' box had shone brightly in reserve games. The knowledgeable Geordies knew that here was a man with scoring instincts.

Graver scored on his debut in a 3-1 home win over Halifax and immediately struck up a profitable partnership with Johnny Garvie, a £750 summer signing from Preston. The pair enjoyed an immediate personal, as well as professional, rapport and spent hour after hour together working out moves together on the training field.

With Finch, Troops and Whittle manning the supply lines, City hit rich form right at the end of 1950. Three wins in a week, with 12 goals, stirred hopes of a promotion push and goals continue to flow. Stockport were drubbed 6-0 (Whittle 4, Graver, Green). Crewe were beaten 4-0 (Garvie, Finch, Green, Troops) in the first game Doug Wright had missed for 18 months. Accrington were blitzed 9-1 (Garvie 3, Graver 3, Finch 2, Windle). After the arrival of Graver, he or Garvie scored at least once in 24 of the next 30 games but City's charge started too late - Rotherham were well-clear - and dwindled away in April with only one win in eight games.

April provided one unique offering in football history; what was to remain Tony Emery's only goal in 402 games for the Imps. During a match at Chester, Emery was concussed early on and - still no substitutes then of course - after having stitches above his right eye was sent back on upfield. Late on, with Lincoln 2-0 down, a Finch shot bounced back off a post and Emery prodded home the rebound.

Lincoln finished fifth. For the second successive year, they applied to transfer to the Third Division South and were rejected. While 14-year-old Lester Piggott was suspended for the rest of the flat season for an offence on Barnacle in the Manton Handicap at Newbury, the Imps signed scouse goalkeeper Jimmy Jones from New Brighton and Hull City pair, full-back John Varney and centre-forward Robert Gibson. Gibson's arrival fuelled rumours, already rife, about the futures of Garvie and Graver. In their first season together at Sincil Bank they shared 40 goals to bring club scouts swarming round like ants round a stricken jelly bean.

To the fans' relief, both strands of the G-force were in the team which opened the new season with a 3-1 home win over York. Not there was contract-rebel Emery, but the defender settled his differences in time for the second match at Bill Shankly's Grimsby Town four days later. With Jones and Varney making their debuts, the G-force moved into overdrive. Graver, Garvie and Green scored as City won 3-2 in front of more than 21,000 people. Anderson's army was on the march. With Wright ever-present at the helm, City unfurled thrilling, attacking football, week after week. Goals flowed. Hartlepool were beaten 4-1 (Graver 2, Varney, Garvie). Lincoln won 3-1 (Graver, Varney 2) at Scunthorpe to become the first visitors to win at the Old Show Ground for a year. Then they beat them 4-1 (Whittle, Graver, Garvie, Troops) at home.

Darlington were smashed 7-2 (Graver 3, Troops 2, Whittle, Garvie). Crewe arrived at the Bank with teenager Dennis Murray making his debut in goal. They were demolished 11-1 - still City's biggest victory. Graver put six - two with his right foot, two with his left, two with his bonce - past the hapless Murray. Also on target were Troops, Green, Whittle, Grummett and George Johnson. A trainee joiner, deputising for the injured Finch, Johnson played just three games but booked a place in history as one of a very short list of players whose only ever Football League goal arrived in an 11-1 victory over Crewe.

A 3-0 win (Finch, Graver 2) on their first League visit to Workington, on December 1, lifted City top. Attendances at Sincil Bank were well into five-figures and crowd-packers were employed for the FA Cup second round visit of Grimsby. In front of 21,757, Graver and Garvie shared the goals as City won 3-1 to earn a third-round visit to First Division Portsmouth. An aeroplane was chartered to take the wealthier City supporters to Fratton Park. Four thousand fans travelled in all as City were beaten 4-0 in front of 41,093.

Anderson's squad had stayed happily injury-free but Varney was clattered during a Christmas Day defeat at Wrexham and ruled out for the season. Anderson wasted no time in spending £3,500 on Doug Graham from Preston. He slotted in smoothly at left-back.

Not even in the 1931/2 title season had there been such joie de vivre about City's football. Crowds flocked to the Bank expecting, and usually getting, goals. Oldham (4-0), Chester (4-1) and Chesterfield (5-1) failed to stem the red-and-white tide. City cruised along on top with only Grimsby vaguely within striking distance. Even when Graver tore knee ligaments, the Imps' progress remained serene. A 3-1 win at Accrington on March 29 included City's 100th goal of the season. A slight wobble, just one win in four games, was steadied by a 4-0 (Finch, Troops, Garvie, Whittle) Easter Monday win over Southport, followed five days later by a 7-0 (Whittle 3, Troops 2, Gibson, Garvie) demolition of Workington.

City approached their final home match - a Wednesday night visit of third-placed Stockport - knowing that victory would secure promotion. Fluency was stultified by tension as Garvie scored twice but then County battled back to 2-1. In the closing seconds, Graham was penalised for handball in City's box. Would it all go to Saturday and an awkward visit to Barrow ? No. Staniforth's penalty was kept out by Jones and the police reached the Imps' goalkeeper just before the 21,501 crowd got there to carry him shoulder-high from the field.

Job done. City were beyond the reach of runners-up Grimsby. Shankly acknowledged: "Lincoln are worthy champions." It had been one of the happiest seasons in the club's history with a club record total of both points (68) and goals (121). Graver scored 36 goals in 35 games and only injury prevented him beating Allan Hall's record of 42 goals in a season. Those torn ligaments also robbed him of a chance to play for England B against Holland. But City's goals arrived regularly from several sources. Whittle 19, Garvie 19, Troops 15 and Finch 14. Whittle, Wright, Emery, Troops and Garvie played 40 or more games. A happy, united, hard-working, talented bunch had earned the Imps another crack at Division Two. Now come on lads. Capitalise.

11.
Mixing with the big boys

ANDY Graver went into Bill Anderson's office and came out smiling. His wages had just gone up from £11 per week in the winter and £9 in the summer to £12 and £10. Johnny Garvie went in and emerged also smiling with the same rise. Next in was Tommy McCreadie, a Glaswegian inside-left on the fringes on the first team. "Son," said Anderson. "We're keeping you on but there's no rise." Why not, asked McCreadie, when Graver and Garvie got one ? Anderson was honest. "They better players than you," he said. "Not in the summer, they're not," replied McCreadie.

There were always limited resources to divide at Sincil Bank. Difficult decisions to make. Lines to draw. Can we afford this ? Could we do without that? How much could we pay this player ? Can we keep that player ?

The club's return to Division Two presented a dilemma. Under-investment after the previous promotion had brought immediate failure. But again, this time, they were far from in a position to throw money around. Bill Anderson's greatest talent - budget-juggling - would be severely taxed. He was a warm, if private, man with a sense of humour and an affectionate Labrador called Sandy but no-one ever called him extravagant. 'Mean' and 'careful,' usually. Or 'tight,' but in the context of City's perpetual penury, 'tight' was essential. The canny Anderson and chairman Charlie Applewhite, a pragmatic, bespectacled farmer, never threw money around.

"Yes, Bill was tight," recalls Andy Graver. "If someone had said to him that one day players would be on £30,000 a week he'd have told them to get a taxi to the nuthouse...or rather a bus because Bill wouldn't pay for a taxi. But Charlie Applewhite was tighter than Bill. Once all the players got invited round to Applewhite's chicken farm. It didn't sound very interesting but we went because we thought at least we'd get a dozen eggs each. We got half-a-dozen."

Applewhite and his board now faced some important decisions. If they wanted Second Division football beyond the immediate term they had to invest. The lesson from 1948/49 - that it was folly to try to compete in Division Two with part-time players - was heeded. The first-team squad went full-time. All the back-room staff got rises with Anderson receiving a £100 bonus and a new five-year contract worth £1,000 per year.

For a while, it worked. Ahead lay City's longest unbroken tenure in Division Two - nine seasons - since the turn of the century. Glory days ? Well, sort of. City finished 15th, 16th, 16th, 8th, 18th, 20th, 19th, 13th and 22nd. Seven of the nine seasons brought relegation worries and it was rarely too comfortable but these were the nearest the Imps have come to glory days. The Sincil Bank terraces were well-populated - sometimes packed. To the Bank came the likes of Tommy Lawton, John Charles, Johnny Haynes, Brian Clough, Billy Wright, Denis Law, Bobby Robson, Ivor Allchurch, Tommy Docherty, Jimmy Hill, Gil Merrick, Jackie Charlton, Ron Staniforth, John Atyeo, Bill McGarry, Harry Gregg, Jimmy Mullen, Jimmy Adamson, Albert Johannsen, Bedford Jezzard, Billy Bremner and Charlie "eeee Flower" Williams. Famous names from big clubs and Lincoln looked them in the eye and mingled with them for almost a decade. The city's ensign fluttered in the top half of the Football League and the population was proud. The Imps' previous four promotions had been followed by Division Two lifespans of two, four, two and one seasons but this time Lincoln got stuck in and gave it a go. Until the dosh, or maybe the sense of adventure, ran out.

In the Autumn of 1952, a gale of adventure blew through Lincoln. It spawned a new supporters' club which soon topped 5,000 members. Of 3,004 season-tickets available at the Bank, 2,076 were bought before a ball was kicked. City's full-time squad was reinforced by signings from, not Willington Quay and Little Poppleton Rovers, but Manchester United and Arsenal. From United came defenders Roy Killin and Billy McGlen. Winger Mike Ryan arrived from Arsenal. These were squad fodder though. When the new season dawned, Anderson stuck loyally to his promotion team. More than 1,000 City fans travelled to watch the opening fixture at Brentford. The London side won 1-0 in front of 27,787 at Griffin Park but Brentford manager Tommy Lawton observed that Lincoln "will finish near the top of Division Two" and singled out Emery for praise.

Boom time. City's first nine games all attracted more than 20,000 people. Graver scored nine goals in the first 10 matches from which Lincoln collected a respectable nine points. There was an uplifting early double over Blackburn (4-1 at home, 2-0 away) while a visit to Huddersfield illustrated the wealth of some clubs with which City now competed. The Terriers' star forward Bill Davie, a £22,000 signing from Luton Town, cost more than the entire Imps team but Graver's double earned a 2-2 draw at Leeds Road. City were holding their own. More than one letter to the local papers began "When we get into the First Division....."

The national press, meanwhile, fuelled speculation over Graver's future, hardly surprisingly as the quicksilver Geordie had netted 65 goals in 79 League games for City. Lincoln fans knew that if opposing defenders or goalkeepers dwelt on the ball, their hero would pounce quicker than a Bolivian Ffig spider.

Pace, that weapon most feared by defences, he had aplenty. Seizing upon a mis-judged back-pass was Graver's own favourite type of strike but it was a headed goal - against Brentford which gave the Imps' arch-predator most pleasure.

He recalled: "We played Brentford one time and their player-manager was the great Tommy Lawton. Well, before the war, when we used to knock a ball around as kids, I always used to be Tommy Lawton - he was my hero. I idolised him. Then, there I was, all those years later, not only being on the same pitch as him but scoring against his team ! Tommy sought me out after the game and said 'Good header, son. You took it well.' You can imagine how I felt !"

Now plenty of youngsters in playgrounds and streets were pretending to be Graver.

But paper talk can be unsettling. The G-force faltered when, with the sea-son 10 games old, Garvie underwent a cartilage operation. Graver badly missed his strike-partner and soul-mate. Of 14 games without Garvie, City won only one. Anderson's search for temporary cover led him to Yorkshire and England fast bowler, and big, awkward centre-forward, Fred Trueman. The rising star, four Tests for England against India already behind him that summer, played several games as an amateur for City's second string. A crowd of 7,328 - a reserve team record - watched him line up against Peterborough in the Midland League but Yorkshire CCC, fearing serious injury for their main asset, pressured Trueman to quit. He agreed and City got the message when Trueman, selected for a Saturday afternoon reserve game, went to open a grammar school bazaar in Horncastle instead.

Anderson was more successful in recruiting inside-forward Brian Birch, a first-generation Busby Babe, from Wolves for £6,000. Birch scored twice on his debut to help earn a 3-2 win at home to Leicester but that was the only victory in November or December and Lincoln dipped into the bottom five. Boxing Day brought brand new visitors to Sincil Bank. Everton, deep in transition after rele-gation from Division One 18 months earlier, brought a young side which created most chances in a 1-1 draw. City's home form was their safety-net. After Christmas they lost just once at the Bank. Garvie returned at home to Swansea in mid-January and scored in a 3-1 win.

A week later came a dark day for English justice. At 9am on a damp Saturday morning, 19-year-old Derek Bentley was hanged at Wandsworth Prison in connection with the murder of PC Sidney Miles on a Croydon rooftop. A plea from 200 MPs, in support of Bentley's devastated parents, for a reprieve was ignored. These were savage times. In Notting Hill, the remains of three women were found walled up at the Rillington Place home of special constable John Christie. Dictator and mass-murderer Josef Stalin and country and western singer Hank Williams, both aged 73, turned up their toes. Sweet rationing ended.

Inflation approached double figures. Louie Williams, mother of actor Kenneth, sent her dog back to the pound because it was too energetic. Rocky Marciano knocked out Jersey Joe Walcott to retain his world heavyweight title. In Sheffield, doctors fought to save the life of former Imps striker Derek Dooley. Infection had set in after the youngster sustained a double fracture of his right leg playing for Sheffield Wednesday at Preston. Surgeons were forced to amputate his right leg. All these occurrences were digested and debated over breakfast tables in Lincoln along with the big question: would City avoid the drop ?

Fortunately, Barnsley were enduring an appalling season with Southampton not far above them. The two promotion places appeared booked from mid-March. Right-winger Jimmy Munro, signed from Oldham in February, settled quickly and helped City to a happy Easter, which brought five points from three games against Hull and Bury. That took them almost to safety and a 3-0 (Garvie, Munro, Whittle) win over Notts County on April 18, guaranteed another campaign in Division Two.

City could relax and enjoy their last three games which attracted more than 59,000 people. On April 22, they visited Goodison Park for the first time and unfurled what Applewhite described as one of their best displays in his 32-year association with the club. Two goals from Birch, separated by a sizzling left-foot strike by Whittle, earned a 3-0 win. The final game at home to West Ham was moved to Friday to avoid a clash with the first FA Cup final live on telly and, after a 3-1 win, the Imps' players were cheered from the field. Those two points lifted Lincoln above FA Cup semi-finalists Everton in the final standings to 15th out of 22. Six points clear of relegation with an average home crowd of 16,693. The team's backbone - Green, Graham, Wright, Emery, Owen, Graver, Whittle and Finch - had negotiated the step up. Anderson had proved himself more than just a Third Division boss. A two-match post-season tour of the Channel Islands was hugely enjoyed. City won 6-1 against a combined Guernsey and Jersey side, beat a Jersey Saturday League XI 1-0 and quaffed a few deserved pints along the way.

Lincoln City Football Supporters Club, meanwhile, quickly gathered momentum. Founded by mining engineer Vic Withers and a group of fellow members of the Castle Hill Club, tucked into the shadow of Lincoln Castle, it's raison d'etre was entirely practical: to generate cash for the Imps. To help ensure the football club continued to exist. From humble origins of its first meeting in Alf Deeks' barber shop, the supporters' club soon spawned an army of collectors and agents out and about every day, in all weathers, round the factories and streets knocking on doors and selling raffle tickets. Bingo sessions and whist drives were established and, within a year, a cheque for £500 - a formidable sum in 1953 - had been presented to the football club. The Supporters' Club also relayed the first live match commentary to patients in Lincoln County Hospital.

In the summer of '53, Emery and Wright joined Graver as the subjects of transfer speculation. Arsenal were rumoured to want Emery, a theory fuelled by the presence of Gunners' scout Leslie Compton at several Imps games during the Spring. But the board resisted all overtures. There was no movement on the transfer front either way. Jeremiah Lowery had arrived from Newcastle in February to compete with Jones for the goalkeeper's jersey but Anderson believed his squad was good enough to hold their own. City stuck with the same personnel, declining to recruit even when the unlucky Garvie was ruled out of the first six months of the season through injury.

Lincoln started the new season at West Ham with exactly the 11 that had finished against the same opposition three months earlier. This time Lowery, Green, Graham, Wright, Emery, Owen, Munro, Birch, Graver, Whittle and Finch took a 5-0 beating at Upton Park. Uninspiring draws - 1-1 at Doncaster and 0-0 at home to Bury - followed with the Bury match drawing heckling from the 14,564 crowd. "I can't understand what all the grumbling is about," said Anderson. "The team has been playing well enough just without clicking. They will do so before long and when they do somebody must look out."

Bill was right. Three days later, Lincoln burst into the headlines by demolishing Blackburn 8-1 at Sincil Bank. Wright was at his most imperious and Finch effervescent on the left. Graver scored four, Munro two, Finch and Whittle one each. As Rovers, including England full-back Bill Eckersley, were handed their biggest ever defeat, Sandy the affectionate Labrador wagged its tail in effusive glee. Extensive wagging of said canine's rear appendage followed as City also won six of the next seven home games to rise to sixth. Rotherham led 3-1 at the Bank but Whittle's hat-trick levelled the score before Graver pounced for a late winner. City were hurtling along gaily but whispers of a promotion drive were stilled by a visit to leaders Leicester City. Without the injured Wright, City gave a daunting debut to youngster Bernard Shaw, signed from Goole Town three weeks earlier. In front of 30,343, the Foxes handed the Imps a 9-2 beating as gargantuan striker Arthur Rowley bulldozed his way though time after time. A 4-1 defeat at Fulham, for whom Bobby "I wish you had been a First Division club Mr Anderson" Robson starred, further emphasised that few off-days were permitted at this level.

In the FA Cup, Lincoln disposed of Walsall at the third attempt to earn a fourth round home tie against Preston, runners-up in Division One the previous season. Here was a true test for Bill's boys and all 25,000 tickets were sold in advance. The magical Tom Finney created Preston's opening goal for Baxter in the 35th minute. Ernie Whittle then squandered a penalty before Preston, with Tommy Docherty and Charlie Wayman prominent, killed the game with a second goal on the hour. It was Whittle's last big match for Lincoln. After four more was his tackling, so precise his positional sense. Six years earlier, Bill Anderson had taken a considerable gamble on the Essex-boy-turned-Geordie, whose full recovery from a war-time leg wound was far from guaranteed. The gambler hit the jackpot - Wright played at least 37 games in each of his five full seasons at the Bank. His benefit of £750 was richly-deserved.

Two games after Wright's departure, Graver scored the winning goal in a 2-1 home victory over West Ham. Then he, too, left. Leicester City, having had a £25,000 offer rejected, upped their bid to £27,000 plus reserve striker Eric Littler. This time the City board could not resist. Within an hour of signing for the Foxes, Graver, diligent to the end, fulfilled an obligation to attend a coaching session with Anderson at Bailgate Youth Centre.

After Graver's departure, Lincoln won only two of 15 games to again flirt with relegation. Anderson ambitiously cabled the Colo Colo club in Santiago to register an interest in former Newcastle United brothers George and Ted Robledo. Bigger fish than City, including Spurs and Arsenal, were involved in that chase so instead, after a brief and unfruitful first-team spell for Littler, the number nine shirt passed to Bob Gibson, Graver's understudy for the past three seasons.

Gibson managed nine goals in 18 games and City finally secured their status with three games to spare by beating Derby 3-0 at Sincil Bank. The match was watched by less than 10,000 however, as were five other home games after Christmas. Even a visit from Matt Busby's Manchester United for a friendly in March was poorly attended. Busby brought his full First Division side except Duncan Edwards who was playing in a Youth Cup game against Plymouth. United won 3-1 with goals from Foulkes, Webster and Albert Scanlon (later to survive the Munich runway disaster and then join the Imps) but only 7,844 paid to see it. The first signs of a post-war waning of interest were evident.

In truth, it had been a season of attrition. Neal and Middleton were effective but in an uncompromising way. They harried and spoiled where Wright and Graver had sparkled and inspired. After one tedious spectacle - a 1-1 draw with Ipswich in April - Lincolnshire Echo reporter Maurice Burton lamented: "Watching football this season it has seemed to me that footballers generally are losing sight of the fact that they are being paid - and well paid - to entertain." The season ended with a depressing 1-0 defeat to Port Vale with slow-hand clapping echoing round the Bank. Again City finished 16th.

Emery's excellence was rewarded with a place in an FA squad to tour the West Indies but there were signs that City were starting to cling, rather than adapt, to Division Two. When Graver, having not settled at Leicester, agreed to return to Lincoln, Anderson was delighted. City paid £14,000, just over half what they had received from Leicester. Graver was glad to be back having spent most

League appearances he plunged himself into Workington Town's third Football League campaign.

City lost form and again dipped too close to the relegation zone for comfort but the Wright, Emery, Owen axis and 14 goals from Graver and fit-again Garvie in the last 10 matches elevated them to safety. A reminder of how much Garvie had been missed was supplied by a hat-trick on the last day of the season in a 4-1 win over Fulham. Largely without him the Imps had managed another season of consolidation and profit. They finished 16th, again six points clear of the drop, and made £2,725. Of that sum, £52 discharged a fine imposed by the Lincolnshire Football Association for fielding a weakened team at Scunthorpe in the County Cup.

Such a profit helped Anderson stave off growing interest in Graver. Sheffield Wednesday, Wolves, Aston Villa, Burnley, Liverpool, Nottingham Forest and Notts County were monitoring the situation closely. "It will take a very attractive offer to tempt Lincoln to transfer him," said Anderson, adding, ominously for City fans, "but there are some kinds of offer which cannot be lightly refused."

Anderson was aware his squad was ageing and now brought in players who could handle immediate first-team football. He hailed experienced goalkeeper Mitchell Downie from Bradford as "one of our most important signings since the war." A non-smoking, dance-loving teetotaller, Downie, 27, was a penalty-save specialist having kept out 11 of 17 he faced the previous season. Joining part-time so he could retain his job in Bradford's confectionery industry, his arrival alerted Sandy to the possibility of a few free choccy-drops. Anderson also brought in two promising young half-backs. Dick Neal, a tall, powerful left-half, arrived from Wolves for £1,000. Fair-haired right-half Fred Middleton, whose tackling came with a health warning, joined from Newcastle for the same fee. Their arrivals heralded the beginning of the end for Wright and Owen.

Emery was unassailable though and when City's third fixture of the 1954/55 season sent them to Elland Road, he took responsibility for dealing with the threat of John Charles. He scarcely gave him a touch as Lincoln went 3-0 up. Graver harrassed young Jackie Charlton into a handball from which Don Dykes lashed home a 25-yard drive for number three and City hung on to win 3-2. After the sixth game, a 2-1 home defeat to Luton, Neal and Middleton replaced Owen and Wright. Both impressed on their debuts at Ipswich, Middleton scoring the winner in a 2-1 win.

Wright, the architect of some of the most attractive football ever seen at Sincil Bank, was not out of the side long before departing. After skippering the Imps for six years, he left by mutual consent to become player-coach of Blyth Spartans. In 233 appearances for Lincoln, Wright was never booked, so skilful of his time at Filbert Street in the reserves. Straight after joining Leicester, he had been told by manager Norman Bullock that: "It's not me who wants you, it's the directors." After scoring on his debut at Chelsea, Graver was dropped as soon as first-choice striker Derek Hines recovered from injury.

Could the G-force rediscover the old magic? To help them, centre-forward Tommy Northcott was signed for £3,000 from Cardiff City. From the other end of Wales came inside-right Tommy Bannan, a tiny, tenacious Scot who arrived from Wrexham for a small fee, plus Littler.

With Northcott joining Munro, Garvie, Graver and Finch in the forward line, City won four of their first five games. Graver scored on his return in a 2-0 win at Blackburn and again in a 2-0 home win over Hull. To Graver's delight, Leicester were thumped 7-1, the Imps moving the ball around sweetly and at pace as Finch 2, Northcott 2, Munro 2, and Graver, from Garvie's pass, shared the goals. In September, Lincoln, for the first time since 1912, sat top of Division Two though realists viewed it less a launching pad for a promotion bid than a solid foundation for avoiding relegation.

The FA Cup brought a shock 3-2 home defeat to Southend United of the Third Division South but with Emery and Neal united at the back, City enjoyed much their best season since returning to Division Two. Graver wasn't part of it for long. He played just 15 games before moving again, this time to Stoke City for £10,000. A quantity of 250,000,000-year-old fossilised grasshoppers were found in a coal-mine in Czechoslovakia while in England football started to emerge from the dark ages. Floodlights were going up. After a 4-1 win at Plymouth, Lincoln stayed in Devon until Monday to play Exeter in a friendly under lights at St James' Park. The Third Division South side won 3-1 in front of 2,015 people. Floodlights at Sincil Bank were felt desirable but the obvious snag was cost. The ever-industrious supporters' club got their thinking-caps on.

In the Spring of 1955, the Football League's management committee included installation of floodlights at all grounds in a five-point plan to reverse a steady decline in crowds since the immediate post-war years. They also recommended that, sooner rather than later, Divisions Three and Four should replace the Thirds North and South. Here was incentive for Lincoln to stay in Division Two. Life in Division Three North was grim but Division Four? Too bleak to contemplate.

Inside-right Colin Gibson, signed from Aston Villa for £6,000 on January, now replaced the fading Garvie. There was just one more appearance in the red and white for Garvie. He slotted in at the last minute for a home game against Forest when Gibson missed his train. Forest won 3-1 and Garvie's charming but injury-plagued Imps career closed on 78 goals from 184 appearances.

City finished strongly. They scored at least twice in each of their last eight games, five of which were away from home. Northcott grabbed a hat-trick in 13 minutes in a 4-0 win over Barnsley. Then he converted two resounding headers in a 4-2 win at West Ham, earning two points which took Lincoln to their highest ever tally in Division Two. Barry Hawkings, a Brummie signed from Coventry City, scored twice on his debut in a 2-1 home triumph over Stoke. A 2-0 win over Liverpool on the closing day left the Imps a lofty eighth in the final reckoning. They ended only six points behind promoted Leeds United and a comforting 18 above relegated Plymouth. Downie, Graham, Troops, Middleton, Emery, Neal, Munro and Northcott all played at least 38 of the 42 games.

Three seasons of hanging on had been followed by a much more convincing effort. Now City reached a crossroads. Would they look forward and spend ? Time, surely, to keep building. Would they invest to refresh the squad and make the push for those extra three wins which could earn a place in Division One ? Could they invest ? Did they have the dosh ?

Cash was spent on just one player. Right-winger Ron Smilie was bought for £2,000 from Barnsley. A part-time footballer, he continued to work as a miner at Grimethorpe Colliery. Garvie departed to Carlisle United and Brian Birch to Barrow. Garvie went on to pass through Boston United, Corby Town, Stamford Town and Ilkeston Town and also became the first ex-Imp to become steward of Corby Trades and Labour Club. Birch set off on a mystery tour of a career which embraced Exeter, Oldham, Rochdale, the Philippines, Mossley, Boston United, Sydney, Malaysia, Ellesmere Port, Blackburn Rovers and Galatasaray, whom he coached to the Turkish championship.

Despite the transfer inertia, auspices were good early in the 1956/57 campaign. Left-winger Alan Withers, former understudy to Stanley Matthews at Blackpool, got his chance after a season mostly in the reserves and hit four goals in two games: a 4-0 home win over Port Vale and a 4-3 triumph, in front of 23,663, at Blackburn. Bannan was also on target in both those games, indeed all of City's first four, from which they took a promising six points. A rarity in September was the presence of an England manager at Sincil Bank. Walter Winterbottom watched City's 1-0 win over Fulham. "We like to get around a bit," revealed Winterbottom. He was there to check out Fulham striker Roy Dwight who was marked out of the game by Emery.

The bright start floundered on the rocks of under-investment. A goal-shortage was City's problem and even when they managed to score six in two FA Cup ties against non-league Peterborough United they still went out. The first match took place in front of a capacity 23,000 crowd at Peterborough's London Road home. Lincoln were 2-1 down entering the last minute when Hawkings' header was allegedly diverted onto the post by a Posh hand. Four minutes furore, debate and consultation between officials followed before the award of a penalty which Troops coolly slotted home. Peterborough, including four ex-Imps - Roy Killin, Billy Hails, Bob Gibson and Bernard Shaw - carried a sense of injustice into the replay at Sincil Bank and were again 2-1 up in the closing seconds. Again, Lincoln equalised, this time through Neal, but Peterborough showed tremendous resilience in extra time and rushed 5-2 up with three goals in seven minutes. Northcott and then Bannan, with a late penalty, dragged it back to 5-4 but Posh went through.

The cup demise further deflated a mediocre season and just two points from the next six matches reeled City down the table. A nadir was reached at the Victoria Ground in February when Stoke, minus the injured Graver, won 8-0. The Potters' outside-right Tim Coleman delivered eight shots at goal and seven of them beat Downie. In desperation, City looked to former Honved coach Josef Somogyi for advice and the Hungarian spent a week organising training in which no tackling was allowed. Then he headed for Columbia, one of the more exotic ships to pass Lincoln in the night.

As City struggled, crowds dropped and the familiar cycle of having to sell, turned again. At Easter, as soon as safety from relegation was assured, Dick Neal was sold to First Division side Birmingham City. Neal had won England Under 23 caps against Denmark, France and Scotland during the season but was cashed in for £15,000 plus tough-tackling inside-right Bert Linnecor.

The sale angered supporters who had seen their side survive narrowly without style or comfort. City's goal-tally of 54 was the lowest in Division Two. To lose Neal's authority and class was, surely, small-time thinking which could only drag City back to the small time. But these were, insisted Applewhite, simply the facts of life for a small-city club in Division Two. The economics of necessity.

Those economics sent the Imps into the 1957/8 season with a squad of players largely ageing, unproven or expendable. City fans feared the worst and for a long time their fears were realised until they witnessed one of English football's great escapes. An escape so great it made Papillon's hair-raising, death-defying leap from Devil's Island look like stepping out of a paddling pool.

12.
Great escape -
but heading for the black hole

SOMETIMES, at the end of a football season, deep joy ends up in surprising locations. A team which suffered an absolutely crap time for seven months, summons, in a matter of hours, an escape which grants supporters, long-resigned to despair, the ecstasy of reprieve. They sing and dance and celebrate like billy-o even though their team has finished only a place or two above relegation. The narrowest of escapes brings a surge of thrill and adrenalin denied to fans of clubs with much better teams, far higher in the table. In the last 30 years, Coventry City have become arch-practitioners of this but even they have never topped the Imps' escape of 1958.

The 1957/8 season had been utterly dismal. Lincoln won only two of the first 15 games despite signing one of the finest players ever to grace Sincil Bank. The purchase of George Hannah, for £4,500 from Newcastle United, was a masterstroke by Anderson who fought off interest from Leeds United, West Ham, Preston, Bolton, Wrexham and Notts County. A skilful, intelligent inside-right, Hannah had played at Newcastle for eight seasons and featured in their 3-1 FA Cup final winning side against Manchester City in 1955. To persuade the 29-year-old ball-artist to drop into a Second Division relegation dogfight was testament to Anderson's persuasive patter. The Imps' numerous Geordie connections helped - as did provision of a semi-detached house.

Predictably, the star recruit was singled out for some rough treatment by opponents. When Grimsby visited the Bank, Hannah was kicked out of the game in the opening minutes. Without their injured star, Lincoln wilted 4-1 to the Mariners' aerial onslaught, prompting the Echo to rage: "This stuff may please the morons but it does the game generally incalculable harm." Hannah missed the next five matches from which City collected one point. They didn't win a game in October, won just one in each of November and December, and none in January, February or March. Bulky inside-forward Roy Chapman, 22, arrived from Aston Villa and, after struggling in a 6-1 home defeat to champions-elect West Ham, became the focal point of crowd abuse.

City raised their game for an FA Cup third round visit of star-studded Wolves, skippered by Billy Wright. After Wolves squeezed to a 1-0 win thanks to a second-half goal from Jimmy Mullen, their manager Stan Cullis was generous.

"How you manage to be bottom of the Second Division beats me," he said. No wins from the next 12 games helped.

On February 6, the air of despondency around Sincil Bank was heightened by the Munich air disaster. One of the journalists killed, Henry Rose, was a close friend of Anderson and had sent a Christmas card urging: "Get out of trouble Bill." Billy McGlen, now City trainer, shared his apprenticeship at Old Trafford with several players killed on that hideous icy runway.

Dark weeks followed for English football. Gloom was thicker than ever at Sincil Bank on March 8. As half-time approached in a home game with Cardiff, the Imps, busily self-destructing again, trailed 3-0. Then the city was hit by a blizzard and within minutes was deep in snow. At half-time a groundstaff worker started clearing the touch-lines and was swiftly instructed to stop by Anderson. With snow still falling, the second half was delayed for 15 minutes before the referee walked into the home dressing room with the magic words: "It's off." Relief for City, though at the time it seemed just a truncation of a bad night. Not the planting of seeds of euphoria.

With City on the bottom, not quite belly-up, Anderson made signings. He recruited centre-forward Ron Harbertson for £2,000 from Darlington. Even that relatively small fee would have been beyond Lincoln without a recent £2,500 injection from the supporters club. Their regular donations were virtually keeping the Imps afloat as City's crowds fell way short of the 12,500 break-even figure.

Harbertson's first day as an Imp was eventful. At 4.15am on Saturday March 15, he and the sprightly 44-year-old Anderson scaled a 10-foot wall to get into the Feethams kit-room for the player's boots. Eleven hours later, after a brisk drive to Liverpool, Harbertson made his debut in a 1-0 defeat at Anfield. Willie Coxon, a left-winger from Norwich City, made his debut on the same day and, on the journey back, City's team bus collected Harry Brook at Manchester. On the bus Brook, a 36-year-old inside forward, completed his transfer from Leeds United. A long and busy day for Bill.

Two weeks later, for a visit to Leyton Orient, Anderson controversially dropped stalwarts Downie and Emery. In came the much less experienced Johnny Thompson and John Capper. City lost 1-0 at Brisbane Road and the Echo reported: "Relegation-haunted Lincoln City obviously regard their position at the bottom of Division Two as hopeless."

Hopeless seemed about right after two 3-1 home defeats at Easter, to Stoke on Saturday and Barnsley on Monday. During the Barnsley game a supporter scaled the flagpole and lowered the Imps' colours to half-mast. After the match Anderson leaned, head in hands, on the old coke stove in a silent Imps dressing room, and moaned: "That's it now." The obituaries were being written.

City simply had to start winning but they had lost nine on the trot and not won in 17 attempts. Apart from Hannah, Linnecor and Harbertson, Anderson's recent signings had failed. Lincoln had fielded an unchanged side just twice since August. With heavy hearts, supporters prepared to dust down the route-maps to Hartlepool and Halifax.

Anderson had to think quickly - City's defeat to Barnsley was followed 24 hours later by the reverse fixture. The boss got drastic. Out went Thompson and Capper and back came Downie and Emery. Coxon and Brook, whose impact on City's fortunes had been as substantial as Ringo Starr's was to be on the Beatles' "Yesterday," were also discarded. Roy Chapman, still the butt of supporters' ire, was recalled to lend support to Harbertson while Alan Withers came back at outside-left. It was last-ditch stuff by Anderson. More than ever he needed heroics from Hannah.

Eureka. Barnsley looked complacent and City took advantage. Chapman responded to the crisis with a stirring performance. Hannah gave City the lead and though Barnsley drew level by half-time, Harbertson struck an opportunist effort a minute after the break. Chapman's cool finish completed a 3-1 win. No celebrations followed though. Lincoln were still well bottom, three points behind Doncaster, five behind Swansea and six away from Notts County. Still deep in the brown stuff but there was just a glimmer of a ghost of a sliver of a chance.

Four days later came a visit to Doncaster, directly above Lincoln and plummeting after 11 games without a win. Rovers took a 14th minute lead but were truly awful and Lincoln wingers Smilie and Withers were soon romping into space. Hannah equalised on the half-hour and two minutes later Chapman capitalised on slapstick defending. Harbertson added a third goal and Lincoln had, in four days, doubled their season's tally of away wins. But at a price. Middleton, with a badly bruised foot, hobbled off Belle Vue and out for the season.

In the bars of the Blacksmiths and the Blue Pig, and the lounges of the Plough and the Millwright Arms, the Second Division table was studied. Yes, City could still stay up. But they still had to visit a strong Huddersfield side and meet Rotherham, Bristol City and Cardiff at Sincil Bank, where they had not won since November 16.

For the visit of Rotherham, Middleton was replaced by versatile local youngster Russell Green. The Millers were safe, but not far above Lincoln after a scruffy campaign. City were always in command. Chapman was again incisive - suddenly the crowd respected him - Green was busy in midfield and Hannah and Harbertson alert and dangerous. The Imps were kept out for an hour then Hannah, Withers and Chapman manufactured a cross which Harbertson headed home. Breathing space was added when Rotherham's goalkeeper Quairney wandered from his line and was caught out by Smilie's dipping shot. At the other end,

Downie was hardly troubled. A 2-0 victory - with three games to go, City were through the escape tunnel. Just the barbed wire, guard dogs and sprint across open, searchlight-scanned heathland to negotiate. Three games in seven days: Wednesday night home duels with Bristol City and Cardiff separated by that awkward visit to Leeds Road.

The city was awakening to a gallant rearguard action. For Bristol City's visit the crowd crept back above 10,000 for the first time in five months. Again, Lincoln were unchanged - Downie, Jackson, Dykes, Green, Emery, Linnecor, Smilie, Hannah, Harbertson, Chapman, Withers - and tension was palpable. Even Sandy the Labrador tied his chew in a knot. What better than an early goal ? In the eighth minute, Harbertson held off two defenders and crossed for Chapman, timing his run perfectly, to net at the far post. Smilie made it 2-0, then before half-time delivered the cross from which Harbertson smacked in number three. Green had a storming game and on the hour more clever work by Smilie was rounded off by Harbertson's rasping drive. 4-0. If Lincoln could take three points from their last two games they would be safe.

From somewhere, City had produced four successive wins. By now the revival was attracting national attention and hallowed scribes reported some good fortune for the Imps. Rising star Denis Law was ruled out of Huddersfield's side by torn ankle ligaments. Still, the Terriers were in the top ten - this was the toughie. Lincoln got the ideal start. After six minutes Chapman's pass sent Harbertson powering through to score his sixth goal in five games. An 84-minute siege followed on Downie's goal but, with Hannah, Linnecor, Emery and Green outstanding, City protected their lead with massive resolve and a disciplined off-side trap. They clung on. After other results came through it emerged that Lincoln required just one point from their rearranged game against Cardiff to send Notts County down by 0.1 of a goal, on goal average.

Bert Linnecor remembers the Huddersfield result as that which really convinced City's players they could complete the escape. "Huddersfield threw everything at us for 85 minutes," he says. "How we held out I don't know - they poured forward all night and had two very good penalty shouts turned down. But we hung on and that left us needing only a point against Cardiff. Funny thing was there was never any talk, from Bill Anderson or the players of going out for just a draw. It was never mentioned. We went out to win the game."

Cardiff arrived in mid-table but with plenty to play for. Officers of the Welsh FA travelled for the game and places in Wales' squad for the World Cup, just a month away, were up for grabs. Hannah said the tension was greater than in his FA Cup final appearance as the Imps kicked off beneath a wall of noise generated by 18,001 people. After 45 minutes of taut probing and jousting it remained goalless. Then disaster. Six minutes after the break Cardiff scored.

With the crowd shocked into momentary silence, the Bluebirds' centre-forward Joe Bonson - later to join Lincoln - turned to Emery and taunted: "That's put you in the Third Division." Suddenly the weight of those terrible first 36 games loomed heavily again, apparently set to crush the late spasm of resistance. But now came the final, unforgettable twist, sparked by a moment of class from Hannah.

In the 69th minute, he skipped past two defenders to the by-line and squared for Chapman to finish. 1-1. Five minutes later, Chapman connected with Harbertson's cross. 2-1. Then, true joy as Harbertson rounded off the recovery with one of the finest strikes ever seen at Sincil Bank. Sprinting between two defenders, he raced forward from the centre-circle and delivered a searing shot which hit the back stanchion of the net, bounced down and up and down, finally settling, unnoticed, on the grass behind the goal-line while the crowd went bonkers. 3-1. There was no way back for Cardiff now. Jubilance bubbled and rippled round stands and terraces which had so often echoed to the sound of slow hand-clapping. Heaven was thanked for that March 8 blizzard !

The great escape was complete. City finished 20th out of 22, one point above Notts County and four above Doncaster. Only one thing remained to do: Party. That's what the City players did - and with some unexpected company.

Linnecor recalls: "We went to the Millers Arms first and then decided to keep on going. We all threw 10 bob into the kitty and got some drinks to take back to my house. As I drove back I saw a group of blokes milling about by the road and thought they looked a bit like the Cardiff players. I carried on home and a few minutes after I got back I answered a knock on the door. Standing there was the whole Cardiff team. They'd heard there was a party going on.

"Well I thought our lads could drink but Cardiff's were in a different league. Within half-an-hour everything had gone. Then a doctor who was present - I don't know where he had come from - said he knew somebody who could help. So he disappeared with some of the Cardiff lads and came back an hour later with a half-bottle of whisky for me, as host, and 72 bottles of beer. The beer lasted three quarters of an hour - and then they claimed back the whisky !"

It took time to digest the astonishing events but Anderson knew the reprieve had only papered over cracks. Two days after the Cardiff game he freed seven players including the veteran Troops and the wizened Brook. The board, too, had no laurels on which to rest. Cash invested in unsuccessful panic-buys had contributed to a seasonal loss of £14,000 and the club was put on financial red alert. Never did City have a greater need to enlist quality players, but Applewhite insisted that they must depend on home-grown youngsters. Seven players out, none in. It was preparation redolent of an army equipping itself for battle by washing the white flag.

In five of the first eight games, City conceded four goals. They lost 4-2 at Grimsby and at home and away to Fulham. Ipswich beat them 4-1 at Portman Road. At home to Grimsby, the Imps led 4-1 after an hour, 30 minutes from a huge morale-boosting derby win, but ended hanging on for a point at 4-4 after Ron Rafferty's second-half hat-trick for the Mariners.

Hannah had stayed loyal but his sale was inevitable. On Friday September 9, he took tea with his family at home in Lincoln, thinking only of City's tussle with Bristol Rovers next day. Three hours later he was at Sincil Bank collecting his boots. Manchester City had bought him for £10,000 plus promising inside-right John McClelland (valued at £12,500). So Hannah lined up for Manchester City at Arsenal instead of City against Rovers. Of course the Imps' fans hated the development. Twice during the game they tried to force their way into the directors' box but their indignation was partly mollified by an impressive debut for McClelland. He scored as Lincoln won 4-1, their first victory in eight games.

Victories remained rare and frank views were exchanged at the club's annual meeting. The sale of Hannah was lambasted. Blame for City's struggles was apportioned in turn to reticence to sign players, the "complete lack of training facilities" and the tendency of players to spend too much time in "a certain cafe." Anderson insisted it was "stupid mistakes" on the field alone that were to blame.

Andy Graver, at 31, returned from Boston United for £2,500. Downie was dropped again as Bill Heath joined from Bournemouth but Heath's seven mid-season appearances in goal included a Sheffield double-whammy: drubbings 6-1 at United and 7-0 at Wednesday. After the Hillsborough game, Tony Emery was relegated to the reserves. The 'True Gent' among defenders had played the last of his club record 402 League games for Lincoln. Square-jawed Don McEvoy, sturdy and experienced but fading a little, was bought for £2,000 from Sheffield Wednesday to take the number five shirt and the captaincy.

Anderson gambled. He signed 28-year-old forward Arthur Fitzsimmons from Middlesbrough. Here was a player, with 25 caps for Eire, whom City had been chasing for three years. Twelve months earlier, 'Boro priced him at £15,000 but their valuation had suddenly plummeted to five grand, a knock-down sum. If that wasn't enough to set alarm-bells ringing, Anderson confessed the Irishman had taken "a good deal" of persuading to join City after nine seasons and more than 200 games for the Teessiders.

Sure enough, Fitzsimmons contributed little and was soon dropped. Graver rolled back the years with a hat-trick at home to Scunthorpe but even that only earned the Imps a point from a 3-3 draw. Again City had to win on the last day - at home to Sheffield United - to be sure of safety. It wouldn't be easy - victory for the Blades would put them third in the final table, earning £660 for their players. They got their mitts on the dosh. City lost 2-1 but Grimsby and Barnsley below them also lost and went down. At Trent Bridge, up-and-coming left-hander John Edrich hit two centuries in a match for Surrey against Nottinghamshire to press his Test claims. City survived by a gnat's whisker.

It had been another austere season. But, almost as if they had grown weary of the challenge of Division Two, the board tightened the financial shackles still further. The club desperately needed fresh money. New directors. The existing board was elderly and tired, their bank accounts and enthusiasm eroded by keeping City going for a decade. "More cuts, please, Bill," was the instruction. Eight players with first team experience, including Emery after 14 years, Finch after 10 and Downie, were released. While the out-door was busy only one man - serving soldier and rookie winger Ken Barrett from Aston Villa - came in.

As the nation prepared take a huge collective gulp of fresh air, hold its nose, hitch up its trunks and pitch itself headlong into the Swinging Sixties, Sincil Bank was far from swinging. Eight defeats in the first 10 matches of the 1959/60 season landed Lincoln on the bottom of Division Two. Slow hand-clapping became a familiar sound at the Bank. During a 6-1 defeat at Stoke, McEvoy was injured so Ray Long, a teaching student from Louth United, was thrown in at centre-half for the next match, at Leyton Orient. Leyton cruised to a 4-0 win. Long's Imps career was over and at last the board had to grudgingly release some dosh. Anderson spent £5,000 on Sheffield United's reserve centre-half Dennis Gratton. He tightened things up and when Aston Villa paid their first visit to Sincil Bank, a 0-0 draw provided only the Imps' second clean sheet in 11 attempts.

Reinforced by Gratton, City improved. At Hull, they lodged their best away win for 13 years, 5-0 (Linnecor, Middleton, McClelland, Harbertson 2). They trailed 1-0 at home to Derby at half-time but hit back to win 6-2 (McClelland 3, Harbertson 2, Smilie). Around the country farmers, tugmen, miners, pilots, joiners and railway dining-car waiters were on strike while City ground 13 points out of 16. With Heath and Thompson injured, sixteen-year-old goalkeeper Bob Graves, from Boston, made an assured debut in a 1-0 home defeat by Rotherham. Graves looked relaxed and competent and went home well-pleased for his tea. As he did so, Rotherham supporters, on their way home, got into a brawl outside Gainsborough Town Hall.

Sustained by the resolute Smith, Jackson, Gratton, Graver, Linnecor and Ron Allen, a right-back signed from Birmingham City, Lincoln surprised a few people. Linnekor scored twice in a superb 4-2 Boxing Day win at Sunderland. A handsome payday came from an FA Cup visit by a Burnley side including nine internationals. Harbertson's second-half equaliser earned Lincoln a replay in which they battled gallantly before going down 2-0 under the Turf Moor lights.

When Lincoln visited promotion-chasing Liverpool, Linnecor became the only Imp ever to bag a hat-trick at Anfield. City won 3-1 and many of the 24,081 crowd had left by the time Linnecor accepted the match-ball from the referee.

With a makeshift, hastily-assembled squad, Anderson had wielded his motivational magic. Though they lost more than they won, this time City were safe from relegation by late March. In the circumstances, a final placing of 13th was a remarkable effort and stupidly the board started to believe they could continue to exist on such a shoestring in Division Two.

When, after decades of devoted service, Applewhite resigned as chairman, his successor Alwyne Mawer immediately stated that Second Division survival was the height of City's ambition. A luxury such as floodlights was certainly not on the agenda so the supporters' club launched an appeal for £18,000 to bring floodlights to Sincil Bank.

In the 1960/61 season, survival was never a possibility. City failed to score in their first four games and were thrashed 5-1 by Third Division champions Norwich on what remains the Imps' only ever visit to Carrow Road. Misfortunes piled in. After an 8-3 County Cup beating at Grimsby in November, Lincoln returned to find Sincil Bank's offices ransacked. Cupboards were pushed over, drawers emptied and glass widely scattered. Worst of all, quantities of booze and fags had been stolen. Attendances dipped to their lowest since the war. The Footballers' Union, calling for freedom of contract, threatened "no pay, no play," but it was City's fans who stayed away. Only 4,397 turned up for the relegation battle with Brighton.

Having started the season with only 16 full-timers, Anderson lost Allen in early December. A broken right leg, sustained at home to Leeds on December 3, effectively ended his playing career. Anderson recruited Ian Greaves from Manchester United for £2,500 (United's Tommy Heron having declined a move) but there was no League win between Christmas and Easter.

Bizarrely, among this dross, for the first time ever Lincoln knocked First Division opposition out of the cup. West Brom were the victims, 3-1, and 18-year-olds Bob Graves and Roger Holmes starred against the stars. Sheffield United terminated cup progress in the next round and slow-hand clapping was back during a 2-1 home defeat to Bristol Rovers in March. This time, there was no hint of a revival. Relegation was confirmed by a 1-0 defeat at Brighton on April 8. To compound the sense of era's end, it was Andy Graver's last first-team appearance for City.

The Imps' Second Division lifeblood trickled away. Relegation now certain, they returned to the less-than-welcoming pastures of Sincil Bank and were beaten 4-1 by Ipswich. For the final away game, at Leeds United, 21-year-old goalkeeper Brian Burden was given his debut. The youngster had impressed with

West Stockwith in the Gainsborough League but facing the likes of Albert Johannsen, Billy Bremner and Jackie Charlton was slightly more taxing. Leeds romped home 7-0. As City's pounded team trudged off the Elland Road pitch, a Leeds director boomed over the tannoy how honourably they had taken their defeat. The curtain descended on City's Second Division life when Leyton Orient visited Sincil Bank. Middleton and Joe Buick scored in a 2-0 win but there were fewer than 4,000 there to see it. The same day, Graver played his last game in Lincoln colours, for the reserves away to Workington. City won 6-3 and guess-who scored a hat-trick.

Relegated, demoralised and losing £250 per week, the heady days of the early Fifties seemed an eternity ago. City were heading for a black hole.

13.
Frank steps in

FOR more than an hour, Frank Eccleshare had been sitting in the manager's office at Sincil Bank listening to Bill Anderson explain the crisis enveloping Lincoln City. The club was clearly in dire straits but there's only so much a man can take in at once and Frank was thirsty.

"I said 'I'm getting hoarse with all this talking,'" recalls Eccleshare. "Any chance of a cup of tea? Bill ummed and aahed then called in the one remaining member of groundstaff and told him to fetch some tea. The chap looked a bit hesitant. It was half-an-hour before he came back with a pot on a silver tray.

"Bill owned up. The bloke had had to go over to a neighbouring house. City's water had been cut off. That's how bad a state the club was in."

In the UK, the summer of 1963 was a maelstrom of social change. Cultural icons were being shattered. Taboos challenged. People started growing their hair long and indulging in drink, drugs and rock'n'roll. There were sex-parties and raves. Order, discipline and conformity gave way to lawlessness, decadence and social rebellion. Everywhere, teenagers would knock loudly on doors then run away before the householder could answer.

It was a time of adventure. A time of excitement. A time of anarchy, freedom and love. The Beatles arrived. "Money can't buy me love," they warbled. Lincoln City needed some love and, even more urgently, money. Or the club would die.

After relegation from Division Two in 1961 they had passed straight through Division Three. Then they finished their first ever Division Four campaign 22nd out of 24 so had, for the first time since 1920, to apply for re-election. In two seasons they won 17 of 88 League games. As spring of 1963 was dragged, kicking and screaming, on to the cold slab of history to be replaced by a bright, vivacious, infant summer, Lincoln City was in total disarray. More than £10,000 in debt - and losing £300 per week - the club had no chairman and no vice-chairman, no accountant or secretary and just a handful of full-time players. Ten years earlier the football club was the city's pride. Now it was an embarrassment. If Lincoln City had been a horse, the screens would have gone up around it.

A succession of directors had lost interest, ran out of money or died. City were kept going, just, by Bill Anderson and the supporters' club. But one determined individual and a hard-working group of volunteers are not enough to sustain a Football League club. Supporters club chief Vic Withers knew that and, in desperation, contacted business leaders around the city to plead for help. Most took one look at the carnage of the Imps' accounts - showing an overdraft of £7,500 - and said: 'No thanks.' All, in fact. Except one.

Frank Eccleshare ran a well-established and profitable building company. He wasn't into football. But, born and bred in the city, he was into Lincoln. And he was convinced by Withers, who he knew through business, that the football club was worth saving; that a famous city institution must not be allowed to perish. That's how he came to be taking tea with Bill Anderson, listening carefully as the magnitude of the pickle City were in became clear.

"It was absolute chaos," recalls Eccleshare. "Nobody knew how much the club owed or who they owed it too. I sat down and asked 'where are the books ?' and really there weren't any. They owed money all over the place - the council for rates, the police, the bank, the water and also to a lot of small traders who had been owed for years. That upset me because small traders were having a poor time of it anyway.

"It was a total mess. But I knew Vic Withers well and trusted him personally. It was his involvement alone that persuaded me to take a chance. Without him, Lincoln City would have died.

"In business I had made money from the people of Lincoln. I saw the football club's plight as a chance to put something back."

Eccleshare moved in after two years of freefall in which City deteriorated from a respectable, if stretched, mid-table outfit in the Second Division to a depressed rabble near the foot of the Fourth. The opening day of the 1961/2 season - City's first in the unified Third Division - had brought ominous signs. Bournemouth, on their first visit to Sincil Bank, won 2-0 and slow-hand clapping echoed round the ground. Early in the season, City sold leading scorer Roy Chapman to Mansfield for £6,000 and right-winger John McClelland, a fans' favourite, to Queens Park Rangers for £14,000. The sales eased pressure on the board, who could not afford to keep the pair, but piled it on to a squad which couldn't afford to lose them. The team looked dishevelled. In the League Cup at Norwich, they led 2-0 with 16 minutes left but lost 3-2. Only five League victories before Christmas chiselled out an immediate pathway to Division Four.

The only light in a season of gloom came from the supporters' club. It was their £16,000 that paid for Sincil Bank's floodlights, erection of which began in October. The lights were still to shine for the first time when boardroom upheaval began. On December 14, Alwyne Mawer quit after 16 months as chairman and 31 years as a director. He insisted that younger blood was needed but there was none available. Edgar Gilbert, more sturdy oak than sapling, took over as chairman.

The long-awaited floodlights switch-on arrived on January 20, for a goal-less draw with Northampton. The way City were playing it would have been kinder to leave them off. To boost flagging crowds, Lincoln experimented with Friday-night home fixtures but four wins from 23 home games explained why attendances were small. Left-winger Albert Scanlon provided some brighter moments. As a Busby Babe, four years earlier, Scanlon had survived the Munich air disaster but his best efforts, along with the hard-working Bert Linnecor and Russell Green, could not salvage City's dreadful season. At home, they went three months without a win. Away, they registered 13 nils while conceding four at Swindon, Grimsby, Port Vale, Newport and Reading and five at Peterborough.

It was Queens Park Rangers who administered the coup de grace. Lincoln had to beat them at the Bank in the penultimate game of the season to have any chance of survival. Rangers scored four goals in 19 first-half minutes and eased to a 5-0 win. Lincoln finished 22nd, sentenced to drop to Division Four along with Torquay, Brentford and Newport. The descent was gathering pace, out of control, and there was no-one was at hand with a parachute.

Lincoln's first ever Division Four fixture brought an encouraging 4-2 home win over Tranmere. Their second was the inaugural Football League fixture at Oxford United, who had replaced Accrington. Scanlon gave Lincoln a fourth minute lead at the Manor Ground but the home side, driven forward by Ron Atkinson, hit back to win 2-1.

Hope sprang from a September uprising which brought 20 goals in five home wins over Newport (6-3), Hartlepools (4-1), Bradford City (3-2) Workington (3-2) and Exeter (4-1). Ex-Wolves and Leicester City striker Brian Punter scored seven of the 20, Linnecor four and Scanlon three. During this fleeting revival, a case at Lincoln magistrates court helped explain why the Imps were in such a financial mess. Into the dock went Anthony Walker who had, despite lacking any relevant experience, been appointed City secretary in the Autumn of 1960. He was sacked the day after City's 2-1 defeat at Oxford and now the reason became clear. During 23 months at Sincil Bank he stole a total of £1,850 18s 1d from the football club. In mitigation he claimed he took the job with no book-keeping experience but received no help from the directors. "They left everything to me," explained Walker before being led off to serve 12 months in one of Her Majesty's one-star 'otels. Dishonest, Walker might have been, but it was reckless of the board to allow a novice such freedom.

Another unfilled vacancy was created on that board when Robert Giles, a director since 1936, died. Troubles crowded in. To the list of City's tormentors was added a steak and kidney pie, the one which four players - Smith, Broadbent, Linnecor and Jackson - ate on the way back from a 1-1 draw at Exeter. They got food poisoning. City's autumn revival also turned sour. Two victories in 21

League games between the ends of October and April dragged them into the re-election zone. Friday morning team-talks by Anderson, never elaborate, were sombre affairs and one contained some horrible news. On the eve of a visit to Doncaster, Anderson was addressing the team in his office when the telephone rang. The venerable boss rarely showed much emotion but by the time he replaced the receiver his face had turned white. Harry Troops had been killed in a road accident in Sheffield. He was 37.

City scrambled past Darlington and Halifax to reach the FA Cup third round and were paired with Jimmy Hill's Coventry City but the weather turned nasty and the match was postponed 15 times. Finally, 63 days after first sched-uled, it went ahead. Coventry's Jimmy Whitehouse scored after 15 seconds and the Sky Blues cantered to a 5-1 win.

In spring 1963, the City ship listing badly, more crew-members bailed out. Vice-chairman William Wright, director Geoffrey Gilbert and club secretary George Key all quit. On May 15, doomed to finish in the bottom four of Division Four, the Imps attracted the lowest ever crowd for a League match at Sincil Bank - 1,993 for a 2-1 win over Gillingham. Six of their last seven home games attract-ed less than 3,000 people. The stadium, shabby and near-deserted, had an atmos-phere like an empty fridge and the team finished 22nd: 90th in the League. In June, Edgar Gilbert resigned as chairman to leave the club's roll of officers even more closely resembling a string vest. Lincoln City, at the grand old age of 79, was close to the point of no return. About, it seemed, to follow Accrington into extinction.

The resourceful Vic Withers, however, was not the type to give up. Since moving from London to Lincoln just before the war he had taken City as close to his heart as any Yellowbelly ever did. He wasn't going to let go. He hitched up his trousers, rolled up his sleeves, got his thinking cap on and made some calls. And that's where Frank stepped in.

Eccleshare agreed to save the club on one condition: that he took control. Full control. With no other saviour in sight who could argue ? Firm decisions and immediate action followed and the principal casualty was Anderson. Having helped prop up the Imps - and almost lived at Sincil Bank - for 16 years he found responsibility stripped from him. A statement from the new supremo revealed that: "Mr Anderson has been relieved of his duties concerning the internal administration of the club and also of his acting position of company secretary." It was the beginning of the end for Anderson at the Bank but Eccleshare, inject-ing his own cash into the rescue, demanded total power and a clean slate.

He said: "I was called dictatorial and, yes, there was only one bloke in charge. That's the way it had to be. Half the previous remaining directors backed away and the other half were no good so I sacked them. Bill Anderson had put a lot into the club - money too - but I had to have full control. There was so much to sort out.

"I don't know how the club was allowed to get into such a state. But I spoke to the major creditors - they knew me and my father before me - and told them I could pay them something, though not all the club owed. I wanted to pay off the small traders first. That's what happened and slowly we started to turn things round.

"I'm not a football man - I don't know the first thing about it. But the club needed someone with a bit of business sense and drive. That's what I provided."

At last, someone had halted the club's aimless drift into ruin and others responded. Within 10 days of Eccleshare's takeover, £1,000 of shares in the club were bought and a further £3,500 worth promised. Eccleshare brought in his company accountant, Roy Chapman (not the former striker). Another of his employees, George Cook, joined the Imps board. So did two business acquaintances, silverware dealer Walter Mant and motor trader Charles Warner. In December, the club's annual meeting was the best attended for years.

"Operation Booster," was launched to heighten public interest in the football club. Ideas spawned action. Eccleshare asked Lincolnshire Roadcar and British Rail to provide more services from outlying areas on match-days. Commercial opportunities offered by the Sincil Bank arena were exploited. The Sixties swung into the Bank with pre-match pop music. Johnny Vee and the Vampires performed before a game against Chesterfield and inspired City to race 4-0 up in 32 minutes on the way to a 5-2 win (Linnecor 3, Bud Houghton 2). The Avengers, before the Brighton game, inspired Brighton, who won 2-0. With Anderson still picking the team, City improved to finished 11th, hardly fabulous but suggesting a bottoming-out of the collapse.

In June, greyhound-racing returned to Sincil Bank, although atrocious weather limited the crowd to 473 and profit to £30. WL Beresford Promotions presented wrestling at the Bank. A profit of £125 resulted and Bradford's Denis Mitchell, despite gaining an early pin-fall, was knocked out by 'The Mask.' The tireless battalions of supporters' club agents and collectors, out and about night after night extracting precious shillings from the community, presented another £3,250 to Eccleshare just before the 1964/5 season.

Anderson faced the challenge of matching this off-field resurgence with a few goals and wins. He brought back the ageing Dick Neal, who had moved on to Middlesbrough, and signed wing-half John Milner from Huddersfield. In, too, came forward Ken Fencott from Aston Villa and outside-left John Hawksby from Leeds United but the squad remained largely devoid of high quality and long-servers. Linnecor joined Boston FC and apart from stalwart full-backs Alf Jones and Jeff Smith, only the versatile, Scunthorpe-born Roger Holmes could confidently expect to see his name on the team-sheet. The skilful Holmes, a regular since he was a teenager in the late 1950s, had, through the lean years, become a firm favourite. Now, at last, he went full-time. There was no full-time goalkeeper on the staff. Part-timers Bob Graves and Malcolm White competed for the number one shirt.

Fencott scored on his debut as City opened with a 4-2 home win over Hartlepools but the Anderson/Eccleshare liaison was one of sufferance. After eight games, which yielded seven points, Anderson was relieved of selection duties. Now offered a nebulous general-manager role, he just sat in his office, not required even to answer the telephone. It was an undignified way for the Geordie - "Mr Lincoln City" - to approach the end of almost two decades service at the Bank. It had not been a great year either for two other major Imps figures; Joe McClelland and Sam Tonge. They both died, aged 79; McClelland at St George's Hospital, Lincoln, and Tonge in Wollaton, Nottinghamshire.

Team selection matters were taken over by the board with tactical guidance from skipper Brian Jackson and a grudging Anderson. It didn't work. City lost 4-0 at Brighton, 7-0 at Newport and 3-0 at Hartlepool. By Christmas they were back in the bottom six. Eccleshare, whose life had contained so many excellent business decisions, so many wise moves and shrewd choices, now dropped a monumental, cast-iron, footballing clanger. He appointed, as first-team coach/trainer, Cornelius Moulson. As news of the appointment spread round the country, a frequent reaction was: "Who?" Lincoln folk knew who. Their reaction was a bewildered: "Eh ?"

'Con' Moulson was a popular centre-half for Lincoln during the 1930s. Rugged and effective, he earned the rare distinction of playing international football (for Eire) while an Imp and was still fit enough to guest in 97 City matches during the war. He had since worked as a full-time machinist at Rustons, a factory esteemed nationwide for its production of reliable, high-quality precision turbines but not as a nursery of football gurus.

Tipperary-born Moulson was more boiler-suit than track-suit but had one thing going for him - he came cheap. "I brought him in and it caused a riot," recalls Eccleshare. "But it was the correct decision to take. We were still almost bankrupt. I couldn't say to a potential manager: 'Right, we're a bit hard-up just now, but we can pay you properly when things pick up.' They wanted the full whack straight away."

So, at 58, Moulson jacked in his factory job and took over training and tactics of the Imps' first-team. For Anderson, if every day vegetating in his office was a slap in the face, the appointment of Moulson was a punch in the guts. The former boss had always kept a dignified silence but admitted: "The duties of Con Moulson, the new trainer/coach, clearly conflict with my responsibilities as manager under the terms of my existing contract." Anderson watched helplessly as Moulson's reign headed for a place in Imps history. A perfect record. 100 per cent. Eight matches, eight defeats.

Con had a plan. For his first match, at home to struggling Bradford City on January 16, he sent out a 3-3-4 formation. "Flexibility," he insisted, was the keynote to the "new method." Sincil Bank's lowest crowd of the season saw a confused City team beaten 2-0 by a Bantams side including 10 free-transfer players.

Next came a visit to Chester. Moulson made four changes including the return of Roy Chapman who, perhaps sensing an imminent coaching vacancy, agreed to rejoin from Mansfield. Con's method failed again as Chester won 5-1 though the scoreline was, according to Moulson, "a travesty of justice. We played really well, especially in midfield and did all the attacking. I wish the supporters could have been there to see the football we played."

Con's plan never came together. City lost 5-3 at Wrexham and 1-0 at home to Torquay. A 3-1 reverse at fellow strugglers Stockport was the Imps' seventh successive defeat and dumped them bottom of Division Four. The supporters were torn. Eccleshare had saved the club but surely he must own up to this mistake. Fast. Moulson pledged to find players who would battle for the club but already the turbine factory was calling him home. City lost 2-1 at home to Crewe and 1-0 at Chesterfield. After a 2-0 home defeat to Doncaster - no points in eight games under Moulson - even Eccleshare, who admitted he knew nothing about football, spotted that this wasn't working.

Chapman took over as player-coach - and also captain, City's sixth of the season. A slight improvement followed - two wins and two draws from the last 10 games - but it was far too late to keep Lincoln out of the bottom four. They finished 22nd, one point above bottom-placed Stockport, and applied for re-election.

Eccleshare was now convinced of the need to turn things round on the pitch too. He insisted that signings would be made and Chapman plumped for experience. Former Sunderland goalkeeper Peter Wakeham arrived from Charlton Athletic. Full-back Geoff Hudson, 15 seasons of League football behind him, and left-half Alec Farrall joined from Gillingham. Barry Hutchinson, son of former Imp Jimmy, moved north from Weymouth for whom he scored 43 Southern League goals in the 1964/5 season. "This will show people we are not merely concentrating on ground improvements," said Eccleshare, alluding to the recent arrival of a supporters' club social club under the South Park Stand. In that social club, little Lee Chapman, son of Roy, was often to be seen in the vicinity of the fruit machines.

With Chapman Senior settling in as player/coach, Moulson, so recently head honcho on the tactics front, painted the dressing rooms. Soon he was clocking on again at Rustons. A valedictory statement from the football club dug deep for a compliment. "Con Moulson has certainly worked conscientiously and to the best of his ability," it said. "His insistence on cleanliness and hygiene have been exceptional."

City fans, down to a 3,000 hard-core, prepared to cringe through another season. Hutchinson started the 1965/66 campaign well with eight goals in eight League and League Cup games but the team was full of strangers. Mid-table in early October, Lincoln started to sink as inexorably as the setting sun. Chapman could not hold it together. Only one of 12 League games was won and after a 3-1 FA Cup home defeat by Barnsley the young coach confessed: "The fans are sick of defeat. I am sick of it and the players are sick of it. Give me £20,000 and I will go and build a good team straight away."

Not even the brilliant supporters' club could supply £20,000 at a moment's notice. Soon after Christmas, City already looked doomed to finish in the bottom four of a division for the seventh time in nine seasons. Finally the players, generations of whom had, through all the troubles, showed remarkable loyalty, grew restless. Bunny Larkin, in and out of the side after joining from Watford, and long-serving Jeff Smith were transfer-listed at their own request. Hutchinson, having scored 18 of City's 31 League goals, asked for a move and, next day, so did Wakeham. Hudson, ever-present at right-back, submitted five transfer requests. Milner, on his way to catch the team coach for the visit to Halifax, paused at a pillar-box to pop his transfer request into the post. Eccleshare was righting the ship but it certainly wasn't a happy ship.

In March, Chapman's problems increased when, during a war of a home game with Doncaster, he sustained a fractured cheekbone, ruling him out for the season. Veteran striker Joe Bonson joined City - his seventh League club - from Brentford for £2,000. Bonson returned to the Sincil Bank greensward he last trod as part of Cardiff's team on that heady night in April 1958. At the other end of the career-scale tall, city-born striker Phil Hubbard, aged 17 years and 25 days, made his debut in a 2-2 draw at home to Chester. Harry Godbold, a recruit from Boston FC, made his debut on the wing. The team was composed largely of wannabees and wantaways. At Crewe, a Lincoln side containing five players on the transfer list at their own request went 6-0 down in the first 38 minutes, eventually losing 7-0. At the Imps' annual meeting in Spring angry shareholders called for Bill Anderson to be reinstated. In an unrelated incident, meanwhile, Sleaford's coroner issued the chilling warning: "Anoraks may be dangerous."

On April 6, 1966, no Lincoln players featured when Alf Ramsay announced his list of 40 'probables' for England's World Cup squad. Five days later, City travelled on the eve of a Monday-night game at Southport. Chapman ordered his squad to a Sunday-night show in Morecambe for a bit of bonding.

Peter Wakeham stayed in the hotel and went to bed early. Next morning he was sent home. Eighteen-year-old Patrick Jeavons got a shock debut in goal, dropped an eighth-minute ricket which cost a goal, had an all-round nightmare and City lost 5-1. Jeavons never surfaced in the first team again. Bonson struck form, hitting 10 goals in the last 12 games but, despite brighter late-season form, City again finished 22nd, albeit with 37 points, 11 more than the previous season.

The summer brought English football's finest moment. Thanks to West Ham wizards Bobby Moore, Geoff Hurst and Martin Peters, England won the World Cup. Euphoria swept the nation. Street-parties were held and lifelong memories forged. From wherever streamers and bunting could conceivably be hung, streamers and bunting were hung. Beer was consumed. Carnivals took a patriotic theme as national pride shone from every orifice of everyday life.

Joy infiltrated Sincil Bank. Its debts being discharged, the football club was now off the critical list. To further tighten up administration, Harold Pepper was appointed secretary. Former chief cashier with Arundel Co-operative Society in Sussex, Pepper was tempted away from the secretary's job at Peterborough United. City signed Welsh goalkeeper Colin Treharne and outside-right Geoff Anderson from Mansfield and wing-half Dick Scott from Scunthorpe. Hubbard turned professional and the board voted unanimously to give Eccleshare another three years as chairman with full executive powers.

The 1965/66 season's late rally - two defeats from the last 12 games - had hinted at a lifting of City's gloom. Corners, perhaps, were being turned, on and off the field. The World Cup was England's. Time to hitch up the trousers, stick out the chin and lick the lips at the prospect of better times ahead. Get ready to party. Oh yes. Er, oh no. For the first time since 1911, City finished rock-bottom of the Football League.

All seemed well when two Second Division sides were dumped out of the League Cup at Sincil Bank. Bonson's header secured a 1-0 win over Hull City then an excellent display accounted for Huddersfield. Tony Leighton gave the Terriers a 15th minute lead but Anderson's spectacular header levelled on 27 minutes. Seven minutes later Bonson's goalbound shot was handled on the line and he converted the penalty. Wingers Godbold and Anderson starred as City held on to win 2-1 amid almost-forgotten levels of noise from the 6,442 crowd.

Three days later the revival was forgotten as Southport eased to a 4-0 win at the Bank. In the closing minutes, cynical City fans cheered on the visiting team. Within a week came the final break with Anderson. Eccleshare announced that "by mutual agreement" Anderson's contract was terminated. He vacated his office immediately, restricting his comments, with great dignity as ever, only to that, at 51, he hoped to remain football. Despite the untidy end to his Imps employment, there was never going to be a shortage of offers. Anderson soon joined Nottingham Forest as assistant manager to Jimmy Carey.

City's League Cup run ended at First Division side Leicester City. Five hundred travelling Imps fans watched Gordon Banks foil Holmes and Tommy Brooks early on before the Foxes, including John Sjoberg, Peter Rodrigues, Derek Dougan and David Nish, took control. A 5-0 defeat at Leicester was acceptable. Ten days later, a 5-0 defeat at Hartlepool was not. By late October, after just one win from 12 League games, Lincoln were bottom again and Chapman was reduced back to the ranks. Appointed manager was the burly, genial Ron Gray.

For Gray, another native of the north-east, it was a return to full-time employment after three years as a freelance scout and physiotherapist. He had been on City's books as a player in the late 1930s but did not make the first team before war broke out. After guesting for Dundee, Grimsby and Notts County during the conflict, his playing career was ended by injury soon after peace resumed. Gray then spent nine years on the back-room staff at Watford and another 12 at Millwall, serving briefly as manager of both clubs. He was offered a position as general manager at Millwall but baulked at a role detached from the players and left to open a physiotherapy clinic, mainly treating cricketers, in Baker Street, London. Aged 45, he accepted a one-year contract with the Imps having just turned down a position with the newly-formed USA soccer administration. Mrs Gray didn't fancy the States. Almost as soon as his cheeks landed on the manager's chair at Sincil Bank, Gray received a best-wishes telegram from Bill Anderson.

A strict but affable disciplinarian, Gray called for 100 per cent effort from his players. His second match brought an encouraging 2-0 victory over high-flying Tranmere. City went out of the FA Cup in the first round, beaten 4-3 at home by Scunthorpe before playing host to fellow strugglers Luton Town. The Imps, having scored 18 goals in 20 League games, went bananas with an 8-1 win. Billy Cobb, a Newark-born inside-right signed by Gray from Brentford, became the first - and still only - player to score a hat-trick on his Imps debut. Chapman and Bonson added two each and Holmes the other.

It was not enough to lift City off the bottom and despite Gray's diligence and hard work, he needed time to mould the disparate collection of part-timers and misfits into a decent side. Two more signings - striker Clive Ford from Walsall and right-half Ray Lancaster from Grimsby - became first-team regulars but the Imps' 5-4 victory at Stockport in the season's final game ended a 15-match winless sequence. City finished bottom, four points behind Bradford Park Avenue and York City.

The big battle, however, had been won. The football club was solvent again. At City's annual meeting on March 21, 1967, Frank Eccleshare stepped down as chairman. "I feel my part in keeping Lincoln City alive has been completed," he said. "The time has come when my dictatorial powers should be relinquished." Under a clause inserted when he took over, Eccleshare nominated his successor as chairman, Walter Mant. Eccleshare stayed on the board for another five months then quit. He had secured Lincoln City's future and now he moved on.

An argument could be made that without any of several men - Dawber, Strawson, Milner, Tonge, Taylor, Anderson, later Heneage Dove and John Reames - Lincoln City might have ceased to exist. But only Eccleshare has stood, alone, between the club and oblivion. And this from a non-football man. Still, in the year 2000, Eccleshare remains active and involved in Lincoln life but, since quitting the Imps' board more than 30 years ago, he has not once been back to Sincil Bank.

"It was never going to be a long-term thing for me," he recalls. "Just a question of getting the club back on its feet so that new blood would come in. And that's what happened. I settled all the debts then moved on.

"I will always want City to do well and always look to see how they have done but I've never been back because that would just reopen the door on a lot of business that has finished. It was always my intention to make the football club safe then walk away."

14.
A resurgence, giant-killing thrills, crowd trouble, Kevin Keegan, Rodney Marsh, Jim Callaghan, Ted Heath, Percy Freeman, many dead goldfish and the Watney Cup

Frank Eccleshare was the catalyst for Lincoln City's survival. He stepped forward and got involved with, crucially, the financial clout to drag the Imps out of crisis.

It was a crisis that he, alone, had both the interest and resources to resolve but many people shared his passion. They hadn't much money to offer but cared deeply. Even through those most joyless seasons a hard-core of supporters stuck by the club. Another generation of a magnificent nucleus of fans, very rarely less than 3,000, who for more than a century have turned up at Sincil Bank whatever the weather, opposition or League status.

Supporters who didn't have enough money to get involved at boardroom level, indeed sometimes struggled to find the price of admission, but found it because they loved the football club. They loved it for its cast of characters, its heritage and its identity; for its dogged swimming against the tide and its homely, familiar stadium. They loved the passion, unpredictability, theatre and the occasional rampant, boil-in-the-bag euphoria but above all, they loved Lincoln City for its Lincolnness. It was their club and they were not about to desert it. In 1967, after seven skeletal seasons, they deserved something better.

The task of delivering something better fell to the avuncular figure of Ron Gray and he decided a new set of players was required. He released 11, including the well-established Jones, Chapman and Anderson, and began rebuilding. Gray tapped into contacts in Scotland. Celtic manager Jock Stein recommended tall, Irish-born goalkeeper John Kennedy, whom he had just freed, and the legendary Stein's word was good enough for Gray. The Imps' boss travelled to London to meet the Celtic party just before they flew to Lisbon for the European Cup final against Inter Milan. At Heathrow Airport, Kennedy signed for the Imps, on a part-time basis so he could continue his teaching career

Gray also persuaded George Peden, a robust left-back, to move south from Hearts. Peden and Kennedy were to prove excellent servants to City well beyond Gray's tenure. Ray Harford, a tall, intelligent centre-half, moved up from Exeter. Speedy winger Lewis Thom joined from Shrewsbury and right-back Mick Brown from Hull.

Mant and his board, meanwhile, laboured to keep the refortified club shored up. Severe loan-repayments still loomed each month. Mant launched the Centurion Appeal: a new label for a familiar device - lobbying the business community for cash. The chairman described the response as "steady but not over-whelming" but the appeal yielded one excellent result. It spurred Collingham farmer Heneage Dove to get involved. An Imps fan for years, Dove, a friend and neighbour of Charles Applewhite, was to be a lasting source of sense and ballast to the club. Less impressed by the new initiative was the supporters' club who criticised its timing. Mant's response was to disassociate the supporters' club from the appeal and an internecine rift formed between the two organisations. Vic Withers stepped down as the supporters' representative on City's board and insisted that all money handed over in future must be for an agreed, specified purpose.

Hearts and Skegness Town offered contrasting friendly opposition at either end of the summer of 1967. City, discarding the traditional stripes in favour of new Arsenal-type shirts, beat Hearts 3-0 at Sincil Bank in May. In August, their visit to Skegness Town attracted 100 spectators. These were all asked to leave, just before kick-off, when someone unearthed an FA rule stating that pre-season matches could only be played in public within 14 days of the new season (August 19). It was August 2. Out the spectators obediently trooped but, one-by-one, all returned over fences and through railings to witness the 1-1 draw.

City's early League results were mixed but attendances moved encouragingly back over 6,000. That hard-core was enjoying a bit more company once again. What was really needed was something special to capture a new generation of fans. Lincoln's youngest football-watchers knew City only as whipping-boys. They wanted the Imps to whup some ass. Some First Division ass, in a rollicking League Cup run, did the job nicely.

After disposing of Mansfield 3-2 (Cobb, Holmes 2) at Field Mill in the first round, Lincoln were drawn at home to Newcastle United. To the Bank came Joe Harvey's famous Magpies with their mighty cup pedigree and fanatical support. Up front were Welsh star Wyn Davies and razor-sharp Bryan "Pop" Robson. In goal, Northern Ireland international Iam McFaul. Plenty of quality but in dodgy form. They arrived in the wake of two heavy defeats, 6-0 at Liverpool and 4-0 at Nottingham Forest, while Lincoln came off the back of a rip-roaring, tub-thumping 1-0 home win over Halifax.

A crowd of 15,454 witnessed the best night at Sincil Bank for years. In a blistering start, Cobb headed against the bar, Holmes' shot was scrambled off the line by MacFaul and Ford's drive struck the inside of a post - all in the first 12 minutes. Ray Harford dominated Davies and for an hour City looked the likelier side to score. Newcastle broke to take an undeserved lead when substitute Ollie Burton fired home a 20-yarder in the 70th minute but Lincoln kept going. Thom's header was fumbled by MacFaul and Grummett pounced to equalise. Five minutes from time, Iley handled in the box and Peden sent MacFaul the wrong way from the penalty. After three minutes of stomach-churning injury-time, the final whistle heralded roars of atavistic delight. City's players hugged each other while Newcastle's took their defeat in the most sporting manner.

The third round draw meted out a home tie against Third Division side Torquay, a hurdle as awkward as it was unglamorous. The Gulls were full of confidence having lost just once in 13 games. Every stand ticket was sold and the 13,532 crowd had its first glimpse of the Red Imps Girls, dressed in red and white, selling autographed photos of City players. Evening dog-walkers, nearby on South Common, found their usually sedate exercise accompanied by an almost constant roar as City raced 4-0 up in 19 minutes through Lewis (2), Holmes and a typically thunderous Peden penalty. Peden, Harford and Grummett then led the resistance as Torquay's tenacious fightback was held to 4-2.

Into the last 16 and a much more mouth-watering draw: A visit to Brian Clough's Derby County. Lincoln's supporters, filling a fleet of coaches and a special train, were given a hostile reception by some Derby followers but, in front of 25,079, on a typical Baseball Ground swamp, the Imps again lifted their game. Undaunted by loss of a 14th minute goal to Barker, they stayed strong and pressed the Rams back. A Jack Lewis "goal" was controversially disallowed for offside but the visiting support became louder and prouder as Lincoln fought tigerishly. Derby grew edgy and a richly deserved equaliser arrived 15 minutes from time when John Gregson's cross was headed home by Thom, the smallest man on the field. The glorious run continued. It was back to the Bank for a replay. The draw for the quarter-finals opened up stunning possibilities. If Lincoln ousted Derby they would be at home to fellow Fourth Division side Darlington in the quarter-final. Remarkably, a place in the League Cup semi-final was a realistic prospect. Clough, looking ahead to the replay, asserted, with typical arrogance: "We'll crush them."

After first being postponed due to fog, the replay attracted 23,196 - still a record - to Sincil Bank. Again Derby took an early lead - John O'Hare striking in the eighth minute - to which they hung unconvincingly. A pivotal moment arrived just before half-time when Gregson's 25-yard piledriver had "onion bag, top corner" written all over it until Reg Matthews, at full stretch, somehow turned it over the bar. City scrapped, resisted and pressed after the interval and their resistance only buckled seven minutes from time. Brown was sent off for head-butting Kevin Hector who, face bleeding, picked himself up, jogged forward and made it 2-0 from the free-kick. O'Hare added a third in injury time. The Imps were out but far from crushed. The city had a frission of pride reading the match reports in the national papers over their bacon and eggs next morning. For the directors, just one conundrum. The players deserved some extra reward but a cup-run bonus was not in their contracts. The board came up with a good old farming-county solution - every player got a sack of spuds.

League form failed to match the cup exploits. Clive Ford scored a hat-trick, including two goals in the first minute, in a 5-1 win over Bradford Park Avenue but, though Kennedy, Peden, Harford and Grummett were ever-present, ten matches without a win in February and March ended promotion hopes. Gray made three deadline signings. Wing-half Jim Smith, a former Sheffield United groundstaff boy, joined from Halifax. From Derby County, for £6,000, came experienced outside-right Gordon Hughes who had played in both League Cup ties against City. Inside-right Peter Kearns moved north from Aldershot. All three settled straight into the side and, although City never climbed above mid-table, brownie points stored by the cup run, allied to seven wins in eight games in April, kept crowds high. More than 8,000 attended the visits of Exeter and Brentford. The Imps finished 13th and reached Wembley - the Empire Pool, that is - for a national five-a-side tournament. They qualified from an eight-strong qualifying section at the Mecca Rolarena in Leeds, concluding with a 5-2 final victory over Halifax. At Wembley, City's interest ended early - a 1-0 first round defeat by Grimsby.

Less frivolous matters occupied Gray during the summer: more scouting, more road miles, more negotiating, more signings. On July 23, 1968, he spent £4,000 on right-back Graham Taylor from Grimsby. Left-winger Dave Smith, a former youth international, joined from Middlesbrough. Wing-half Graham Parker arrived from Rotherham for £7,000. The articulate Taylor was appointed captain and netted a spectacular 25-yarder on his debut in a 5-0 opening-day win over Notts County. Further victories - at Halifax (1-0) and at home to Newport (1-0) and Southend (2-1) - put City top of Division Four. Next came a 5-0 defeat at Darlington, revealing a fragility that was to surface too often. City stayed in the top half but were always just off the promotion pace. Unhelpful were serious injuries which ruled out Holmes and Kennedy for much of the season. On November 16, Yoko Ono had a miscarriage at Queen Charlotte's Maternity

Hospital, London, and the Imps knocked Northern Premier League leaders Macclesfield out of the FA Cup. The 3-1 (Kearns, Thom, David Smith) win at Moss Rose was City's first cup victory over non-League opposition for 23 years. They then overcame Chester to earn a visit to Second Division Birmingham City in round three. Cheered by raucous travelling support among 31,429 people in the huge St Andrews bowl, the Imps earned high praise from a 2-1 defeat.

Again, though, they could not peak often enough in the League. The team, built round Jim and Dave Smith, Peden, Harford, Grummett and Hubbard, clung to the tail of an 11-club scramble for promotion. The versatile Hubbard found himself wearing shirts 6, 9, 2, 9 again, 8, 12 and 2 again as Gray toyed with turning the striker into a right-back. Seven points from 10 games before Easter dropped City out of contention. Rod Fletcher, schoolteacher and centre-forward, became the "new darling of the terraces." His nine goals in nine games included a hat-trick at home to Workington, but City finished eighth, five points short of a promotion slot. Parker joined Exeter City after starting just four games for Lincoln. A poor investment. As Gray might have said: "You can't knock over a coconut every time."

Two weeks after the League campaign closed came a unique occurrence: two future England managers in opposition at Sincil Bank. Lincoln, including Taylor, played Scunthorpe in the County Cup final. A tiny striker called Kevin Keegan put Scunthorpe ahead in the 14th minute. Alick Jeffrey equalised then extra time goals from Dave Smith, Jeffrey and Jim Smith earned a 4-1 victory. Jim Smith's goal was with his last touch as an Imp. He had already - along with Kearns, Thom and young goalkeeper David Tennant - been told he was to be freed. The decision perplexed many supporters who appreciated Smith's commitment.

Less appreciated was the behaviour of some supporters during the 1968/69 season. Football-related violence flared for the first time since the sport's earliest days. In Lincoln City's infancy, way back in the 1890s, players and supporters often ended up as brawling gangs, committeemen frequently exchanged blows and referees were routinely thrown into rivers. But this new outbreak of misrule, after decades of orderly spectating, was more sinister. Less spontaneous: more organised and vindictive. City's home match against Southend in August attracted their first five-figure crowd for six years but was marred by fighting fans. On the way to a League Cup tie at Scunthorpe, Lincoln supporters wrecked most of the 10 carriages of a football special train. BR's response, hardly surprisingly, was to "seriously consider" not bothering with specials in future. A Lincoln supporters' bus was attacked by Scunny fans. Most home games brought problems with the police forced to increase their usual presence of an inspector, a sergeant and eight constables. Mant vowed to ban trouble-makers from Sincil Bank while Home Secretary Jim Callaghan, aware of a national problem, "declared war" on football thugs, just the sort of aggressive rhetoric they relished.

League football was more attractive than ever to hooligans but also to aspiring members. In 1969, Bedford Town, Cambridge City, Cambridge United, Hereford, Kettering, Nuneaton, Romford, Wigan, Wimbledon and Worcester all sought entry but the closed shop remained secure. Bradford Park Avenue, Grimsby, Newport and York were re-elected. Cassius Clay launched "champ burgers," Nobby Stiles underwent knee surgery and Allan Clarke, an Imps manager-to-be, moved from Leicester City to Leeds United.

City's pre-season friendlies - a 2-2 draw at Derby and, in Ireland, a 2-1 win over Glentoran and a 2-2 draw with Ards - were promising but Gray's men started the 1969/70 season badly. They failed to win any of their first eight games and crowd problems again dominated. City's supporters' club stopped taking buses to away games because they often came back damaged. In York, Lincoln fans appalled locals by "fouling" the lake in a public park causing the deaths of many goldfish.

Flame-haired Fletcher, once rejected by Don Revie at Leeds, continued his rise and, after 22 goals in 30 games for City, signed a new two-year contract in early December. Graham Taylor was less happy. Dropped by Gray for a match at Newport on November 8, he immediately lodged a written transfer request. Already owner of a full FA coaching certificate, Taylor was reportedly unhappy with City's tactics but returned to the side after missing six games. Again, the Imps were too inconsistent to force their way into the promotion shake-up and again they finished eighth. They enjoyed two valedictory meetings with Bradford Park Avenue, winning 5-2 and 3-0. Park Avenue finished bottom of Division Four for the third year running. Not since 1967 had they managed to scrape above a club - Lincoln - in the final reckoning. Now even the highly insular League members lost patience. Avenue were out, replaced by Cambridge United.

At Sincil Bank, there was a change at the top. Mant relinquished the chair and power transferred to a group headed by Heneage Dove. With him were Charles Warner and Dennis Bocock - big cheeses in the city's motor and building trade respectively - and Roy Chapman. Warner had joined the board at Eccleshare's invitation in 1964 while Bocock arrived three years later. The new board agreed to circulate the chairmanship every year.

Dove had first go and a month later Gray, with 14 months left on his contract, was sacked. It was a harsh decision. Gray was a victim of his own success. Having arrived when City were rock-bottom, he improved the side to one capable of promotion but was dismissed because they failed to achieve it. Subsequent managers were to be deeply grateful for Gray's astuteness in the transfer market.

His ability to spot potential was beyond dispute and he went on to unearth key players to help Ipswich Town to domestic and European success in the late 1970s and early 1980s.

Not for the first time (Martin, Strawson, Fraser, Moulson) City looked within. Bert Loxley was elevated from trainer to team manager/coach. After a long playing career with Notts County and Mansfield Town, Loxley had joined City, at the invitation of Roy Chapman [the player/manager, not the director] as trainer/coach in July 1966. His boots had been hung up but came down again in an injury crisis in the autumn. He partnered Jimmy Grummett in seven games at the heart of defence before a dislocated shoulder ended his playing career for good. Now came the 35-year-old's first stab at management. It was a job he had never chased and did not cherish but, flattered by the offer, accepted. Among his first moves was to sign Derek Trevis, a central striker or defender, from Birmingham for £6,000. He also unearthed, pursued and signed a man who was to pass into Imps legend.

Loxley said: "I was at Lilleshall on a course and this bloke from West Brom was telling me about a striker on their books. He sounded interesting so I went to have a look. He didn't look a great player but useful and what really impressed me was his build. I saw his physique and thought 'by golly.'" The player was former lorry driver Ronald Peter "Percy" Freeman and that physique was to become the bane of many an Imps opponent.

Loxley's first game in charge was the inaugural Football League fixture at Cambridge United's Abbey Stadium. Trevis scored on his debut in a 1-1 draw. Next came a 2-0 home win, Freeman scoring both, over Brentford, the match held up for 45 minutes near the end when the goal-posts at the Railway End collapsed. City ousted Barrow, Bradford City, Grimsby and Sunderland to reach the third round of both cups but lacked consistency. Their erratic form was summed up in the FA Cup third round at Torquay where they led 3-0 but lost 4-3. Fletcher scored eight goals in 10 games in the autumn but then one in 15. After a winless February, with the team in low mid-table, Loxley reverted to back-room duties. He was delighted to be out of the hot-seat.

"I had known within two or three months that it wasn't my cup of tea," he says. "I like training and physio work but I hated making the tough decisions like telling a player he was not good enough. I had a good set of players under me and we did OK but I was glad to be replaced. I think I was a bit too nice to be a manager."

In a quantum leap of policy, the City board switched from the homespun Loxley to former Scotland, Arsenal and Manchester United star David Herd. It was Herd's first crack at management after a glittering playing career. A polished forward, he established himself at the highest level with Arsenal, with whom he won five Scottish caps, before joining Manchester United for £37,000 in 1961. Seven seasons followed alongside the likes of Best, Charlton and Law in Matt Busby's United side before his playing career wound down with short spells at Stoke City and, in the League of Ireland, Waterford. Confident and debonair, Herd was the nearest Lincoln manager yet to 007 material. He arrived with vast experience of top-flight football. But how relevant was that to the challenge of getting Lincoln out of Division Four ?

He used the rest of the 1970/71 campaign to browse through his squad. Lincoln-born striker John Ward, a prolific striker in local football with Adelaide Park, was given his debut 11 days before his 20th birthday and scored in his second match - a 5-4 home defeat to York. City won two of their last 15 games to finish 21st, requiring their 14th application for re-election.

Herd's browsing spawned some surprising decisions, notably the release of skilful left-winger Billy Taylor and the transfer-listing of Trevis, Fletcher, Branston, Harford, Grummett, Svarc and Holmes. The fans were surprised that so many first-team players were deemed expendable and Dove made it clear that the list was drawn up by Herd - the board was simply backing the manager. That statement was one of Dove's last duties as chairman before the board rotated. Warner took the chair with Bocock vice-chairman.

Herd recruited some pals. He brought in three former team-mates: ex-miner Frank McMahon, a ginger-haired midfielder, from Waterford, and right-back Mick Bloor and right-winger John Worsdale from Stoke. He also signed David Kennedy, a centre-forward freed by Leeds United. Kennedy scored on his full debut, in a 4-2 defeat at Stockport in September, but never again for Lincoln and started just six games for the club. Instead, an established duo were most influential as City started strongly. Hubbard and Freeman - one all alertness and pace, the other intransigence and power - struck up a fruitful partnership and shared 11 goals in a five-match run in September and October. Off the field, the capable Dick Chester arrived as secretary.

There was another encouraging League Cup run. Alan Gilliver's goal accounted for Scunthorpe at the Old Show Ground in the first round. The second round brought a visit to Blackburn, just relegated to Division Three. After drawing 0-0 at Ewood Park, the Imps stormed to a 4-1 win in the replay, Hubbard rattling in a hat-trick in front of 7,638. Next came a visit to Queens Park Rangers, a Second Division side but, containing Phil Parkes, Dave Clement, Ian Gillard, Terry Venables, Gerry Francis and Rodney Marsh, ranked one of the most promising teams in the country.

Again, City raised their game against quality opposition. Marsh, the idol of Shepherd's Bush, tormented Taylor but, after Morgan's diving header put Rangers 1-0 up, City responded belligerently. Smith's 34th-minute corner was forced home by Freeman. Within seconds, Marsh's expansive dribble earned a corner which McCulloch scrambled home and when, three minutes after half-time, a needless handball by Taylor offered Marsh a penalty, City seemed dead and buried. Freeman had other ideas. His 70th minute surge earned a free-kick which MacMahon delivered at pace into the box. Hubbard pounced. 3-2. More Marsh magic created space for Venables to cross and Frank Saul headed home to finally kill off the pesky Fourth Division side but QPR manager Gordon Jago was full of praise. "This," he said of Lincoln, "is not a Fourth Division side."

City approached Christmas well-placed for a serious push for promotion. Midfielder John Kurila arrived from Colchester and impressed with some fierce ball-winning but Christmas Eve brought a pressie the Imps' fans did not desire: the departure of Phil Hubbard. The 22-year-old had just scored both goals in a 2-1 win over Stockport and fully expected to be part of that promotion push but at lunchtime on Christmas Eve the tinsel-bedecked telephone tinkled at Sincil Bank. It was Norwich City. Within two hours the clubs agreed a deal. Hubbard signed for the Canaries that night subject to a medical which he passed on Christmas Day.

The £20,000 that landed in City's bank account didn't stay there long. Within a month, in came rugged centre-half Tom Spencer for £10,000 from Workington, and striker Dixie McNeil for £9,000 from Northampton. McNeil's arrival was well-received - he had already bagged 17 goals for the Cobblers in the first half of the season - and both new men scored on their debuts in a 4-1 win over Brentford. While Prime Minister Ted Heath tried to fend off a power crisis, a miner's strike and Tory spin-doctors' attempts to get him married, Herd collected a gallon of whisky for being Division Four manager of the month for January. During an 11-match unbeaten run, more than 18,000 gathered at Sincil Bank for a top-of-the-table clash with Scunthorpe. The Iron included ex-Imp Rod Fletcher but it was Gilliver's header which pinched the points. Sadly, the after-noon was marred by fighting between fans. There were skirmishes on the pitch before kick-off and brawling on the terraces during the match and later at the bus station. An ugly minority had attached itself firmly to football. A week later, at Reading, Trevis and Gilliver raced to protect referee Tony Morrissey when he was attacked by a Reading fan at the final whistle.

A five-way pursuit developed for four promotion places. Lincolnshire trio Scunthorpe, Grimsby and Lincoln were involved, plus Brentford and Southend. One of these would miss out. Two crucial lapses in April - a 2-1 reverse at Hartlepool then a 1-0 home defeat to Darlington - meant that it was City. They finished fifth, a point behind Scunthorpe.

Despite the proximity to promotion there was unrest among the squad. They disliked some of Herd's methods and a delegation of players met the board to outline their concerns. These included time spent by the manager in Manchester on business other than Lincoln City's. Not all Herd's training methods were appreciated. His participation in five-a-sides, in which he enjoyed proving what a fine player he still was, appeared self-indulgent, while he sometimes appeared to forget that he was no longer mixing with the likes of Charlton and Best.

Graham Taylor recalls: "David would get us in training and say, 'right, now at Manchester United, Paddy Crerand would take a throw-in like this, then Bobby Charlton would dip his shoulders and do this with the ball.' I said, 'David, most of us can't even dip our shoulders like Charlton, never mind do what he could with a football.' It was a valuable lesson to me. It's as important to understand what players can't do as what they can do."

The board (which had rotated again: Bocock now chairman, Dove his deputy) considered a proposal to sack the manager. That was heavily defeated but two days before the players reported back from their summer break, Graham Taylor was elevated to player-coach, essentially to improve liaison between Herd and his flock.

Into that flock came another two men from the League of Ireland: midfielder Jimmy McGeough, from Waterford, and striker Brendan Bradley from Finn Harps. Bradley, 21, cost £8,000, plus another £2,000 if he played for Northern Ireland. A hefty sell-on clause was attached to the deal. Herd hailed him the best striker in Irish football. Manchester United evidently agreed. They had watched him closely but dithered and it was for the Imps that Bradley signed, with savage irony, at Manchester Airport.

Lincoln's impressive form under Herd earned them entry to a new competition in the close-season. The Watney Cup was contested by the two top scoring teams (excluding promoted sides and UEFA Cup entrants) from each of the four divisions. On a boiling hot July afternoon, City took on Burnley, of Division Two, at Sincil Bank. An excellent crowd, 7,425, saw teenage sensation Leighton James slot home the Clarets' winner with 30 seconds left. As Burnley centre-forward Frank Casper trudged, tired and sweaty, from the pitch, how could he know that one day, 25 years later, his sportswear company would supply first-team kit to Lincoln City FC ?

City started their Fourth Division programme with a 2-1 home defeat to Hartlepool. "Pathetic," raged Herd who responded by spending £5,000 on Welsh utility player Terry Cooper from Notts County. History was made on August 30 when Lincoln City travelled to a match by air. For the visit to Workington they chartered a 78-seat Viscount. Supporters were invited to help fill the plane and the players responded with a 3-0 win (Bradley 2, McNeil).

Two Imps legends embrace: Graham Taylor and Percy Freeman.

Lincoln City, 1977/78: managed by George Kerr (front, centre).

The Imps fans that visited Roots Hall on April 11, 1981, were labelled "quite an unpleasant lot" by Southend police. This lot don't appear too unfriendly do they ?

What am I bid?
Manager George Kerr auctions a picture of himself at a fund-raising
event on May 4, 1986. The snap fetched £15.

Demolition day: the St Andrews Stand bites the dust in June, 1986.

Seconds out: another frank exchange of views during the Conference season. Wealdstone provide the opposition.

Kindly leave the stage:
Barnet manager Barry Fry is escorted from the Sincil Bank
pitch during a tempestuous Conference tussle.

That'll do: Phil Brown (left) and Dave Clarke celebrate after Brown has made it 2-0 against Wycombe to effectively seal Lincoln's re-entry to the Football League.

Mission accomplished: Colin Murphy enjoys the moment. But within hours he was thinking: "Should I stay or should I go?"

Back where we belong:
Lincoln's 1987/88 Conference champions start the
party.

What's in 'ere then ? Brian Clough investigates John Reames' pockets as Nottingham Forest visit to open the new St Andrews Strand on May 8, 1988.

Lincoln's two most famous assets:
its cathedral and, pictured on a training run in July 1989, its football
team.

Magnificent milestone: on April 6, 1991, the total sum donated to Lincoln City by Lincoln and District Football Supporters Club reached £1 million. In the centre are Vic Withers and John Reames, chairmen of the two organisations.

Great servant: Defender Grant Brown joined the Imps in 1990 and is enjoying a testimonial season in 1999/2000.

Jason Lee: never won the Lincoln fans over but netted City a six-figure profit when he joined Southend for £150,000 in 1993.

Day in the spotlight: Manager Keith Alexander chats to Sky TV's Andy Gray as City prepare for their televised FA Cup match against Bolton in 1993.

Club captain and player of the season in 1993/94: John Schofield.

Stadium in transition: June 1994, the Stacey West Stand has arrived but the Sincil Bank terrace is soon to disappear beneath an impressive new stand.

"This is what we'll do": John Beck meets supporters in the Centre Spot, at Sincil Bank. The bucket is for donations towards buying Kevin Austin from Leyton Orient.

Near miss: John Beck applauds supporters after 6,495 turned up to see Rochdale thwart the Imps' play-off hopes on May 3, 1997.

Mutual admiration:
Gareth Ainsworth swaps applause with City's supporters.

Calm down chaps: referee Mike Reed sorts out a fracas during Lincoln's
FA Cup first round replay with Gainsborough Trinity at Sincil Bank in
1997. City scraped through 3-2 - but Emley were waiting!

Carrying the burden: John Reames.

Freeman, Bradley and McNeil formed a potent strike-force. In a 4-0 win at Bury, Freeman's hat-trick was completed in trademark manner; a mighty run from deep followed by a crashing shot which shifted every hole in the onion bag. Even the Bury fans applauded. A familiar voice - Jim Smith's - came through on the Sincil Bank telephone. He had stepped up into Football League management at Colchester, after cutting his teeth at Boston United, and immediately tried to take John Kennedy to Layer Road on loan. Herd said no. It was one of his last decisions at the Bank. Promise remained unfulfilled. After an eight-match winless sequence, including an FA Cup first round exit to Blackburn Rovers, Bocock flew back from holiday in Jamaica to confront growing grumbles from players and fans. Herd was "invited" to resign, which he did.

Bocock said: "The board deeply regret that things have turned out the way they have but results speak for themselves and after all the careful pre-season planning we made, to see Lincoln City Football Club only an average side with regard to points tally to date is bitterly disappointing."

So much for the Glamour Boy. The City board reverted to type and looked within. They interviewed Derek Trevis, Terry Branston and Graham Taylor. Taylor impressed them most and, at 28, became the youngest manager in the Football League.

15.
Taylor-made record breakers

ON December 7, 1972, Graham Taylor became manager of Lincoln City. A vast odyssey of a career, including more vicissitudes than you could shake a stick at, lay ahead of the fresh-faced son of Worksop but, for now, all that occupied him was the Imps. Lucky enough to get an early stab at management, he moved into the gaffer's chair, took the top off his pen, hitched up his trousers and left nobody in any doubt about his enthusiasm for the job.

"I shall play in the first team only when it is absolutely necessary," he said. "I am under no illusions to the task facing me. My job is to realise the potential with the club and that commits me totally to the welfare of Lincoln City. I am hoping this will be my first and last official statement because there is work to be done."

Taylor's elevation to manager was an adventurous move but the board - Heneage Dove in particular - believed they had spotted a unique potential. Taylor was never going to pull up any trees as a player. A victim of the classic backhanded compliment "steady," he had to work hard to make the best of limited ability. But hard work was something he relished and, presented with an early chance to tackle team management, he applied to it the same level of commitment. Now, freed from the limitations of that green oblong, he could wrap his industry round greater talents. Taylor was intelligent, inquisitive, eloquent, confident, assertive and ambitious. He thought about the game and, unlike many footballers, he thought about the future. A journeyman player, he was a manager waiting to happen. Dove spotted that.

Born in the Nottinghamshire mining town of Worksop, Taylor, from the age of two, was brought up in Scunthorpe where his father was a journalist. At Scunthorpe Grammar School, young Graham was a diligent pupil. A prefect, he was looked upon as potential head-boy material but football was soon his all-consuming passion. After a brief spell linked to Scunthorpe United as an amateur he joined neighbours Grimsby Town. By the summer of 1968, Taylor had played 189 League games in the Mariners' defence when Lincoln boss Ron Gray - searching for a right-back after Mick Brown joined Cambridge United as player-coach - made him an offer he didn't refuse.

Already, Taylor's interest in coaching was deep. At 21 he had become the youngest ever FA Staff Coach. He served as secretary of Lincoln and District Football Coaches' Association and coached the Lincolnshire League team and City School Old Boys XI. He had ideas, energy and drive. These were evident during four years as a player at Sincil Bank and now, at 28, he had control of a Football League side. He was the gaffer, with the confidence and security of a three-year contract.

The taking off of his pen-top was not simply an act of showmanship. Immediately, he furnished the board with a lengthy document outlining his vision of the Imps' future, on and off the field. He had ideas about football tactics but also plenty of original thoughts about the broader operations of a professional football club. Lincoln City, he insisted, must integrate itself into the community. The supporters' rapport with the players had to reach beyond a Saturday afternoon here and a mid-week night there. Players, he felt, must be ambassadors. Get them out into schools, hospitals, youth clubs, factories and offices. Supporters, surely, will feel more warmth towards players they felt they knew. Instead of blandly pleading for cash from the business community, Taylor thought along more mutual lines. What could the football club give as well as take ? Ideas teemed. Plans crowded on to the drawing board but the ultimate barometer of any manager - results on the pitch - showed, in the immediate term, "stormy."

Taylor's reign opened in front of 1,200 people at Boston United's York Street ground where City lost a County Cup tie 2-0. A victory was a long time coming. The first League game - a battling 2-2 draw at Newport County - was encouraging enough but, by the end of January, City had met Barnsley, Doncaster, Aldershot, Exeter, Crewe and Hereford and still not won. The supporters had their doubts and enunciated some of these, in colourful fashion, toward the rookie manager as he stood near the dug-out.

"I remember one of my early games when we had still not won," recalls Taylor. "We were standing in front of the dug-out which, for some reason, had been moved over to the Sincil Bank side. I was getting some terrible stick from somebody in the crowd. 'Taylor out, Taylor out,' they were chanting. I could understand that - I had not been an exceptional player and now here I was as manager, with a poor record so far. Our physio, Bert Loxley, turned round to one of these guys, pointed to his red medical-box and threatened to stick it somewhere. It doesn't sound very pleasant now but I needed that sort of support in those early days and I was very grateful for it." The happiest of working relationships - and a lifelong friendship - was forged between Taylor and Loxley. The red box, almost used as a weapon all those years ago, remains with Loxley at his North Hykeham home today.

Taylor was still hunting his first win when Reading came in for Percy Freeman and the board felt the £11,500 bid was too good to refuse. A glut of injuries added to the new boss's problems and forced Taylor to pick himself for three games: a defeat at Hereford and draws at Northampton and at home to Bury. In February, Taylor completed "the best signing I am likely to make." George Higgins, 47, joined from Grimsby as trainer/coach. The familiar presence of Higgins, who had been at Blundell Park throughout Taylor's time there, strengthened the manager's cordon of security against unconvinced fans. Taylor knew that in Dove, Higgins and Loxley there were people close by who had faith in him.

The travails continued. At Hartlepool, 23-year-old right-back Dennis Leigh made his debut after a £4,000 move from Rotherham but City lost 1-0. Next came a 2-0 home defeat to Newport before, at last, at the 12th attempt, came that first League win. On a blustery Wednesday night, bottom-of-the-table Darlington visited the Bank. It was another ordeal of a match and plenty of the 2,479 crowd had already headed homeward for tea and crumpets with lashings of hot butter, when Branston's 87th-minute header finally broke the deadlock - and Taylor's duck. City's sequence of 19 League and Cup games without a win was over and. To ice the cake, the Imps immediately recorded their first away win for six months, two goals from McNeil earning a 2-0 win at Colchester.

There was a flurry of deadline-week transfer activity. Skilful left mid-fielder Alan Harding arrived from Darlington. The Quakers rated him at £25,000 but, on appeal by City, the Football League brokered a deal under which Frank MacMahon and £7,000 went to Feethams. Centre-half John Cottam arrived on loan from Forest, impressed on his debut in a 1-0 home win over Chester (Harding scored on his debut) then was briskly recalled by Forest boss Dave McKay. Brendan Bradley, after 12 goals in 31 games for city, returned to Finn Harps. The Irishman, and especially his pregnant wife Marie, never settled in England.

In the season's closing weeks, those who had expressed faith in Taylor started to wear knowing looks. City beat Fourth Division leaders Southport 3-1 (Ward 2, McNeil) and promotion-chasing Stockport 5-3 (Ward 3, Harding 2). Sincil Bank was transformed from mausoleum to fortress. A 2-1 Easter Saturday victory over Cambridge was City's seventh successive home win. McNeil scored both goals, taking him to 20 for the season. A powerful recovery - nine wins from 12 matches - lifted Lincoln to 10th in the final standings. Peden was player of the season. Branston and Trevis, so recently interviewed for the manager's job, were among seven players released.

Summer was a time for Taylor to take, not a break, but stock of his first six months in charge. Troubled by a hip injury, he cancelled his own registration as a player (Bobby Charlton and Tostao also retired). City recorded a £1,244 yearly profit - and reduced their overdraft by £1,400 - so Dove supported his protege with funds.

Ian Branfoot was signed for £7,500 from Doncaster to wear the number two shirt, Michael Bloor having been released. Abrasion was enlisted in the formidable shape of Sam Ellis, a £7,000 capture from Mansfield. Seven years earlier Ellis, aged 18, had played for Sheffield Wednesday against Everton in the FA Cup final. There was back-room recruiting too. George Kerr, after a long playing career with Barnsley, Bury and Scunthorpe, replaced George Higgins as trainer. One of Kerr's principal tasks was to strengthen the Imps' youth set-up which all but ceased to exist during the 1960s. A junior team was entered in the Northern Intermediate League.

No PR opportunity was missed. When City players visited Lincoln County Hospital, "many a young lads' eyes lit up." Lincoln took a strong side to play Sleaford Town as a thank-you to fans based there. "From very early on," says Taylor, "I took the view that a football club was part of its community. Footballers did not have just an ordinary job. They represented the club and place they were from. A lot of people talk about the community initiatives I set up at Watford but I always remind them that I first put the ideas into action at Lincoln."

As the new manager, backed up willingly by his players, targeted unity in the community there was further division close to home. The split between the football and supporters' clubs widened. The supporters' club detached City's name from its title and rechristened itself Lincoln and District Football Supporters' Club, which it remains to this day.

Reverting, much to the fans' approval, to traditional red and white striped shirts, City warmed up with a 10-1 win over Bishop Auckland and a 2-0 conquest of a Forest side including Liam O'Kane, John Cottam and Duncan McKenzie. The Imps started the League campaign slowly with just two wins in seven games. Taylor failed to persuade Everton to release striker Rod Belfitt on loan but, again well-resourced by the board, bought stylish forward Peter Graham, for £12,500, from Darlington. John Kennedy passed 250 games between City's posts and received a joint benefit with Peden. Chelsea were the chosen opposition and a Blues' squad including Ron Harris, Alan Hudson, Peter Osgood, David Webb and Ray Wilkins won 4-2 at the Bank in front of 6,591.

City consolidated. Decent home form kept them out of trouble, poor away form kept them out of the promotion picture. New Year, 1974, brought the first Sunday football to Sincil Bank. A power crisis, caused by striking miners, meant that electricity resources were drained on Saturdays when industry operated. The League invited clubs to switch to Sundays when floodlights would tax a less stretched supply. Taylor protested that this would rob players of their only day of the week with their families but to no avail. On January 27, the first Sunday match at Sincil Bank, a 2-1 win over Rotherham, attracted 6,157 - almost 2,000 above average. There were 7,150 present, seven days later, for the visit of second-placed Gillingham.

Even better news on the finance front came from a good result with Lincoln City Council. The Imps' board wrote to the council pleading for financial help. The current directors, they said, had already made interest-free loans and personal guarantees of more than £55,000 to the football club. Now they needed help to shoulder the burden. The council stumped up a loan of £30,000 at 5% interest over a 20-year period. Councillor Clodagh Wilkinson, evidently not a football fan, accused her fellow councillors of spending money "like drunken sailors."

Midfielder Dennis Booth arrived from Southend but City faded badly, winning only four of their last 18 games. A 1-0 home defeat to Hartlepool was described by Lincolnshire Echo reporter Maurice Burton as "an interminable spell of 90 minutes of non-action from a Lincoln team who should be thoroughly ashamed of themselves. Graham Taylor has spent many hours thinking about his problems - and yet they are as acute as ever." None of the last six home games attracted more than 3,000.

The jury was still far from unanimous on Taylor who had, in Fourth Division terms, spent heavily. Due mainly to transfer spending, City lost a mammoth £40,565 year-on-year. Warner replaced Bocock as chairman and increased the pressure a notch or two on the manager. Taylor, said Warner, had "given maximum effort and concentration to build an acceptable team. He has suffered disappointments, some of which I hope will stand him in good stead. He will now have to operate with a much-reduced budget. It will be a real challenge."

Taylor now had to sell to buy. Dixie McNeil, after 53 goals from 96 starts for City, was the surprise departure - to Hereford United for £20,000. Welsh international winger Dick Krzywicki, eight full Welsh caps behind him, arrived for nothing from Huddersfield, four years after the Terriers paid West Brom £45,000 for him.

Patti Maynard ("Twenty Stone of Song") performed at the Imps social club and John Kennedy ("Twelve stone of goalkeeper") retired after 251 games for Lincoln. Even the buxom Maynard could not fill the void left by Kennedy's retirement and it was too soon for 18-year-old Jimmy Gordon, signed from Luton, to be pitched in to the first team. A 'keeper search became increasingly frantic, ending only three days before the season's opener at home to Chester. West Ham's Peter Grotier, displaced from the mighty Hammers' first team by Mervyn Day, agreed to join on loan until the end of September.

City beat Chester 2-1 and, in the next home game, walloped Exeter 5-0. Three draws followed and then a 5-0 defeat at Cambridge in September but it wasn't all bad news that day: Con Moulson, wielding a four-wood, hit a hole-in-one on the fourth at Southcliffe and Canwick. By late September, Grotier had done enough to convince the board to break City's record by buying him for £16,666. West Ham were patient for the full amount and supporters were asked to help out. Lincoln and District Football Supporters' Club and the Red Imps Association (another fund-raising force of loyal Imps fans) launched a 'Pay for Peter' campaign. LDFSC kicked it off with £3,000.

City's direct, positive style now started to click. In late Autumn a settled team - essentially Grotier, Branfoot, Leigh, Booth, Ellis, Cooper, Krzywicki, Ward, Graham, Smith, Harding - strung together a 12-match unbeaten run. Taylor pledged all-out attack and, on successive Saturdays, City won 4-1 (Graham, Krzywicki, Branfoot, Smith) at Darlington and 4-0 (Krzywicki, Graham, Smith, Ward) at Shrewsbury. Supporters were involved in the push for success. Taylor urged the Sincil Bank audience to chant each player's name before games. After a 3-1 Friday-night win over Torquay, the manager insisted: "The size and attitude of the crowd was a great talking point in the dressing room after the match."

With City fourth in the table, Taylor collected the Division Four manager-of-the-month award for November. His prize was a king-size bottle of Bells whisky and after a 1-0 home win over Scunthorpe, he took it into the social club and invited supporters to have a tot.

Ade Coker became the first African-born Lincoln player, making six appearances on loan from West Ham, but Luton Town striker Rodney Fern rejected a loan deal. Percy Freeman returned. Reading had tried to change his style, asking him to work, back-to-goal, holding the ball up. It was like trying to use a battering ram as a tooth-pick. City got one of their favourites back and, paying just £1,500, recorded a nice ten-grand profit.

Lincoln stayed unbeaten at home until March when Swansea won 3-1 at the Bank. That heralded a sizeable running-out of steam. They won only one of six games which included a 4-1 defeat at promotion rivals Chester. With Mansfield, Shrewsbury and Rotherham assured of promotion it was now a race between City and Chester for the fourth slot. Lincoln had been around the top four all season but the momentum was with the Cheshire club. A 5-2 home win (Krzywicki, Harding 2, Ellis, Cooper) over Newport got City going again but a 3-1 defeat, in front of 14,392, at Mansfield gave Chester the edge with two games left.

The Imps faced two tricky away games - at Workington and Southport - in three days. At Borough Park, Workington, in front of a 1,531 crowd dominated by travelling Imps fans, Ellis and Branfoot scored in a 2-0 win. Celebrations were cut short by news of Chester's 1-0 win at Crewe. That meant City had to go to Southport, in mid-table with a strong home record, on Monday night and get a point. One point for promotion.

Taylor selected an unchanged team. Within 17 minutes they were 2-0 down. Krzywicki pulled one back straight away but Southport reinstated their two-goal lead by half-time. After the break, amid constant noise from City's travelling faithful on the open Haig Avenue terraces, it was one-way traffic. Home goalkeeper Kevin Thomas pulled off a string of fine saves. Graham hit the bar from 18-yards and was then sandwiched by two defenders in the box. Ellis converted the penalty.

Seventeen minutes to go. Lincoln were one strike from promotion. They probed, hustled, humped, chased and drove forward without creating a clear chance until, two minutes from time, Freeman's cross split the home defence. Ward, two yards out, blazed the ball over the bar. At the final whistle, City's players sunk to the knees, the cheers from the handful of Chester fans present ringing in their lug-oles.

Taylor's troops returned, desolate, to the dressing room. Poignantly waiting there was the pile of good-luck telegrams, opened in such anticipation two hours earlier, now looking sad, discarded and splashed with spilt tea on the dressing room table. Several players were in tears. Chester took the last promotion place by 0.0383 of a goal.

This, however, was not a fragile bunch of players. Next day, Taylor fielded the same team for the County Cup final against Grimsby at Sincil Bank. They lifted themselves to win 2-0 with Ward and Freeman on target. The supporters, too, responded positively to the disappointment of 24 hours earlier. The spectators present that night take their share of credit for glory soon to follow.

"We had been expecting to be celebrating promotion," said Taylor. "That wasn't the case but about 2,000 people turned up and gave us a great reception. That gave me a great lift and also convinced me that I didn't need to change too much." He kept the cast together. They spent the summer practicing their lines. The dress rehearsal was over. The Sincil Bank theatre of dreams waited. Next up was the real thing. The 1975/6 season. Hold on to your hats.

***

Only one player - midfielder John Fleming, released by Oxford United - was recruited during the close-season. Taylor believed his squad was good enough. And he was right.

After an opening-day 3-1 defeat at Newport, City went into overdrive. Hugely entertaining, attack-attack-attack, muck-and-nettles, all-for-one-and-one-for-all, magnificent, boil-in-the-bag overdrive.

First there was a summer of boardroom shift. Heneage Dove, keen to return as chairman, gathered together a new consortium. The supporters' club favoured Dove and his new men and pressure grew on Warner and Chapman to quit as chairman and general manager respectively. Bocock had already resigned from the board. At a special meeting of directors, Warner and Chapman, bowing to public demand, submitted written resignations. Dove retook the chairmanship he coveted and five new directors were co-opted. Now the Dove-Taylor alliance dovetailed.

Admission prices rose for the new campaign but that was not the board's decision. A League directive, opposed by City, ordered an increase in minimum admission from 40p to 65p. Never mind. Sincil Bank devotees got plenty of good 65p worths. First visitors, Chesterfield, in the League Cup, were beaten 4-2 with Ward scoring all four. The first League visitors, Torquay, also conceded four, including Fleming's first goal for Lincoln. In each of the first five home League games, Lincoln scored at least three goals. Eight different City players scored in the first four matches.

After completing a 6-5 aggregate win over Chesterfield, the Imps faced First Division side Stoke City in the League Cup second round. It was one of those evocative nights of high passion somehow unique to floodlit occasions. The atmosphere from a 13,472 crowd was throbbing as City prepared to line up against a Stoke side including £350,000 goalkeeper Peter Shilton, midfield superstar Alan Hudson, arch-predator Jimmy Greenhoff and Republic of Ireland winger Terry Conroy. Top, handsomely-paid players but this Lincoln team feared nobody, especially at Sincil Bank.

City stormed forward from the first whistle. Harding was twice denied by Shilton. Wherever Hudson went, Booth was there too, harassing him. Ellis was a tower of strength while Freeman bludgeoned around testing out Corporal Jones' hallowed theory: "They don't like it up 'em." For 18 minutes, Stoke hung in there. Then they got a break. Fleming delivered a back-pass to Greenhoff instead of Grotier. The striker capitalised and Stoke's supporters roared with relief. But relief was brief. Within 60 seconds, Lincoln were level. Harding dodged two tackles and let fly with a rasping low shot that left Shilton flailing. Fourth Division was looking First Division squarely in the eye. Stoke were happy to reach half-time still level.

Ten minutes of sanctuary in the dressing-room did the Potters some good. They opened the second half with much greater composure. Grotier denied Greenhoff and Ian Moores. Cooper, Ellis, Branfoot and Leigh dug deep to deal with the barrage before the passion in the cauldron spilt over. Weight of people on a wall at the South Park End caused it to collapse, propelling spectators on to the pitch. Nobody was seriously hurt but 18 people required hospital treatment.

After a five-minute hold-up the match, 25 minutes left, resumed and almost immediately Lincoln took the lead. Shilton could only parry Smith's shot and Booth dived in like a hairy Scud missile to head home the rebound. The eruption of sound almost stirred Robert Dawber in his resting-place a mile to the south-east. He would have loved this. Stoke battered away. Grotier denied Greenhoff. The Potters' best chance fell, fortunately for City, to right-back John Marsh, scorer of just one goal in more than 200 games. It was a sitter but he fired wide and after 95 minutes the final whistle installed a famous evening into Imps folklore. How good was this Lincoln team ? How good was the up-and-coming manager ?

Three days later, back in Division Four, City travelled to Huddersfield. After the Lord Mayor's show ? No way. They gritted out a 1-0 win, Fleming the scorer. Against Stoke, the Imps had proved they could handle a big occasion. When they visited Southport on a damp, galeswept Wednesday night, it was a very small occasion. There were 871 paying spectators, the first time since April 2, 1935, (773 on another galeswept Tuesday night at Southport) that an Imps League game attracted less than 1,000 people. City exorcised painful memories of Haig Avenue four months earlier with a 2-1 win (Ward, Freeman).

When the League Cup third round - a visit to Leicester City - arrived, Lincoln were still in fine form, having taken nine points out of 10. They also beat Qatar 3-1 in a behind-closed-doors friendly at the Bank. Qatar fielded a weakened side - weakened, literally, because most of the team were nearing the end of a one-month religious fast.

Six thousand Lincoln fans travelled for the League Cup tie at Leicester and shouted their socks off at Filbert Street. Leicester, in the top half of Division One, included Mark Wallington, later to play for Lincoln, Steve Whitworth, Keith Weller and Frank Worthington, later to play for England, and Brian Alderson, later to die tragically young in a car crash in the United States. Again Grotier, Branfoot, Leigh, Booth, Ellis, Cooper, Fleming, Ward, Freeman, Smith and Harding battled brilliantly. Weller sent an early 25-yarder against the Imps' bar but City were unfazed by the occasion and took the lead through Smith's crisp volley. In front at half-time, they took a huge ovation from the red and white hordes.

Weller equalised early in the second half but Lincoln were five minutes from a richly-deserved replay when controversy flared. As Grotier caught a cross, Foxes striker Chris Garland hit the turf. Referee Gordon Kew pointed to the penalty spot. Jon Sammels accepted the gift. Heartbreak. The last five minutes, as is traditional when you're a goal down in a cup tie, elapsed in 10 seconds. The Imps were out. Now came overdrive.

Of 15 League and cup matches, Lincoln won 14 and drew one. Nine games in November and December brought City eight wins and 26 goals. Graham's hat-trick secured a 3-2 win at Crewe. Lincoln visited a Doncaster side in the thick of the promotion race and, in front of 14,343, Ward and Freeman notched two each in a 4-2 win. Taylor's method was simple, well-practiced and effective. Load the ball forward quickly and let warriors Freeman and Ward get hunting. Harding was menacing, Fleming tidy and industrious and Graham, until hit by injury, classy and alert. Dave Smith, so quiet off the field, was hugely influential on the left. When Smith was on song, the team ticked. At the back, Ellis and Cooper patrolled City's box, hating it when the ball got close to Grotier. Before Christmas, Dove challenged Taylor: Give me 100 goals and 70 points.

Another intoxicating day-out awaited the Imps fans. For the first time since 1961, City reached the FA Cup fourth round. They negotiated three tricky away ties: at Boston United (1-0), Mansfield (2-1) and Aldershot (2-1). Victory at Aldershot was a tribute to Taylor's resilience - after watching Exeter v Bournemouth the night before, he was shaken up when his car left the road on the way back to Hampshire. Next day, his pain was eased by Ellis's penalty which clinched City's passage through to round four and a visit to Second Division promotion-chasers West Bromwich Albion.

Johnny Giles' West Brom side could play a bit but were also happy to mix it physically if necessary. City would have to show more than belligerence to rattle the Baggies. The home side imposed heavy early pressure and Tony Brown fired them ahead but this Lincoln squad was made of stern stuff. They weathered the storm and seven minutes from half-time Ally Robertson pushed Freeman in the box. Ellis converted the penalty, his eighth goal of the season. Five minutes later, Smith and Leigh linked on the left, Leigh crossed, goalkeeper John Osborne dived at Krzywicki's feet and Fleming lashed home the loose ball. There was still time before the interval for Smith to volley inches over the bar. The intriguing half-time score, read out in debonair fashion by Frank Bough, on Grandstand, and Dickie Davies, on World of Sport, was West Brom 1 Lincoln City 2.

Giles offered a few strident thoughts at half-time and Albion again started strongly. They levelled 10 minutes after the break when Grotier sliced a punch and Mick Martin looped a spectacular shot into the net. Albion stood up to the Imps' battering and earned the right to play their superior football. It was youth international Bryan Robson - only playing because Len Cantello was suspended - who sent a low 30-yarder past Grotier with 14 minutes left. No heads dropped. Freeman, inspired on his old patch, tested Osborne with two headers - but City went out, heroically, 3-2.

There was no deflecting Lincoln from their League domination. They eased through February top of the table, with games in hand. When flu swept through the squad, Taylor contacted Nottingham Forest (Bill Anderson had been sacked as assistant manager a year earlier, straight after Brian Clough's arrival as manager) and brought in Tony Woodcock and Bert Bowery on loan. Both made their debuts at home to Southport and both scored in a 6-0 win. Ward was also on target - his 22nd goal of the season - as was left-back Phil Neale a hugely promising product of City's youth scheme. Northampton were now the Imps' only rivals for the Fourth Division title. They were beaten 3-1 (Fleming, Krzywicki, Smith) at the Bank in front of 13,880. In successive games, Lincoln trounced Watford (5-1), Bradford City (4-1 at Valley Parade) and Newport (4-1).

Home crowds regularly hit five figures and, on April 7, a 2-1 home win over Darlington clinched City's promotion with seven games to spare. After 14 seasons, including some of the most wretched in the club's history, in Division Four, City were upwardly mobile again. Five days later, when Smith scored the third goal in a 3-0 win at Stockport, City reached 100 goals for the season. Two points took the total to 66. Two games later, a 5-0 drubbing of Doncaster took them to 70. Dove's double challenge had been met.

A 1-1 draw at Bournemouth in the last game left City with an all-time record of 74 points. They set Fourth Division records for most wins and fewest defeats and were the first team for a decade to score more than 100 goals in a season. They totalled 111 in 46 League fixtures. Their home record was sensational: 23 games, 21 wins, two draws, 71 goals scored, 15 conceded.

Grotier and Branfoot were ever-present. Cooper and Smith missed just one game each. Ellis missed two, Booth four and Ward five. Ward scored 24 goals, Freeman 23, Graham 11 from 13 starts before injury and Ellis 12 goals from centre-half. Grotier and his resolute defence kept 19 clean sheets and conceded just one goal 16 times. The players had performed brilliantly on the pitch and because of Taylor-made community policies the fans felt truly part of the success. They knew the players, had met them, nattered to them. Everyone with affection for City had been invited in on this good thing. Made to feel important. Part of the set-up. Part of the success, not just witness to it. Lincoln City Football Club was hailed across the nation as a happening, happy, far-sighted, go-ahead organisation. Dove, Taylor, Kerr and Loxley had done the biz and, as a nice little tangent, City made more than £40,000 profit on the season.

"It was a smashing season," recalls Taylor. "We had a team full of personalities. There was Sam Ellis - a leader. A character but a challenge to manage. We taught Sam to run up and blow kisses to the crowd after he scored - in those days the referees allowed celebrations of a goal to run their course. Percy Freeman could shoot and miss the stand, never mind the goal, but it would lift everyone. Then there was Dennis Booth - another big personality. Teams were petrified of coming to Sincil Bank.

"We knew we were the best side in the division and looking back I think that was the best side - at its respective level - that I ever managed. We had a perfect chairman/secretary/manager combination which is so important: Heneage Dove, Dick Chester and I worked very well together. It was a smashing time. The club was like one big family."

At last, back in Division Three, the Imps' family could again savour a more interesting fixture-list. Sheffield Wednesday - a First Division side six years earlier. Brighton, under new boss Alan Mullery. Crystal Palace, with Terry Venables fresh in the job as manager. Swindon Town, who had visited the Bank only once before.

Despite stepping up a division, Taylor again showed complete confidence in his squad. Again there was just one summer recruit, Hubbard returning from Grimsby for £6,000. City acclimatised quickly with only one defeat in their first eight League games. That long-awaited Swindon visit provided a 0-0 draw. When Sheffield Wednesday attended the Bank for the first time in 18 years, almost 15,000 saw Freeman's goal earn Lincoln a 1-1 draw. In the first 11 games, City conceded more than a single goal only once as Neale slotted in seamlessly alongside Branfoot, Ellis and Cooper in the back-four. After a 3-1 win over Reading on October 23, Lincoln rose to fourth.

There was another decent FA Cup run. Non-League pair Morecambe (1-0) and Nuneaton Borough (6-0) were ousted at home to earn a crack at Second Division strugglers Burnley. After holding them 2-2 at Turf Moor, City perished 1-0 in the replay. In the New Year, hopes of a second successive promotion were still realistic but form flagged during a crazy run-in to the season. Bad weather in mid-winter meant that Lincoln played only eight League games in December, January and February - then 18 in March and April. Eighteen matches in 59 days took its toll. City won nine of them but a four-match winless streak in mid-April detached them from the top five - Mansfield, Brighton, Crystal Palace, Rotherham and Wrexham. Still, sustained by more mighty home form - two defeats in 23 games - City finished a highly satisfactory ninth.

Neale was now a first-team regular and some of Kerr's other youth products got chances to shine. Dean Crombie played 13 of the last 14 games at left-half. Jimmy Gordon, Glenn Cockerill and Brendan Guest surfaced in the first team. So did midfielder Jackie Gallagher, for the final game, a 1-1 draw at home to Peterborough. It was Gallagher's first and last game for Lincoln. It was also somebody else's last game.

As speculation intensified about this talented young manager's future, the ever-astute Dove persuaded Taylor to sign a new three-year deal. The contract included a compensation clause entitling Lincoln to £20,000 if Taylor moved to another club. West Brom and Watford were known to be highly interested. Leicester City, having just sacked Jimmy Bloomfield, joined the chase and Dove gave them permission to approach Taylor. Leicester, like West Brom chairman Bert Millichip, hesitated at paying so much compensation. Elton John, at Watford, however, coughed up. In June, Taylor switched to Vicarage Road.

Taylor recalls: "Heneage Dove was a very shrewd man. He believed he had a manager who would go on to bigger things and realised that there was only so much I could do at Lincoln. Some people might say it was a lack of ambition but he felt there was only a certain level at which Lincoln City could operate. He got me to sign a new contract which would bring the club £20,000 if I left - and that was a lot of money in 1977 ! I think you could say that Graham Taylor and Lincoln City were good for each other."

Watford, backed by the musician's millions, offered Taylor a lucrative five-year contract and serious spending money. The ambitious young manager took the next step along his busy career, accompanied by only good wishes from Lincoln. Dove said: "The offer from Elton John was such that no young man with responsibility to his family could refuse. The Graham Taylor era is finished and we must now forget Graham Taylor and concentrate all our efforts on the new manager - whoever he may be."

Taylor rejuvenated and revolutionised every nook and cranny of Lincoln City Football Club. He chose to move down the League - Watford were in Division Four - because Elton John's fortune was accessible to him. A step backward into a position to leap forward. Which direction, next, for Lincoln ?

16.
"This place needs a bomb under it - and I'm the one to drop it."

THE trouble with achievements is they have to be followed. That can be hard enough when the main architect of the achievement is still around but if the driving force departs then it's not just a case of "Follow that!" but of "Follow him!" On June 20, 1977, the loss of Graham Taylor's dynamic presence left Lincoln City with a void. Many worthy initiatives were in place. Proven, well-honed systems and good players - the instruments of success. But the conductor had taken his baton elsewhere. To fill that void, three days after Taylor headed for Watford, George Kerr was promoted from assistant to head honcho.

Kerr, 34, had been Taylor's assistant for four years. He knew the methods, the tactics and the people which steered City to two fine seasons. Continuity seemed the logical option. Brother of Bobby Kerr (an FA cup winner with Sunderland in 1974), George had played for Barnsley, Bury and Scunthorpe. He scored 36 goals in 159 games for the Iron before Taylor tempted him on to the coaching staff at Sincil Bank. Kerr held the FA's preliminary coaching badge, for which his examiner had been Taylor. Although he was a popular choice to take over, the board gave themselves a safety net by awarding him only a one-year contract. Ian Branfoot stepped up to assistant boss and John Ward took over the captaincy as City anticipated life under their 17th manager.

Not just at Sincil Bank was this a time of flux and excitement. Taylor was new to Watford, Don Revie resigned the England job and Tommy Docherty was sacked by Manchester United. Micky Walker was appointed Boston United supremo. Ken Shellito took over at Chelsea and Nobby Stiles at Preston. Kevin Keegan scored on his debut for Hamburg, Alan Hudson and Malcolm MacDonald were sent home from Arsenal's summer tour of the Far East, Pilkington Recreation prepared for a crunch FA Vase first round visit from Ossett Albion, Groucho Marx rolled a seven and, to cap it all, Harlow-based inventor Robin Palmer announced that he had perfected "the world's first space-age doorbell."

Another bell tinkling was the telephone in George Kerr's office. On the other end was Graham Taylor, soon back in touch to buy Sam Ellis for £15,000. Deprived of Ellis's vast experience, it was in youth that Kerr put his faith. Following a tip-off by a friend of Alan Harding, City signed three youngsters - Michael Smith, Keith Laybourne and Mick Harford - from Lambton Boys' Club in the north-east. Smith was given his debut in the first fixture of the new season - a 1-0 League Cup win at Mansfield.

Kerr found "Follow that!" a tough assignment. After six games, City were rock-bottom with just one point. Left-half Clive Wigginton from Scunthorpe (£5,000) and right-winger Alan Jones from Chesterfield (£11,000) arrived but a £20,000 deal agreed with Bury for big striker Wayne Entwhistle collapsed when the 19-year-old chose Sunderland instead. More teenagers - Alan Cork, on loan from Derby County, and Alan Eden - were pitched into the team but another significant loss was Dennis Booth, who followed Ellis to Watford.

The anticipated continuity was not there. After a 2-0 defeat to Sheffield Wednesday - Jack Charlton's first match as the Owls' boss - in October, Kerr received an improve-or-be-sacked warning by the board. On FA Cup first-round day, Lincoln travelled to Preston badly needing a lift after just five victories from 18 League games. Goals by Harding and Wiggington put them in command at Deepdale, 2-0 up with 27 minutes left, but Nobby Stiles' side fought back to win 3-2. With too many youngsters blooded too quickly, the team lacked resilience. A 2-0 home defeat to Gillingham in mid-December left City with only Plymouth and Sheffield Wednesday below them in the table. The board voted 6-2 to sack Kerr. How quickly it had gone wrong - proof that success and confidence, which invariably take seasons to build, can evaporate in months.

City advertised in the Express, Mail, Mirror and Sun for Kerr's successor. For eight days, with the trusty Loxley as caretaker boss (Branfoot rejected temporary charge), the board considered their options. Applicants included Derek Trevis, who made a public pitch for the job from Philadelphia, Ipswich defender Colin Harper, Sheffield Wednesday reserve boss Ken Knighton and Leicester's Keith Weller. The board drew up a short-list of just two names: Bristol Rovers' striker Bobby Gould and Willie Bell, recently sacked as manager by Birmingham City. Gould's inexperience counted against him so City plumped for Bell.

William John Bell, like David Herd, had played football at the highest level. He figured in Leeds United's classy squad of the mid-1960s and then moved to Leicester City before joining Brighton as player-coach. At the Goldstone Ground, he teamed up with Freddie Goodwin and when Goodwin moved north to manage Birmingham, Bell accompanied him. After five years as coach at St Andrews, Bell replaced Goodwin as manager in September 1975 and lasted two years before five successive early-season defeats secured him the sack. "Bitterly disappointed," he combined scouting for Bobby Robson at Ipswich while hunting for a quick return to management. Ten weeks after getting the boot from Birmingham there he was, casting a curious eye over the elephant's foot hat-stand in the manager's office at Sincil Bank.

Bell immediately put more experience back in the team and stopped Lincoln losing. He started with six successive draws, then victories over Port Vale (3-0 at home) and Peterborough (1-0 away). Mick Harford scored twice in the Port Vale victory and, at 19, became a regular in the side. Physically strong, already with an attitude to match, he scored twice in a 4-1 victory over high-flying Cambridge United, in which young Sheffield-born winger Gordon Hobson scored on his debut. Bell guided City to safety with only six defeats in 26 games after Christmas. Third Division status was secured with two matches to spare. Grotier was player-of-the-year and Harford young player-of-the-year.

The courteous and dignified Bell had prised City from the mire in singular style. He was rare, possibly unique, in the swaggering, macho world of football management - here was a man who never swore. In football, like most sports, oaths and curses are common currency in the heat of the moment and the passion of the dressing room. Footballers' native tongue. When you're 6-0 down at half-time and being taken apart, a "come-on-cheps-this-isn't-quite-the-ticket-you-know," sort of approach won't often work. But Bell, a devout Christian, was always civilised. He was Sergeant Wilson. Pleasant and dapper. He treated people with respect and hoped to be treated the same way.

A few eyebrows were raised when, with his first full season in charge approaching, Bell disappeared, off to America for two weeks. A strong link with the Taylor years was broken when Dick Chester failed to agree a new contract and resigned after seven years as secretary. His replacement - 26-year-old John Sorby - arrived from the madcap, febrile world of agricultural ironmongery. One of his first duties was to organise, following a League directive, an increase in minimum admission to £1 for the 1978/79 season. Bell returned to England in time to attend a County Cup match between Scunthorpe and Grimsby, a dull affair enlivened only by two dogs striding on to the pitch during play and copulating.

Bell's attempts to sign players met with frustration. He signed rookie centre-half Billy Wright from Birmingham and veteran winger David Sunley from Hull, but his showpiece swoops all fell through. He spoke to former Leeds colleagues Paul Reaney and Allan Clarke but Reaney, having appeared interested, decided at the last minute to stay at Bradford City. Clarke landed the manager's job at Barnsley. Birmingham City's Welsh international defender Malcolm Page talked to Bell but demanded wages beyond Lincoln's reach.

The Imps began with a 2-1 home win over Tranmere, watched by only 2,835 due to rival attractions at Nottingham Forest where Argentinian stars Ossie Ardiles and Ricky Villa made their debuts for Tottenham. A few days into the season, Branfoot quit to join Southampton as youth coach. Veteran midfielder Ian McCalliog (former Scotland, Leeds, Chelsea, Sheffield Wednesday, Wolves,

Manchester United, Southampton, Chicago Sting, Lynn Oslo) was enlisted as player-coach. Bell's inflexibility, meanwhile, deprived him of one of his best players. He disciplined and dropped Phil Neale for reporting back late from cricket duties with Worcestershire.

After beating Tranmere, City lost the next four matches before welcoming Graham Taylor's Watford to Sincil Bank. It proved a momentous evening. Elton John became the first chairman ever to arrive at the Bank wearing gold, high-heeled boots. The 90 minutes brought him great pleasure but left Willie Bell feeling it might be 'Easier to Walk Away.' With Harding injured, Bell picked 17-year-old trainee winger David Burrows for his first - and only - game for City. The Imps were overwhelmed 5-0, Luther Blissett scoring twice. Watford unfurled a power, organisation and cohesion which the home fans recognised and as the rout unfolded, some Lincoln supporters started cheering for Taylor's side. As more joined in, the match took on an unreal atmosphere. Bell could hardly believe his shell-likes. "I was disappointed with the result," he fumed, "but doubly disappointed with some of our fans." Taylor added: "I was saddened to see what was happening. I got the impression that quite a lot of people were wanting Watford to win." Bell's rapport with the fans was irrevocably shattered.

To the board's credit, whatever doubts they had, they backed their manager with serious cash. Bell spent £15,000 on midfielder Graham Watson from Cambridge United, then, at half-time in a 1-1 home draw with Walsall, unveiled the big one. The Imps' record signing; £33,000 striker Tommy Tynan from Sheffield Wednesday. Tynan's mission: to beef up City's puny ratio of seven goals in 11 games. On this player - a former Liverpool apprentice under Bill Shankly - Bell pinned his reputation. Tynan's debut was a drab goalless draw at home to Colchester. The next home match - an appalling 3-0 defeat to Swindon - was the Imps' 13th game without a win. "City Disgrace Themselves And Club," raged the Monday-morning headline. Bell resigned.

His summer trip to the US, it now transpired, had not been spent frivolously jettisoning his hard-earned cash in Las Vegas or engaged in riotous, Terpsichorean revelry at the Armadillo Festival, in Arkansas. Bell revealed he was off to the States to become football coach with the Campus Crusade for Christ, a Colorado-based religious organisation. His Christian vocation had always been apparent, not just in his reticence to blaspheme but in frequent visits to sick and elderly people around the city. Payment for his column in the local paper had, on his instructions, been split between the Campus Crusade for Christ and Gideon International, a bible-distributing group. All very Christian and laudable, but how fair was it to the Imps to pledge himself to the club, make all the customary, manager-type noises, splash out a record transfer fee, then quit ?

McCalliog served briefly as caretaker manager but didn't want the job long-term. Trevis flew in from Philadelphia to apply in person but City were in dire straits at the bottom the Football League. They needed someone with experience. Someone with grit and determination who could kick ass and pull things together. Someone who, in an emergency, if all the circumstances demanded it, would even swear. Colin Murphy got the job.

Croydon-born Murphy achieved little as a player, his career at full-back spent mostly in the Southern League with Tunbridge Wells, Folkestone, Gravesend and Hastings. Like Taylor, he was always a more gifted coach than player. By the age of 27, Murphy was already coaching Hastings and, within a year, moved north to join the back-room staff of Nottingham Forest. A man of strong opinions, but also a voracious learner, he linked up with Dave McKay at Forest and when McKay moved to Derby, Murphy accompanied him as reserve team boss. When Derby sacked McKay, Murphy took charge for almost a year before he was sacked to make way for Tommy Docherty. Next came a move to Notts County to assist Jimmy Sirrell before Murphy's East Midlands peripatetics took him to Sincil Bank.

City's new manager was a tough cookie who knew how many beans made five. He would, said Dove, supply "honesty, integrity, first-class coaching knowledge, organisational ability and, above all, complete dedication." Murphy pledged total commitment to Lincoln City and demanded the same from everyone around him. He inherited a mess. City were bottom of Division Three and had forgotten how to win. Most of the squad were long in the tooth or wet behind the ears. At 35, the squad was also in need of serious pruning. "This place needs a bomb under it," said Murphy, "and I'm the one to drop it."

His first match in charge, on November 11, brought City's first away point of the season - a goalless draw at Sheffield Wednesday. A first round exit, 2-1 at Blackpool, torpedoed the players' admittedly slim hopes of pocketing a £500 bonus each if the Imps won the FA Cup. Lincoln became harder to beat, although with several matches postponed through bad weather, they still went into Christmas bottom of Division Three. Boxing Day brought a 1-0 victory at Peterborough, the Imps' first win since August 19.

Tynan was offloaded to Newport County for £20,000. Wherever his long career was to take him in the future, Tynan's goal ratio was to impress but Lincoln fans will forever remember him as a hugely expensive misfit. Few tears were shed for the departure of "Taxi" Tynan, who managed just one goal in nine starts but earned local fame for flamboyant use of cabs on the club's account. After one reserve game, watched by the usual crowd of about 12, Tynan emerged from the dressing-room to ask where the taxi was to take him home ? A fleet of taxis waiting to ferry Lincoln City's reserves home to their cosy firesides ? Get real !

Bell's legacy was a tatty, disunited squad and there was, in the short-term, little Murphy could do. Young central defender Tony Loxley, son of Bert, was given his debut at Swindon. City lost 6-0 and Loxley never surfaced in the first team again. Four days later at Chester, the Imps led 1-0 with 21 minutes left - and lost 5-1. As a short-term measure, Murphy recruited veteran ex-Leicester City defender Graham Cross.

McCalliog left, after serving a three-week suspension for twice refusing to train under Bert Loxley. In nine games for Lincoln, all under Bell, McCalliog was never on a winning Imps side. Mick Harford supplied some hope with five goals in five games late in the season and young Cockerill impressed throughout all the adversity but, with home crowds below 2,000, the season could not end soon enough. City lost seven of their last eight games to finish bottom, 15 points adrift of safety. Seven wins and 41 goals from 46 games laid the fast track to Division Four. Watford, 24 wins and 83 goals, climbed to Division Two.

Serious shuffling of the pack was required. Radical changes - and Murphy was never afraid to be radical. By the end of the season, Clive Wigginton, Alan Harding and Alan Jones had already departed for Grimsby, Hartlepool and America respectively. Dennis Leigh, after 201 appearances for City, was freed. Hubbard followed Jones out west to Columbus Magic, USA. Bradford City paid £10,000 for Terry Cooper and Watford forked out £15,000 for John Ward. The potential of Harford and Cockerill was evident though and they signed new contracts.

Murphy delved into the Southern League. Burly striker Tony Cunningham joined for £15,000 from Stourbridge Town. Cunningham, claimed Murphy, could be "another Cyrille Regis." From Nuneaton Borough, for £15,000, came central defender Trevor Peake, at 21, rated the hottest property outside the Football League. To partner Peake at the back, 28-year-old John Saunders arrived after being released by Barnsley. Midfielder David Carr cost £20,500 from Luton Town while the manager restated his own commitment to Sincil Bank by rejecting a two-year coaching contract in the United Arab Emirates.

Murphy identified Neale as an important squad member and allowed him leeway in his football/cricket dilemma. In contrast to Willie Bell's intransigent approach, Murphy explained: "It's not his fault that he happens to be good at both." Young left-back Nigel Crouch was enlisted on loan from Ipswich as cover until Neale's scheduled return in mid-September. The new signings got a chance to bond during pre-season work at Bovington army camp in Dorset. Back at the Bank, a new gymnasium was added thanks to a £30,000 Sports Council grant while, inside the ground, 600 metres of crash-barrier and 1,000 tons of concrete were laid.

Murphy's self-belief was highly motivating and City opened the 1979/80 season promisingly. Against Allan Clarke's Barnsley in the League Cup, the Imps were beaten only on penalties after holding the Third Division side 3-3 over two legs. When, four days later, City started their Division Four programme at home to Peterborough only two men - Grotier and Hobson - in the starting XI had figured in the opening fixture 12 months earlier.

After a 1-0 defeat to Peterborough, the new men gelled. Cunningham and Harford comprised a powerful up-front cocktail, prompting the manager to set them a target of 50 goals between them for the season. Peake - calm and classy - was thoroughly at home at the higher level. Carr was clearly an astute recruit. City stayed unchanged for the first seven games and then only brought back Neale for Crouch. They lost two of the first 13 League fixtures.

Murphy continued to wheel and deal. Cockerill was cashed in. He joined Swindon Town for £110,000. Immediately, City spent £33,000 of that on gutsy striker Derek Bell from Barnsley. Lincolnshire-born, at Wyberton, Bell had slipped through the Imps' net as a youngster and now found his way to Sincil Bank at last after passing through Derby County, Halifax, Sheffield Wednesday (on loan) and Barnsley. He scored on his debut in a 3-3 home draw with Hartlepool and City ended the first half of the season in the middle of Division Four. Not bad for a reconstituted side - but not good enough for Murphy. In the New Year, he reconstituted it again, investing heavily.

Right-back Trevor Thompson arrived from Newport for £10,000 and the versatile Nolan Keeley from Scunthorpe for £7,000. A club record £45,000 was spent on attacking midfielder George Shipley from Southampton. Peter Grotier joined Cardiff so Eric McManus, whose considerable experience included UEFA Cup action with Coventry City, was drafted in on loan from Stoke City. Phil Turner, a tidy, left-sided midfielder and product of the Imps' Sheffield nursery side, was given his chance and held his place for the last two months of the season. Centre-half Steve Thompson arrived for £15,000 from Boston United, but was kept waiting for his first-team bow.

McManus and his back-four - Trevor Thompson, Neale, Peake and Carr - conceded just two goals in 10 games. Four of those matches were 0-0 draws and there were few spectacles of great excitement but Harford's return from injury helped City finish with a flourish: victories 4-0 at home to Halifax and 5-2 at Torquay. Murphy's first full season had seen major advances. City finished seventh, seven points short of promotion.

The flurry of signings, however, so soon after Willie Bell's squandering of almost £50,000 just before he left, alarmed the bank manager. The wage-bill was now double the sum received through the turnstiles and, after two years of heavy losses, the club was put on amber financial alert. Expenditure over the previous season was more than £300,000 while gate receipts totalled £87,000. "From now on we have to be nett sellers in the transfer market," warned Dove. During the summer, Murphy bought in just one senior player - experienced former Derby County goalkeeper Colin Boulton, while Stuart Naylor, 17, a highly promising 'keeper from Yorkshire Amateurs, turned pro.

The components of a powerful Fourth Division side were already in place, among them Steve Thompson who lined up alongside Peake at the heart of defence when the 1980/81 campaign opened. City started with a League Cup two-legger against Third Division side Hull and raised a few eyebrows with a 7-0 aggregate win. Harford scored five of the seven and added another three goals in the first two League fixtures. Gordon Hobson scored five in three games. The Imps raced to the top of the table with nine points out of ten. Murphy collected the August manager-of-the-month award and Cynthia Payne walked out of HM Prison Holloway pledging: "No more parties."

Fighting spirit, imbued in his troops by Murphy, manifested itself during an early-season visit to Crewe. With Lincoln leading 1-0, still in the first half, Boulton was involved in a sickening collision which left him with a broken right leg. He was stretchered off - and out of professional football. Thompson took over in goal but the Imps' problems grew just after half-time when David Hughes was sent off. 'Thommo' led belligerently from the back, punching extravagantly whenever the ball arrived in his box, and the ten Imps responded with such brio that they stretched away to win 3-0.

Murphy moved quickly to fill the goalkeeping vacancy, enlisting 20-year-old David Felgate on loan from Bolton Wanderers. Previous loan spells with Rochdale and Crewe meant Felgate was used to the rough and tumble of Division Four and, even with the expensive Bell sidelined by a knee problem, City made happy progress. Their first ever visit to Plough Lane brought Murphy a satisfying 1-0 win over Wimbledon, managed by Dario Gradi, his former number two at Derby. The excellent Felgate conceded just three goals in eight games and even in City's grim financial state, that form justified investment. He joined for £25,000 and soon watched, untroubled, as Northampton were routed 8-0 (Hobson 4, Harford 2, Shipley 2) at the Bank.

Southend and Lincoln broke away at the top and when they met in late October, City lodged a bristling 2-1 home victory. Harford hit a hat-trick as Torquay, with former Scottish international Bruce Rioch in the back-four, were thrashed 5-0. City beat Bury 2-1, a margin only restricted by Neville Southall's heroics in the visitors' goal. The Imps delivered relentlessly efficient football. In only one of 22 games did they concede more than one goal.

In December came an amicable boardroom reshuffle. Dove requested some deserved respite from the formidable grind of perpetuating a loss-making business. In a long explanatory statement, he explained he would happily stay on the board but needed a break from the chair. This man of great wisdom and perspicacity also unveiled one of his less wise and perspicacious suggestions: To save football clubs cash, trim the teams. "Why do we need 11 players on the field?" he argued. "I would like to see the game played with, say, nine men. This would cut down the financial commitment of all clubs and it could well lead to more attacking football." Well, he needed a rest !

Dennis Houlston, a potato farmer and builder from the village of Eagle, near Lincoln, became chairman. Navenby builder Maurice Green became vice-chairman with the rest of the board comprising Dove, Allan Davey and Harold Sills. One of Houlston's first moves was to sanction the sale of Harford. City had just rejected a £70,000 bid, from an unspecified club, for Peake but on December 23, Harford, after 40 goals from 109 starts for the Imps, attracted a £160,000 offer from Newcastle United boss Arthur Cox. For a club losing money hand over fist, the bid, a record for a Fourth Division player, was "too good to refuse" said Houlston. But could Lincoln, five points clear along with Southend at the top, maintain momentum without their main man ?

A superb display to grit out a 1-0 Boxing Day win at Port Vale suggested they could. Refreshed by an early-January break to Jersey, City resumed normal service. Unveiling few frills, but making few mistakes, they passed efficiently through December, January and February unbeaten in the League. Murphy's reward was a five-year contract. Felgate's was a call-up into Wales' senior squad for a visit to Republic of Ireland in February.

At the start of March, City were 12 points clear of fifth-placed Bournemouth. There was to be no slip-up. The top two kept their nerve and when, both virtually sure of promotion, they met at Roots Hall in April, 12,391 watched a 0-0 draw. Southend police called Lincoln's 2,500 travelling fans "quite an unpleasant group" though the Essex club's decision to charge City fans £4 for a seat - the home fans paid £2 - was hardly pleasant.

Despite the rush towards promotion, attendances at the Bank stayed low. None of the last four home games attracted more than 4,000. It was success built on organisation and parsimony. Never mind extravagance, look at the League table. In the last 14 games, City scored just nine goals but conceded only six. They conceded 25 goals - the fewest ever in a Division Four season - on the way to finishing second, two points behind Southend. It wasn't sexy football but, in less than three years, Murphy had taken Lincoln from bottom to promotion.

17.
Eluded by triumph, consumed by turmoil, engulfed by tragedy

SHORTLY after the 1980/81 season, Colin Murphy, flushed with promotion success, bumped into Malcolm Allison in a lift. "Well done," offered the flamboyant ex-Manchester City boss. "Now your problems start."

Allison was referring to challenges ahead. A higher division with higher standards. Better teams with better-organised, more talented players. Well, those problems, City mostly solved. They finished their first season back in Division Three just one point short of promotion to Division Two, denied only on a heart-rending May night at Craven Cottage. The Imps raised their game and excelled at the new level but that achievement was to be overshadowed by two years of unprecedented off-field turbulence. Bickering, posturing, boardroom bloodletting, savage cost-cutting, furious protests, alleged death threats, players in dispute, throbbing egos, "nasty medicine" and, most disastrous of all, country and western music at Sincil Bank. These factors combined to weaken the football club to within hours of folding.

Such angst seemed far away as City prepared for their return to Division Three. Three senior players were signed. Steve Cammack, a striker, arrived from Scunthorpe in exchange for David Hughes. Left-back David McVay, freed by Peterborough, joined City the same day that Prince Charles married Diana Spencer. Said mismatch was still functioning happily in August when Glenn Cockerill returned to Lincoln from Swindon for £40,000. Murphy took a summer break from the Bank, though it was hardly restful: Two weeks assisting Fiji's national squad then further coaching assignments in Canberra, Sydney, Hawaii and Alaska.

The Imps' pre-season thrills and spills came from the new Football League Group Cup in which they failed to qualify from a group containing Notts County, Norwich and Peterborough. They quickly acclimatised to Division Three though and lost only one of the first six games. First visitors to the Bank were Fulham for whom midfielder John Beck scored in a 1-1 draw. At the time, Beck's strike appeared just a simple point-earner. In May, its consequences were colossal.

When Newport earned a 2-2 draw at Lincoln, Tommy Tynan scored twice as many goals in an afternoon as he managed in his entire Imps career. A week later Wimbledon goalkeeper Dave Beasant took a pasting as the Dons were hammered 5-1 (Cockerill 2, Cunningham, Cammack, Hobson). City were among the early front-runners and Cardiff City came sniffing around for Murphy but the manager responded by signing an extension to his contract, binding him to Lincoln until May 1985.

After thrashing Wimbledon on October 10, five games without a win sent City down to 20th - maybe it was to be a relegation battle instead. In his ever-eclectic programme notes, Murphy warned that now was the time to "discoidulate the clevage." After playing only once in six weeks due to a big freeze, City, with John Pickering now on the coaching staff, re-emerged in style. Steve Thompson and Trevor Peake formed a daunting central defensive blend of strength and style. Wayne Turner, on loan from Luton, and Steve Hibberd, a youth product, settled productively into midfield alongside Cockerill and Phil Turner as City embarked on a 16-match unbeaten run.

On January 15, City were 17th. On March 24, after a 2-1 win at Exeter, they were top after harvesting 25 points from 16 games. They were still top at Easter, though Carlisle, Oxford, Burnley and Fulham would all overtake them if they won games in hand. This they did, to suck Lincoln back into the pack. Hampered by Gordon Hobson's absence through injury, City lost 1-0 at Swindon and Gillingham. But they were still well in contention with three games to go: away to Chester, home to Exeter, then away to promotion rivals Fulham. A second successive promotion would be secured by three good results.

The visit to Chester presented Phil Neale with a dilemma. Murphy selected him, but so did Worcestershire CCC whom Neale was due to skipper in a Benson and Hedges Cup tie against Yorkshire at Headingley. This was the first test of a 'gentleman's agreement' between the two clubs, allowing Neale's release by one if the other was involved in significant end-of-season fixtures. "He is expected to report at 2pm to Sealand Road," insisted Murphy and, loyally, Neale did. After Cockerill and Shipley scored in a 2-1 win, Lincoln knew that victories from their last two games would ensure promotion. On the final Saturday they beat Exeter 2-1 so it was all down to Craven Cottage on Tuesday night. Lincoln had to win. If Malcolm MacDonald's Fulham took a point, they would be promoted.

More than 2,000 City fans joined a bumper crowd of 20,461 in West London. Former Imps boss Ron Gray was present. Willie Bell wasn't, still off coaching in the Colorado sunshine. As the teams ran out, founding fathers Robert Dawber, Sharpley Bainbridge, William Mortimer and Jack Strawson looked down with their celestial season-tickets. Could their creation - almost 100 years old - seize this opportunity ?

During a tense, full-blooded first-half, Lincoln more than held their own. Peake and Thompson coped competently with Fulham's much-vaunted front two, Gordon Davies and Dean Coney. Approaching the hour-mark that tension still dominated, but the 58th minute was a decisive, cruel, loaded minute. Davies raced forward but was hauled back by Thompson. It was the defender's second booking so off he went. As he trudged, desolate, along the touchline, Tony Gale delivered Fulham's free-kick into the box. It was the sort of set-piece that Thompson was built to deal with but, in his absence, the Londoners' centre-half Roger Brown rose to head home. City poured forward. On 71 minutes, a free-kick from substitute Dave Gilbert was flicked on by Cockerill and Carr arrived to head the equaliser past Gerry Peyton. One goal from promotion. City battered away but Fulham clung on. If only Beck had not scored that goal, back in September.....

At the final whistle, Craven Cottage rose to acclaim promotion. City knew that, almost certainly, their dream was over. It hung by a thread for another 24 hours until Carlisle won at whipping-boys Chester to clinch the final promotion place. By then, Dennis Houlston had quit as Lincoln chairman.

***

Fifteen minutes after the final whistle at Craven Cottage, as the champagne corks popped and Fulham embarked on celebrations long and loud, Houlston sought out Heneage Dove and handed him an envelope. Inside was his resignation, not only as chairman, but from the board. The promotion quest had masked ongoing boardroom infighting and Houlston cited, as the main catalyst for his resignation, a lack of support from his fellow directors. Solicitor Gilbert Blades, after seven years on the board, found himself thrust into the role of chairman.

Blades, still a lawyer in Lincoln, recalls: "I lived for Saturday afternoons at that time. I had been a supporter since I was a boy and on the board since Graham Taylor's first season as manager. But I never had any ambitions to become chairman. Really I took over because there was no-one else - it wouldn't have been right to land it back on Heneage." The reluctant Blades seized the helm just as, immediately ahead, on collision course, loomed an iceberg so big and treacherous it made the 'berg that sank the Titanic look like an ice-cube.

City's debts were spiralling. Despite finishing fourth, attendances at Sincil Bank had been relatively poor - only twice exceeding 6,000 in the League. End-of-season players' bonuses, pitched at a level the club could ill-afford, increased the financial pressure. A substantial injection of capital was essential but an event planned to supply exactly that, catapulted the crisis out of control instead.

Commercial officer David Mitchell had an idea: A Country and Western music festival at Sincil Bank. A scheme with potential, perhaps. Some big names were booked and the thought of Billie Jo Spears, Skeeter Davis and Don Everly warbling away to serried ranks of check-shirted, dungaree-clad, straw-chewing C&W enthusiasts in a packed stadium on a balmy early-summer evening was one to excite the club's bank manager. Sadly, that's not quite how it worked out.

The two-day event, in mid-June, was dogged by ill-luck. On the first day, torrential rain caused the stage to collapse, delaying the start for three hours. As the unseasonal deluge persisted, an emergency roof had to be erected over the sodden, rebuilt stage. Saddest of all, hardly anyone was there anyway. Only 100 people turned up on the first day with large, specially-arranged car-parks remaining empty. A few more punters attended on day two but less than 1,000 visited the whole event. "I love Lincoln," declared Billie Jo Spears, "but I'm looking forward to going back to Texas."

Her affection for Lincoln probably dipped when her cheque was stopped. The festival lost £40,000, pushing City's debts over £400,000. Mitchell, having failed to organise sunny weather, was first suspended, then dismissed by the football club. An event designed to dig City out of a hole had deepened the hole, nay fashioned it into a grave. One step from bankruptcy, just one option remained for the board. To sell the club's home.

The City board had been aware for some time that this drastic action might be necessary. Talks with a potential buyer had been underway for several weeks. Now, urgency was injected into negotiations and a deal was soon struck. Sincil Bank was sold, not to a developer, though. A sympathetic buyer was at hand. Lincoln City Council agreed, through chief executive John Thomas and a delegation of councillors, to buy the ground, then lease it back to the football club for 25 years. The relevant procedures were hurried through and within days, the full council met to consider the matter. Given a free vote, they decided by a narrow majority - 16-14 - to buy the Bank for £225,000.

Clearly, plenty of councillors were less than enthusiastic and not only in the council chamber was support far from unanimous. Some traders, accusing the council of bulldozing the decision through, called for the district auditor to investigate. The local authority took some stick for spending so much rate-payers' money but its action had saved an organisation which had been hugely important to many of its rate-payers for almost 100 years. In similar situations around the country, other authorities turned their backs on football clubs whose earlier successes they were happy to exploit. Lincoln City Council got stuck in when the chips were down and the game was nearly up. The Imps' lease was soon extended to 125 years. And Billy Jo got her cheque.

Blades still believes that selling up was a sound move. "I think it was the right thing to do," he says. "Not just because it raised some much-needed capital at the time but because it brought the city council into the club. It was a turning point. We hadn't always had the best of relationships but after they bought the ground, they were involved. They started pulling in the same direction. Since then, the council has had a lot of important input into areas like redevelopment of the ground."

The sale was attached to conditions: that a public appeal for cash must be launched and, here's the rub, there must be staff cuts, including players. A record annual loss of £259,524 was a reminder that even with the council's cash, the club remained in the red. It lost money every week. Yes, there had to be cuts. Unpleasant decisions for Blades and his board. The ship had been righted - it wasn't going down with all hands - but there would be men overboard. Just one more goal at Craven Cottage in May would have sent the Imps to Newcastle, Wolves, Leeds and Chelsea in the Autumn. Instead, they headed for a season of bitter squabbling, leading to another boardroom shift. There was mutiny ahoy.

After-shocks from the ground sale rumbled on. Dennis Bocock, still controlling a third of City's shares, claimed the club should have consulted its shareholders before flogging Sincil Bank. Bocock, Blades, Houlston and Dove conducted a tawdry public debate though the local press. Bocock's parking space at the ground was painted over. Meanwhile, those cuts took effect. Assistant manager Lenny Lawrence departed for Charlton Athletic, his workload having shrivelled in the face of reductions to the playing staff and youth system. City opened the 1982/3 season with just 15 senior players of whom one - Gerard Creane - was committed to play in Finland until October and another - Phil Neale - still had cricket obligations. The players were angered by 45 per cent cuts to their bonus system. There was a crackdown on complimentary tickets - players' wives got a free pass but everyone else had to pay. The laundry budget was trimmed. To save electricity, the minimum of night matches were planned for the reserve and youth teams. A memo instructed that phone calls must, whenever possible, be made at cheap-rate (after 1pm). While City agonised over every penny, Watford, new to Division One, announced a £400,000 sponsorship deal with truck and bus giant Iveco.

Five games into the season, the squad was pared still further when Tony Cunningham was sold to Barnsley for £80,000. Yet, somehow, City started superbly and, after seven matches, were top of Division Three. Next came a visit to Newport County and Murphy found an outrageous way to make a point about his vestigial playing resources. With Cunningham sold, and Hobson and Bell injured, Murphy was striker-less. On Saturday morning, he summoned young goalkeeper Stuart Naylor from his Wetherby home and sent him out at Somerton

Park in the number nine shirt. County's veteran centre-half Keith Oakes - later physio at Sincil Bank in the late 1990s - easily contained the young keeper-turned-striker and City lost 1-0. No points collected, but a point made by Murphy.

The board did agree to release £2,500 to buy aggressive midfielder Marshall Burke from Blackburn. He made his debut in a thrilling 2-0 Milk Cup second round first leg victory over First Division side Leicester. The giant-killing was completed at Filbert Street where Derek Bell's late goal completed an aggregate 3-0 win. Felgate's handling was superb, while Peake and Thompson shut Gary Lineker and Alan Smith out of the game. At the start of November, City were five points clear at the top of Division Three and ready to face West Ham in the Milk Cup third round. Murphy's magnificent skeleton staff was not just surviving but thriving.

West Ham were taken to a replay and then, grippingly, to extra time at Upton Park before the Hammers scraped through 2-1. City's last home game before Christmas was against crisis-club Bournemouth, the Cherries' first match under caretaker boss Harry Redknapp. Murphy warned: "Lets not get complacent." On a frozen pitch, the Imps won 9-0 (Hobson 3, Bell 3, Cockerill 2 and an own goal) and only the heroics of Bournemouth goalkeeper Kenny Allen kept the margin down. The Imps pulled their Christmas crackers top of Division Three, five points clear of a chasing pack led by Bristol Rovers, Cardiff and Newport. All this, achieved on a budget which made a shoestring seem positively lavish.

While the players performed heroics on the pitch, their grievances festered. Not just over the bonus system but also that no investment was made in the squad. With such a lack of depth - and injuries and suspensions bound to occur - they could see all their good work going to waste. Murphy constantly lobbied the board for spending-money but to little avail. Supporters, paying their hard-earned spondoolik at the turnstiles, naturally wanted to see their team fulfil its potential. The board, on the other hand, had to be wary. Very recent experience proved the extreme dangers of over-spending. Slowly, the austerity package in place, City were inching their way toward solvency. The "nasty medicine" was working, said Blades. You could see both sides.

After the players returned from a four-day New year break to Magaluf, those injuries and suspensions began to bite. Murphy publicly stated he wanted £30,000 for new players and as the board refused to budge, the rift became more public, more bitter and more of a distraction. After five matches without a victory, a home match with Plymouth, on the last Saturday in February, was chosen for a supporters' demonstration. Leaflets, calling for a mass protest against the board, were circulated and on the eve of the match Murphy stoked the discord. He took his players to a hotel where their grievances were aired with the press. As a melodramatic protest at lack of investment in the squad, Trevor Peake lodged a transfer request. Steve Thompson, on behalf of the team, said: "It seems that the chairman and directors are not prepared to help the manager and us gain promotion. The directors have to ask themselves if they want to go into the Second Division. If they don't, they should stand down and let others do it who want to go up."

After City lost 2-1 to Plymouth, some 400 fans lingered to demonstrate. Protests got out of control during the weekend when abusive graffiti was daubed on garages at Blades' home. A police guard was posted there. After receiving death threats, Blades decided enough was enough and quit, followed immediately by the rest of the board. The outgoing chairman launched a scathing valedictory attack on Colin Murphy. "I blame all this hysteria on the manager," he raged. "He started it all by orchestrating the players to talk to the press and he is entirely at fault. It was the most diabolical thing a manager could do. He thinks he is managing Manchester United. He should look at our gates and relate things accordingly."

Since he quit the Imps on February 27, 1983, Gilbert Blades has attended just one football match - a European Cup tie between Dinamo Moscow and Ujpest Dozsa. Like Frank Eccleshare, Blades has never been back to the Bank.

"I've never regretted coming out," he says. "It was difficult to run the football club when, usually, the board were there together only once a week. Really, it's a full-time operation but we all had to do it alongside separate, full-time jobs. It was wearing.

"The cuts we had to impose were unpopular but absolutely necessary. I don't think Colin Murphy really understood that. By the nature of football, there will always be conflict between the manager and board. The manager wants the players to know he's getting everything he can for them, irrespective of finance. The board has got to somehow generate that finance.

"We did our best but we were putting in a lot of time and energy and getting abuse in return. It got pretty unpleasant toward the end and I didn't need all the aggro from something that should have been a form of recreation. I was just grateful to get back all the capital I had put in."

The manager, players and supporters had got what they wanted and, 12 days later, a new board completed a £125,000 takeover. Houlston returned as chairman with directors John Reames, Michael Pryor and Derek Overton. Reames (a Folkingham corn merchant) and Prior (a Lincoln solicitor) - friends since their schooldays at the City School in Lincoln - each took major stakes in the club alongside the chairman. The new board immediately expressed "complete faith" in the manager and within days Murphy enhanced his tiny squad. Ex-Wolves and Birmingham defender Colin Brazier and veteran striker Ernie Moss arrived on short-term contracts. Midfielder Chris Thompson joined, on loan from Bolton, as cover for the injured Cockerill.

They could not correct City's loss of momentum. When Newport visited the Bank for a vital clash in March, Tynan scored twice in a 4-1 win for the Welsh club. Lincoln's promotion hopes were finally extinguished by a 1-0 defeat to Bournemouth, including George Best, at Dean Court. For the first time ever, Lincoln reached the final of a national competition - the Football League Trophy - but the tournament made even the Milk Cup look prestigious. The final - a 3-2 extra time defeat to Millwall - attracted only 3,142 to the Bank. A campaign that promised so much concluded with fewer than 2,500 present for the last home game. City finished a turbulent season in sixth place. Murphy again signed an extension to his contract but his first spell at the Bank had peaked.

Throughout all the conflict, Peake's consistent quality warranted promotion and his progress up the League at last arrived. He joined First Division Coventry City for £100,000. Felgate, Thompson, Turner and Hobson all signed new contracts but Shipley hesitated, hoping to follow Peake to loftier climes. To replace Peake, Keith Houghton was bought, for £25,000, from Carlisle United. Two strikers arrived: former Everton trainee Ross Jack, for £15,000, from Norwich, and John Thomas, a long-time target for Murphy, for £22,500, from Chester.

City opened the 1983/84 season with three conclusive defeats in four games. The third of those - 3-0 at Brentford - triggered a lengthy inquest in the temporary cabin that was the visitors' dressing-room at Griffin Park. Murphy and Pickering issued a 100-minute bollocking to the players before letting them out for a bath.

Reinforcements arrived in the considerable shapes of striker John Fashanu, on loan from Norwich, and centre-half Alan Walker. Walker cost £21,500 from Telford United whom he had captained to FA Trophy final victory at Wembley six months earlier. Lincoln lifted themselves for a two-leg Milk Cup meeting with Tottenham Hotspur. They took plenty of credit from a 3-1 first-leg defeat at White Hart Lane. Steve Archibald fired Spurs ahead and, before half-time, Glenn Hoddle and Tony Galvin created a cross which reached the net off Houghton's heel. Spurs appeared in command but eight minutes after the break, the Imps' fans rose to acclaim a quality goal. Shipley ran on to Jack's perfectly-weighted pass and shot low past Ray Clemence. Galvin's 87th minute goal eased Spurs' anxiety but those City fans had another moment to cherish. When Steve Thompson and Graham Roberts - two of the hardest "hard men" around - went into an earth-shuddering challenge, it was Roberts who stayed down for treatment. Roberts had plenty of defending to do in the second leg. In front of 12,239,

Thomas and Jack beat Clemence as Lincoln won 2-1 to go out, gallantly, 4-3 on aggregate.

Fashanu was signed permanently for £15,000 but the Centenary season was mediocre. Thompson suffered a broken leg in collision with Port Vale striker Eamon O'Keefe on FA Cup first round day. Deprived of both halves of the mighty Peake/Thompson defensive axis, City won only one of nine mid-season games. Promotion aspirations dwindled, then disappeared at the end of February after a 4-0 defeat at Burnley for whom Wayne Biggins, released three years earlier by Murphy, scored a hat-trick.

On deadline day, Cockerill moved again, this time to Sheffield United for £140,000. His transfer helped the club record an annual profit of £88,000 but, while the club's existence had been stabilised, the team won only three of the last 15 matches. Only two of the last eight home games attracted more than 2,000 and when Thomas hit a hat-trick on the last day of the season, in a 3-2 win over Port Vale, only 1,372 were there to see it. Arthur Scargill was arrested as police and pickets clashed at Orgreave Coke Plant, in south Yorkshire, and Lincoln finished a desultory 14th.

Murphy could not correct the slide. His sixth full season in charge was charmless. There was FA Cup embarrassment with first round defeat to Telford United. City were held 1-1 at Sincil Bank by the Shropshire side and then perished 2-1 at Bucks Head. Lincoln won none of their first seven League games and, after a brief occupation of bottom spot, spent the season hovering around the relegation line. While the team struggled to retain its place in Division Three, there was another change of chairman. Houlston and Murphy began to agree on fewer and fewer things. Their rapport cooled, then froze. Houlston's interest in running a football club waned and in March, he resigned. In a letter to the remaining directors, he confined his explanation to "personal reasons." A potato plantation in Argentina awaited him.

John Reames was the only director with sufficient financial clout to take over as chairman and that is what, on March 18, 1985 he did. The fresh-faced, short-trousered, little boy who, back in the 1950s, had so often stood with his grandfather on the shale of the Sincil Bank side, now controlled the club. A year after joining the board as director with responsibility only to liaise with Red Imps Association, the grain merchant now had his finger on the button. Within weeks he recruited a new board member. Geoff Davey was a lifelong Imps fan who had just returned to Lincolnshire after years spent travelling in Europe, then based in London, as an agent in the music industry. Back in Lincoln he become a vice-president of his home-town club before his step-up to the board was conceived, by chance, on a beach in the Algarve.

Davey recalls: "I was lying there on the beach when some lads came along kicking a football. I recognised them from Lincoln and one was John Reames. Us meeting like that was totally by chance but he said he'd just taken over the club and to give him a ring when we got back if I fancied joining the board. I did."

Back in frosty England, the season limped towards its conclusion. City made some progress in the Freight Rover Trophy, reaching a northern semi-final at home to Wigan Athletic on the last Wednesday of the season. In front of 1,782, Lincoln lost 3-1 and a forgettable campaign was almost over. Crowds often below 2,000 had watched City scramble their way above the relegation zone. They were safe from the drop when they travelled for their final fixture to Bradford City, already Third Division champions. This forgettable season was to end in the most horrible, unforgettable way.

Valley Parade was full of happiness as Bradford's supporters arrived to celebrate their championship triumph. The Third Division trophy was presented before kick-off, then the season started to wind gently down with 34 minutes of untaxing, end-of-season football. When a small quantity of smoke began to rise from a corner of the grandstand the incident looked curious but containable. Few people took much notice but soon the smoke turned dark and grew thick. Beneath it was a fulminant blaze which, in seconds, burst free. Feeding upon years of discarded litter beneath the stands, fire consumed its starting point, G Block, in seconds, then swept through tinder-dry stands along the length of the pitch. Spectators, shocked and horrified - how could this horror be unfolding at a football match ? - clambered forward, scrambling for the safety of the pitch. Those who chose, or were forced, to go the opposite way - to the rear of the stand - found hell waiting. The turnstiles had been padlocked and people seeking escape out into the street behind blundered instead into a fog of blinding, suffocating smoke and a hail of burning debris.

Fifty-six people lost their lives. They included two long-time Lincoln supporters, Jim West (70) and Bill Stacey (72) who had travelled to the match together, just as they had done for many years, on the Red Imps Association supporters' coach. Two empty seats on the coach offered a grievous poignancy to the stunned supporters on the journey back to Lincoln. The Stacey-West Stand, at the old Railway End of Sincil Bank, now perpetuates the memory of Lincoln's two victims of the Bradford fire. Two loyal supporters and good men - the essence of the English football follower - who set out that sunny May day to attend a match and never came home.

18.
A police-dog sticks its snout in

THE Bradford fire concentrated minds throughout the country on the safety of football grounds. Obviously, such a tragedy must never be allowed to happen again but it also brought the dishevelled state of many football stadia in England into sharp focus. Many grounds, built around the start of the 20th century, were primitive, uncomfortable and decaying.

Sincil Bank had certainly seen better days. Few improvements had been made to it since the 1930s. Now, ground development was forced high on the agenda, adding to the challenges facing a freshly-composed Lincoln City board. The Bank's St Andrew's and South Park stands were principally timber-based, exactly the sort that had encouraged the Valley Parade inferno. The South Park Stand was closed for the 1985/86 season and longer-term planning, leading eventually to redevelopment of all four sides of the ground, began.

Another matter requiring urgent attention was the position of Colin Victor Murphy. Two seasons of stagnation suggested the playing-side of Lincoln City might need freshening up. Murphy's leadership, so inspiring and successful at first, had run out of steam, drained, perhaps, by years of political infighting around him. After six and a half years in charge, he left by mutual consent. Murphy's adventurous mind needed a new challenge. The board wanted a clean slate.

Now came a big test for the novice board. From the copious applicants for the manager's job, select the best. A swift decision was required to give the new man time to get organised and sign players. Trouble was, while the directors collectively boasted considerable knowledge of grain, music, law and plant machinery, when it came to football, they were simply supporters. Committed, loyal supporters but without experience or expertise within the game. John Major and Dennis Waterman are both avid cricket fans but you wouldn't want them opening the batting for England would you ? Inexperience brings mistakes. The City board were soon flailing outside off-stump.

Geoff Davey recalls: "In our first year as a board we made some terrible, terrible decisions. We made a big effort to make a profit - and we made a substantial profit - but we got relegated to Division Four. We wouldn't pay the wages demanded and lost the likes of Steve Thompson and Gordon Hobson. We were a new board you see and you think you know it all. But you don't."

Short-listed for manager were Asa Hartford, Leighton James, Larry Lloyd, Ray Train, Eddie May, Colin Todd, and John Pickering. Hartford was offered the job but decided to stay in the Manchester area. As the board vacillated, the selection process lasted most of the summer. Finally they promoted Murphy's assistant, John Pickering, on a two-year contract. Mistake.

"After Colin Murphy left in May, we blathered about all summer," said Davey. "We interviewed people and offered the job to one or two of them and they turned it down for various reasons. In the end we went back to John Pickering. A nicer man you couldn't wish to meet but if he had been the right man for the job we would have appointed him in May. By Christmas we sacked him."

While the board blathered, several key players took advantage of new 'freedom of contract' legislation and left. Gordon Hobson joined Grimsby. Steve Thompson and George Shipley moved to Charlton. John Thomas went to Preston and Alan Walker to Millwall. Their departures brought in more than £110,000 but decimated the squad. Pickering, appointed with the new season almost upon him, had almost no time to build. Some bodies had to arrive though, in the interests of getting 11 out against Gillingham on the opening day. Former England striker Bob Latchford, at 34 and near the end of a career which brought him 12 England caps, joined from Coventry. Centre-half Gary West arrived from Sheffield United for £35,000 and midfielder Andy Toman, for £6,000, from Bishop Auckland. Pickering signed young striker Warren Ward, another graduate of Yorkshire Amateurs. Former Liverpool striker Phil Boersma arrived as coach.

City beat Gillingham 1-0, 20-year-old midfielder Neil Redfearn scoring the goal, but Latchford hurt his back and was out for two months. Ward scored on his debut, in a 3-3 draw with Doncaster, and Pickering steered his hastily-assembled side to sixth place after 11 games but the fans were unconvinced. Home games against Brentford, Bournemouth and Newport all attracted less than 2,000. As the bleak talons of winter closed round the season, City's youngsters began to struggle. They had not won in seven attempts when they made the short trip to Derby County in mid-November. Derby - Football League champions only 10 years earlier - were on hard times but their slump was bottoming out and they roasted Lincoln 7-0. Four members of that Imps team - full-backs Robert McNeil and Mark McCarrick and loan pair Alan Judge and Ian Measham - never appeared for Lincoln again while another, defender Gary Richards, started only one more game.

Confidence, particularly in defence, was shattered. Pickering enlisted experience in the shape of former Hull City, Wolves and Minnesota Strikers midfielder Peter Daniel, for £23,000 from Sunderland. After Daniel's second game - a 4-0 home defeat to Cardiff, on December 14 - the Imps had lost 10 of 11 League and cup matches and conceded 18 goals in four games. Pickering was sacked. So was Boersma.

For their third manager in seven months, City turned again to George Kerr. Since his first dismissal by Lincoln, Kerr had enhanced his reputation by coaching Grimsby to the Third Division championship. He then spent two seasons managing Rotherham and it was to there that Kerr looked to fortify Lincoln's callow squad. Midfielder Bobby Mitchell and striker Kevin Kilmore, who both played under Kerr at Grimsby and Rotherham, signed for him again. Teenage midfielder Ian McInnes also moved across from Millmoor. In a flurry of transfer activity, in too came young full-back Simeon Hodson, from Lincoln United. Latchford was farmed out on loan to Newport and soon moved permanently. City welcomed £100,000 into their bank account by selling Stuart Naylor to West Bromwich Albion. His bargain-basement replacement was the veteran former Carlisle goalkeeper Trevor Swinburne.

Hodson, McInnes and Kilmore made their debuts in a home match with Bury and McInnes had a dream start, scoring both goals in a 2-0 victory. Kerr changed the side drastically and March brought a revival with successive away wins at Newport and Reading, then a 4-1 home victory over Swansea. But the appalling pre-Christmas form had left no margin for error. City could not afford another dip and that's what followed. Relegation was confirmed by a 2-1 defeat at Cardiff in the penultimate game. The last fixture brought Wolves to Sincil Bank. Mighty Wolves, one of the great clubs of English football, were accompanying City down to Division Four. Warren Ward scored in a 3-2 defeat - despite starting only 15 games, Ward was the Imps' joint top scorer (alongside Redfearn) with eight goals.

The Imps' board had achieved its objective of making a profit - a record surplus of £100,000. Mistake. Reames now looks back quite candidly. "I took it over and ran it like a business," he says. "I hadn't learned that at that level it is impossible to run a football club successfully at a profit."

Down the slippery slope went the Imps, arriving back in the Fourth Division at an intriguing and dangerous time. For the 1986/7 season, the Football League finally acceded to years of lobbying by senior clubs outside its hallowed portals and scrapped the re-election vote for its bottom four. This time, whoever finished bottom of the Fourth Division would face automatic relegation to the GM Vauxhall Conference. In an instant, the lower reaches of Division Four were transformed from a depressing, but fairly secure, corner of the Football League to the environs of a treacherous trapdoor.

Kerr looked to Grimsby again and enlisted striker Gary Lund, in exchange for Phil Turner. Lund had scored freely at Blundell Park and, at 22, had his best years in front of him. Steve Buckley, at the other end of the career scale at 33, joined City from Derby County. Buckley was an accomplished full-back and, in West and Strodder, the Imps had a reliable central defence, but it was hard to find much quality elsewhere around the squad. The powerful Redfearn was sold to Doncaster for a ridiculously low tribunal-set fee of £17,500.

If the team required serious renovation, the stadium's need was just as great. Redevelopment was still very much at the planning stage as the board investigated possible grant-monies available. During the summer of 1986, the St Andrew's Stand, so new and shiny back in 1932, but now just a wooden anachronism, was demolished. With four shabby sides, Sincil Bank, for players and spectators alike, was depressing. The 1986/7 season was to take depression to a new dimension. Scenes, still fresh in the mind, from Bradford offered a stark reminder that words like tragedy and disaster can never truly apply to a sporting context but, in football terms, the Imps were heading for wretchedness. The plot that took them there, particularly its tangled closing acts and outrageous last twist, any fiction editor would have rejected as far too fanciful.

City started respectably with just two defeats in eight games. They won 2-1 at Molineux on the way to a Littlewoods Cup first round conquest of Wolves. When Swinburne got injured, Lee Butler, a 20-year-old from Harworth Colliery in Yorkshire, deputised capably in goal. City registered successive 1-0 victories at Torquay and Peterborough then beat Tranmere (3-1) and Crewe (2-1) at home. Four successive wins propelled them into November among the promotion contenders. Kerr, it seemed, had learned a thing or two since first time round at Lincoln.

History was made when Kevin Kilmore picked up a hamstring injury. That, in itself, was not historic but his replacement, Shane Nicholson, became the youngest Imps player ever when he appeared at Burnley, aged 16 years and 172 days. City lost 3-1 at Turf Moor but beat Wolves 3-0 in a pea-souper at Sincil Bank then hammered Swansea 4-0, Lund contributing a hat-trick. Eight goals in seven games from Lund helped keep the points tally ticking upwards and after a 2-1 home win over struggling Burnley on January 3, City nestled sweetly seventh in Division Four. Colin Murphy, recently installed as manager of Stockport County, had the problems. County, along with perennial strugglers Torquay, occupied the bottom two positions at the start of 1987.

The arrival of New Year intensified the fear-factor. That final, fatal 24th spot in May looked ever more sinister and gruesome as it drew closer. Who would carry the stigma of being the first club to be relegated to the Conference? Of course, once down, there would be no way back. The victim would languish, forever, in the nether regions of English football. Lost and, after a period of ridicule, forgotten. Yesterday's men with no tomorrow. Adrift with no lifeline. That was the irrational but all-consuming fear of the threatened clubs. Still, it was nothing to do with Lincoln. The Imps, just three defeats in 13 matches, were up there in seventh, eyeing promotion.

Suddenly they encountered a brick wall. The next five matches brought five defeats and not a single goal. After seven defeats - and three goals - in eight games, the promotion zone had receded rapidly from view. The scramble to avoid bottom spot was still remote but, on March 2, Kerr was summoned to a board meeting at which concern was expressed at the steep slump. The manager admitted that automatic promotion was now unlikely. The play-offs, however, he insisted were still a realistic aim. Reames, Davey, Pryor and Overton had their doubts and kept their finger on the trigger. Six days later, after a 2-1 home defeat to Peterborough, said digit twitched. They voted unanimously to sack the manager. City sat 18th in Division Four.

Now, hindsight is a wonderful thing. In hindsight, the promotion of Peter Daniel to caretaker player/manager for the rest of the season was a monumental error. His appointment was economically sound, saving the price of hiring a new man from outside, but, in football terms, represented a colossal gamble. Great managers can struggle to turn things round if a team has lost the winning habit. Daniel, with no managerial experience to call upon, was asked to halt a most ominous slide. Four months earlier, he had told Kerr he was unsettled in Lincoln and fancied a player-coach position somewhere. Now one had fallen into his lap. He was keen - but so is a mouse when it sees a mousetrap.

Early conclusions were hard to reach after Daniel's first three games all ended in 1-1 draws. The middle of these - at home to Torquay, watched by just 1,186 - was Gary Strodder's last appearance before being sold to West Ham for £100,000. Lincoln had won just one of 12 games and, now deprived of the influential defender, supporters were getting twitchy. At a board meeting on March 23, Pryor asked Daniel whether he envisaged City finishing bottom. A categorical "No" was Daniel's reply. It would have been a strange manager indeed who said "Yes."

Transfer deadline week allowed Daniel, now assisted by former Hull team-mate Chris Chilton, a last chance to enlist trump cards and he brought in three players. Striker Jimmy Gilligan, who had struggled to live up to six-figure moves to Grimsby and Swindon, joined for £35,000 from the Wiltshire club. On loan came centre-half Glenn Humphries, from Doncaster, and veteran midfielder Derek Hood from York. The trio were given immediate debuts - replacing the transferred Strodder and the dropped Kilmore and Lund - at Hartlepool. After six minutes, Humphries was sent off. Final score: Hartlepool 2 Lincoln 1. The Imps' next three home games were woeful: a 2-0 defeat to Aldershot, a goalless draw with Hereford and a 1-0 defeat to Dixie McNeill's Wrexham. The Wrexham game prompted scathing criticism. "Pathetic," raged the Lincolnshire Echo. "City just didn't have the guts." The rookie manager was struggling to motivate his troops and unwisely elected not to confine his thoughts to the dressing room. After the defeat to Wrexham, he singled out Kilmore, Hodson, Hood, Gilligan and Lund. "They let the club down," he raged.

With five matches left, City travelled to Stockport who were still not free of danger but in a much healthier position than when Murphy took charge in November. Daniel opted for blanket defence at Edgeley Park, but Andy Hodkinson's 71st minute winner lifted Stockport to a 1-0 victory and their highest position of the season. They climbed to 20th. Lincoln, for the first time, slipped into the bottom four.

Next came a Sunday visit to Sincil Bank by champions-elect Northampton. Out of nowhere, Lincoln summoned up, not just a victory, but a performance of zest and power. Assisted by a bizarre 30-yard own goal from the Cobblers' Phil Chard, City blitzed their complacent opponents, won 3-1 and received a standing ovation. The points sent Lincoln into May with six teams below them. All six had games in hand, but one point from any of the last three games - at Wolves, at home to Scunthorpe and at Swansea - would almost certainly ensure Lincoln's safety. Daniel felt confident. "I've said all along that that we would not go down," he purred, after the Northampton game. "The belief was apparent as soon as the players went out. I think it is safe to say we are reasonably safe."

Foolish words. At Wolves, it all went pear-shaped early on. After 90 seconds, Steve Bull seized upon Shane Nicholson's errant back-pass to score. Bull struck again on 12 minutes and Wolves won 3-0. In the penultimate game - a Monday night visit from Scunthorpe - the Imps blundered spectacularly. One point short of safety, they led 1-0 with seven minutes remaining. Then Gary West, who before kick-off had collected the Imps' player-of-the-season award, gave the ball away to Andy Flounders who equalised. A minute later, Flounders pounced again as defenders dithered. Scunthorpe won 2-1. City had been so, so close to safety. If they had held on, even for a draw, all the pressure would have lifted. They could have sat back, nice and relaxed, travelled to Swansea without stress and monitored the big issue from afar. Instead, the pressure tightened. City remained one of five clubs still within reach of the Conference's tentacles. Lincoln, Burnley, Torquay, Tranmere, Rochdale. Who would be dragged under ?

Not Rochdale. They had a game in hand and, on Wednesday, beat Stockport 2-1 to slice themselves free of that tentacle. Out of relegation's grasp. Now there were four candidates left. Alfred Hitchcock never directed anything this tense. Agatha Christie never wrote anything this tangled. Tony Hatch never composed theme music for anything this dramatic.

On Friday night, Tranmere played Exeter at Prenton Park. Defeat would have left the Birkenhead club highly vulnerable and made Lincoln safe for sure.

But Ronnie Moore's side won 1-0 to save themselves. When the last Saturday of the season dawned, three clubs still teetered on the brink: Lincoln (away to Swansea), Burnley (at home to Leyton Orient) and Torquay (at home to Crewe). Spread around three diverse, far-flung locations - the gritty mining territory of south Wales, Lancashire's industrial heartlands and the genteel Devon coast - this complex plot would resolve itself and someone, somewhere, would be devastated. Years later, relegation to the Conference is a heavy blow to bear, but demoted clubs know others have bounced back. That first time, it was unthinkable. Fear of failure married to fear of the unknown. "We'd never get back." That type of emotion.

Burnley were bottom, a point behind Torquay and two behind Lincoln. Of the three, the Imps were favourites to stay up - if either of the other two lost, obviously, City were safe. Burnley, under Brian Miller, had to get a result against Leyton Orient, who were already assured of a place in the play-offs. The Clarets' famous history meant that most publicity on this fateful day went their way. More than 17,000 packed ghoulishly into Turf Moor, attracted by the prospect of a historic funeral. While Burnley were the prestigious, potential fall-guys, Torquay, meanwhile, had, all season, been expected to plummet. They had finished bottom in the last two seasons as chairman David Webb implemented savage cost-cutting. The arrival of Stuart Morgan as manager triggered a miraculous turnaround. The Gulls had wallowed in the bottom two until spring after which they suddenly hit promotion form. Momentum was with them. On the last day, they faced a Crewe side in low mid-table but including David Platt, Geoff Thomas, John Pemberton and Peter Bodak, all later to play top-flight English football.

Lincoln City travelled to Swansea. It could have been much tougher for Daniels' side. Swansea's push for promotion had floundered with just three victories from 18 games. Not much to play for, perhaps, but Swansea manager Terry Yorath was a good friend of Stuart Morgan's from their days together in the Welsh national squad. On Saturday morning, Yorath telephoned Morgan to say: "Don't worry, we'll beat 'em for you."

Rarely, nay, never in the history of world football has 3pm so closely resembled High Noon. Lincoln City, cheered on by the customary wonderful, phenomenally-loyal travelling support, lined up to kick-off at Vetch Field. Butler, Daniel, Buckley, Cooper, West, Humphries, Hodson, Lund, Gilligan, Franklin, McGinley. In these men lay the Imps' fate. City were awful. Swansea weren't much better but, after half-an-hour, former Scottish international Tommy Hutchison aimed a cross into the Imps' box. He sliced the ball which veered away from the onrushing strikers but also evaded the confused Butler and nestled in the corner of the net. Swansea 1 Lincoln 0. A chill ran through those travelling fans. More bad news: Neil Grewcock and Ian Britton had put Burnley 2-0 up against Orient but wait a minute...what about this? After half an hour, Torquay 0 Crewe 2. Platt and Bodak had scored to terrify the home fans packed into Plainmoor. Lincoln had done nothing to earn a reprieve but one seemed at hand.

A hint of dramas to come arrived just before half-time. In Devon, Jim McNichol pulled a goal back for Torquay. Burnley were next to get a scare when Alan Comfort's 56th-minute strike for Orient trimmed their lead. Miller's men had 34 minutes to survive. Torquay still trailed. City still had time to take matters into their own hands but they huffed and puffed without pattern or inspiration. Twelve minutes from time, substitute Phil Williams headed Swansea's second goal. The Lincoln fans, unable to extract any hope from their own powder-puff team, could only hope. Burnley were hanging on at 2-1. Torquay were still 2-1 down. City were still okay. But now events at Plainmoor ventured into the realms of the bizarre.

After 75 minutes, full-back McNichol cleared the ball up the line and stumbled into touch. His momentum took him on to the perimeter-track which, due to the large crowd, was being patrolled by police officers with dogs. McNichol landed beside one of these dogs, a sturdy animal called Bryn. The pooch, thinking his handler was being attacked, efficiently recalled its training procedure "Handler: Protection of" and bit McNichol on the thigh. The defender collapsed in a combination of pain and shock. There was uproar. Confusion. Laughter. Then, during a 12 minute hold-up while McNichol's bite-wound was treated - the Gulls had already used their substitute - tension reasserted itself. Oblivious to this pantomime, Lincoln's fans watched the limp spectacle at the Vetch Field peter out to its conclusion. Swansea 2 Lincoln 0. Burnley held on to win - their summer-long celebrations were launched. Now it was Torquay or Lincoln.

When the final whistle sounded at the Vetch, there were still, due to Bryn's intervention, 15 minutes left at Plainmoor. Morgan now knew Yorath had fulfilled his promise and the Gulls' boss was screaming from the touchline: "Come on lads, all we need to do is score." Crewe did Lincoln proud. They fought hard. Torquay battered away, driven by desperation and fear, deep into injury time. They were two minutes from the Conference when Crewe defender John Pemberton collected the ball in his own penalty area and tried to dribble his way clear. He lost control. Paul Dobson took possession and rifled the ball into the net. Plainmoor went bananas. Desperation turned to mad, spine-tingling, disbelieving, throw-yourself-indiscriminately-in-all-directions-at-once, glorious euphoria. When, seconds later, the final whistle sounded, the roar was so loud that a cricket match, two miles away at Barton, was halted by the noise. True joy and relief. At Burnley, joy and relief. Torquay, Burnley, Tranmere and Rochdale had got themselves embroiled in this mess of a lottery of a farrago and survived.

Lincoln had perished. Seventh in the Fourth Division in January, City had not been bottom of the Fourth Division all season - until after the last whistle of the last game of the season. Now they were bottom. Bottom, down and out.

The news filtered through to Swansea like a bereavement. Lincoln's players were in tears. Supporters and directors were in tears. The bizarre details were barely known but anyway they were irrelevant. City's proud Football League status was gone. The club felt belittled and humiliated. On this big day, for this huge game - perhaps the biggest in Lincoln City's history - the team had put in a small, timid performance. Daniel implicitly acknowledged his failure to motivate his players. "The truth is we played bloody awful," he confessed. "That first goal went in and the players sat back and thought: 'That's it.'"

After the match, the Swansea directors showed their Lincoln counterparts into a quiet room, sent in four bottles of whisky and left them to it. At 7.30pm, Geoff Davey wandered out, alone, into the centre-circle of a deserted Vetch Field and wept. City's supporters embarked on the long journey home. For more than an hour, on the first Red Imps Association coach, not a word was spoken. Instead of the usual hubbub and chatter, there was silence. Thick, depressed, incredulous silence. Then, towards the back of the vehicle, a lone, young voice broke into song. Firmly, defiantly, it began a chorus of "You'll Never walk Alone." Others joined in and soon every supporter on board was singing. Defiance in sadness. The process of recovery was already starting but it was a black, bleak night for Lincoln City Football Club. Out of the Football League for the first time since 1921. In Torquay, an evening of riotous celebration ended with supporters forming a joyful conga round the harbour.

19.
Murphy's Mission

LINCOLN was a city in shock. Everyone connected with the football club was numbed, not just by the magnitude but the melodrama of its demise. Loss of Football League status for the first time since 1921 was a stunning blow to a proud organisation and for days a state of near-disbelief existed. Then, incredulity gave way to acceptance of the harsh reality and there, rising quickly to the surface, was determination. Fierce determination. Lincoln City had to bounce straight back. There was no time for self-pity or recrimination.

Within days of relegation, City's four-strong board - Reames, Davey, Pryor and Overton - was sending out positive messages and making positive decisions. The football club would continue to operate on a full-time, professional basis. A full youth system, with 13 trainees under the senior players, was retained. The club would press on with construction of a new St Andrew's Stand, due to open in the autumn of 1987. Lincoln City were down but they refused to think 'down' or act 'down.' They had no intention of staying down but, who, as manager, could lead them straight back up ?

Peter Daniel lobbied hard to take the job full-time but City's advertisement for a new manager in national papers, within 36 hours of relegation, suggested he had two chances: Slim and None. And Slim had just left town. Daniel's temporary reign hardly coruscated with glory and City were in dire straits. They needed someone with experience. Someone with grit and determination who could kick ass and pull things together. Someone who, in an emergency, if all the circumstances demanded it, would even swear. A street-fighter. Sound familiar ?

There were 120 applications for the manager's job. Twelve of these, the board considered realistic and some were impressive - Martin O'Neill was interviewed - but the job went to a man who did not apply. A man whose attributes were already well-know to the City board. Step forward - again - Colin Murphy. The Imps poached him from Stockport with four months of his contract to run. They agreed to pay compensation, confident they had the right man for the job.

Lifting Lincoln out of the Conference - that was Murphy's Mission. He immediately pledged: "I am going to win the treble. I want to win the GM Vauxhall Conference, win the FA Trophy and get the club back into the Football League at the first attempt." Astute supporters spotted that his treble was, in essence, a double, but the gung-ho rhetoric was just what they wanted to hear after City's lily-livered surrender of Football League citizenship.

Since his first departure from Sincil Bank, Murphy had spent a year coaching in Saudi Arabia, sandwiched between two spells as manager of Stockport. He returned to the Cheshire club in November 1986 when they were bottom of the League and steered them clear of the fate that ultimately engulfed Lincoln. But Murphy was saddened and, in professional terms, intrigued by the Imps' plight from the moment it unfolded on May 9.

"I knew how John Reames, Geoff Davey and Mike Pryor would be feeling," he recalls. "The fact that they had been bottom for only one day meant it was not a true representation of the facts. I felt really empty inside on their behalf. When the chance arrived to go back I went because I knew it would be a challenge - a tremendous challenge."

Murphy took over in slightly different circumstances, second time around. First time, back in 1978, he inherited an unhappy, unwieldy and unsuccessful squad. Now he hardly inherited a squad at all. Football League regulations allowed players to became free agents if a club dropped out of the League. It was legislation designed to protect players in the rare case of a club failing to gain re-election, and had not been updated for the arrival of automatic relegation. City's players had until July 15 to find themselves another club. Only Nicholson, Buckley, McGinley and Gamble declined to jump ship.

"The Football League wasn't prepared for the change," said Murphy. "Subsequently, things have been put right, but in that first year we paid the price for being first. By cancelling players' contracts, they ripped the guts out of the club." The Imps' sense of injustice heightened when the fixtures were published. City were allocated the toughest possible start - away to Barnet, runners-up to Scarborough the previous season, and big-spending Weymouth, in the first four days. Welcome to the Conference!

Ahead lay a very different sort of season for Lincoln City and, in at least one way, unique. For the first time in their history, the Imps were the team to beat. Top dogs. City slickers. Every club combed the fixture-list to see when they played Lincoln. They all wanted to turn the full-time, ex-League, hoity-toity big knobs well and truly over. City would be exposed to aspiring "giant-killers" every week. This was unchartered territory. Hostile territory.

Murphy recalls: "We were the first Football League team to be relegated and, make no mistake, the Conference wanted to rub our noses in it. Everyone was desperate to beat us. They just wanted to get at us. I knew every match was going to be a battle, so the players I brought in had to be fighters. Not just good players but good types. We couldn't afford to have any players that would hide."

Murphy got the backing he wanted from the board. Reames had learned lessons from under-investment in his first two years as chairman. He pledged that City would stay full-time for at least two seasons. Driven by fear of becoming trapped in the Conference, Lincoln hurled money at their escape-bid. Geoff Davey admitted it was a "mercenary job" with the club paying Third (now Second) Division wages to attract players. Forced to start with almost a clean slate, Murphy faced a bit of a task: Build a Conference-winning side virtually from scratch. His powers of persuasion were taxed to the limit - he was, after all, asking players to drop out of the Football League. Unprecedented levels of player-traffic followed through Sincil Bank. There were more ins and outs than you could shake a stick at.

Murphy plundered mainly Stockport and Grimsby. His assistant at Stockport, Gordon Simmonite, accepted the equivalent position at Sincil Bank. Simmonite knew Lincoln from three years spent there as a defender in the early 1980s. Also from Edgeley Park came strikers Phil Brown and Mark Sertori and rugged central defender Trevor Matthewson. City picked up Matthewson for a snip - a tribunal-set fee of £13,000. Stockport wanted £50,000.

From Grimsby came Bob Cumming, Andy Moore and Nigel Batch. Cumming was a buccaneering, skilful midfielder with more then 350 games in 14 years with the Mariners behind him. Batch, too, was vastly experienced, having played 205 consecutive games in goal for Grimsby during 11 years at Blundell Park. He had first impressed Murphy as an apprentice at Derby in the mid-1970s. Cleethorpes-born defender Andy Moore was the most expensive summer recruit at £34,000. Cash was also released to recruit midfielder Les Hunter (£8,000 from Scunthorpe) and striker Mick Waitt (£17,500) and utility player David Clarke (£5,000) from Notts County.

With Batch on board, City cashed in young goalkeeper Lee Butler. The 21-year-old joined Graham Taylor's Aston Villa for £100,000. The departure of Gary West - a good servant for City - to Gillingham for £35,000 was regretted but those of Peter Daniel, to Burnley, and Jimmy Gilligan, for £20,000, to Cardiff, not so much. Gary Lund, leading scorer with 13 goals during City's slide into the Conference, joined Notts County for £27,000. After 21 years with Lincoln, physiotherapist Bert Loxley was sacked - and to this day is not sure why.

It was a bewildering level of movement. The supporters waited and wondered. They analysed the fixture list. It contained some decent, strong, ambitious teams. Barnet, Weymouth, Maidstone, Altrincham and Enfield all considered themselves potential Football League members, though who would have thought City would ever visit Fisher Athletic, Sutton United and Bath on League business? To add to the adventure, the Conference was selected by FIFA as guinea-pig for an experiment with the offside rule. For this season only, players could remain on-side when receiving the ball directly from a free-kick. Everywhere, there were unknown quantities, not least the Imps' reconstructed team.

Supporters, nationwide, watched with interest to see how the Football League's first fall-guys would fare. When the curtain went up, key pieces were still to be fitted into Murphy's jigsaw and City lost those first two games - 4-2 at Barnet and 3-0 at Weymouth. It was just the welcome the Conference had hoped to offer Lincoln. "That was the lowest point of all," recalls Reames. "We had spent heavily and all stayed as upbeat as possible yet there we were with two defeats and seven goals conceded. At no point had we contemplated failure but it's hard to keep the thought totally out of your mind when you're sitting there with no points from two games."

Murphy stayed calm though. He not only had more cards up his sleeve and further irons in the fire, but also other fish to fry. On the eve of the third game - against Dagenham, he brought in another ex-Stockport man David Mossman. The big midfielder scored twice on his debut and City won 3-0. They were up and running.

Two days later, on Bank Holiday Monday, Runcorn were beaten 1-0 at the Bank. Waitt scored the only goal in a mean, uncompromising brawl of a match. Murphy relished it. "An excellent test," he said, but Runcorn boss Johnny King was unhappy at his side's "shabby treatment" from Lincoln. "I found the people there very unfriendly," he protested, accusing City of thinking they were too big for the Conference. Meanwhile, Barnet manager Barry Fry claimed that if his side deprived Lincoln of the title they would be the most popular Conference champions ever. It was increasingly clear that the Imps were not welcome at this party but the criticism bound them together. In adversity, supporters warmed to the cause. Besieged, City circled their wagons.

Murphy completed two more transfer swoops. Paul Smith, a pacy left-sided striker, was signed for a record £48,000 from Port Vale. He made an eye-catching debut in a 4-1 win at Stafford Rangers in which Waitt hit a hat-trick. When Murphy returned, yet again, to Stockport for right-back Clive Evans, the cast for the 'Mission' was almost complete. Evans' debut match was a 4-0 home victory over Enfield in which Smith, quickly settling in, scored twice. A Tuesday night visit to Runcorn's Canal Street ground reminded Lincoln why they needed out of this division. Hospitality was sparse, so was the crowd (970) and, to round off a rotten evening, the Cheshire club won 4-1.

Simmonite quit as assistant boss in October to join the police but, the following day, Lincoln won 2-1 at Maidstone to move into fourth place, two points behind Barnet, Weymouth and Kettering. Forced to compete in the FA Cup fourth qualifying round, City negotiated a trip to north-Lincolnshire side Brigg Town, with ease, winning 4-1. Murphy wanted battlers and battlers he got. Lincoln were not to be intimidated and more brawling followed when Barnet visited Sincil Bank. Fists flew and the Londoners' Noel Ashford and Herbie Smith were sent off - the latter after just seven minutes on the pitch as substitute. After an on-pitch free-for-all, in which Reames and Davey got involved, Barry Fry was escorted from the field. At the end of the bout, City emerged with a 2-1 win. Three days later they thrashed Cheltenham 5-1. The victory was marred by a broken leg for Waitt from an innocuous collision with Cheltenham goalkeeper Alan Churchward. The crack, and Waitt's yell of pain, was audible throughout the ground - he was ruled out for the season - but City's fans ended the day singing "We're going to win the League."

On November 14, the day of an FA Cup first round visit from Crewe, the new St Andrew's Stand was opened. Funded principally by Lincoln City Council and the Football Trust, the £650,000 structure housed 1,400 seats and, on the ground floor, a community centre. From a football point of view it was impressive - as far as it went, which was roughly to the edge of each penalty area. Spectators near either end were stuck with restricted views and there were a few traditionally obstructive pillars but it was a step forward from the building site of the last two years. The stand was officially opened seven months later when Brian Clough's Nottingham Forest paid a visit.

Watched, for the first time in 18 months, by spectators on four sides, Crewe's visit offered City a chance to embarrass a League club. They seized it with McGinley and Cumming scoring as Crewe were beaten 2-1. A less uplifting cup occasion was an FA Trophy first-round visit to South Liverpool. City drew 1-1 in front of 307 people and required three attempts to see off the tough-tackling Northern Premier League side.

Murphy was full of ideas. For a Boxing Day visit to neighbours Boston United, he decided that Simmonite, who had been playing for Gainsborough Trinity in the Northern Premier League, was the man to spring on the Pilgrims for the big derby. But time was short. The deal was still to be registered when Christmas arrived.

Murphy said: " I wanted to be absolutely sure the transfer was complete because everything we did - every transfer, every loan move - the Conference went through with a fine-tooth comb. Geoff Davey phoned the Conference secretary Peter Hunter a couple of times on Christmas morning to make sure Simmonite was registered. Geoff was told 'yes he was' but I wanted to make trebly sure - the last thing we needed was points deducted for playing an unregistered player. So I phoned Peter again and he said 'Look, this is the third time I've been bothered on Christmas morning. I'm just taking the chicken out of the oven!' I said 'well you want to be considered parallel to the Football League don't you ? They have staff working on Christmas Day. Put the chicken back in the oven and check the registration has come through.'" It had - and, next day, Simmonite starred as Lincoln won 2-1, thanks to Phil Brown's exquisite 89th minute chip, in front of 5,822 at York Street. And the chicken was lovely !

City steamed their way through a 15-match unbeaten run. After a 3-0 victory over Fisher Athletic on January 9, they moved alongside Barnet, five points clear of the rest. January brought Murphy his second Manager-of-the-Month award of the season. Most matches brought excitement, tons of passion and, invariably, some aggro. City's fighting spirit overflowed during a 2-1 FA Trophy win at Maidstone when McGinley was sent off for apparently head-butting his team-mate Smith. There was crowd trouble at Enfield where City's FA Trophy trail ended with a 1-0 defeat. Matthewson was sent off during another war of a game at Kidderminster - a 3-3 draw. It was heady stuff. This Lincoln side never rolled over and the supporters liked it a lot. Crowds at the Bank rose 80 per cent on the previous season.

Into the last third of a bruising campaign, injuries started to bite. Nicholson, Batch, Cummins and Smith missed 33 games between them during the vital closing months. But City dug in. Richard Wilson, nephew of former Arsenal and Scotland goalkeeper Bob Wilson, deputised capably for Batch. City beat Altrincham 5-0 (McGinley 2, Clarke, Moore, Brown). In front of a Conference record 7,542, Boston were beaten 5-1 at the Bank after another audacious transfer swoop by Murphy. He signed midfielder Paul Casey from Boston five days before the two clubs met.

There was still a thick residue of hostility toward Lincoln. They arrived at Macclesfield in mid-April to find inches of water on the dressing room floor and no hot water for the players. Macclesfield had decided to reciprocate the austere conditions they found at a half-rebuilt Sincil Bank earlier in the season. Never mind the frosty welcome - what really hurt City was the 2-0 defeat at Moss Rose. It left them four points behind leaders Barnet with just one game in hand. City beat Wealdstone 3-0 - again including a mass brawl - but defeats, 2-1 at Bath and 2-0 at Kettering kept the initiative with Barnet. Reames confessed: "I'm a bag of nerves. This is far worse than being at the foot of the Fourth Division," and even the experienced Murphy felt the heat.

"In the closing weeks I did feel a lot of pressure personally," he says. "I knew that, with everything that had gone on and us having had so many new players, second place would be a real achievement. But I also knew that would cut no ice - in the supporters' eyes that would be a failure."

A 1-1 home draw with Maidstone only increased the nerves. With two games left, City trailed Barnet by one point. Just like a year earlier, Lincoln needed results elsewhere to be kind. On April 30, Lincoln, thanks to goals by Phil Brown and Clive Evans, beat Stafford 2-1. This time, news from afar was greeted by mighty cheers. Barnet had lost 2-1 to Runcorn. If Lincoln won at home to Wycombe on Monday night, they would be back in the Football League.

Another Conference record crowd of 9,432 - City's largest attendance for more than five years - squeezed into Sincil Bank. Wycombe were 18th in the table. Beatable, surely, but nerves can flare up when the winning post is in sight. An early worry arrived when McGinley hobbled off injured but his replacement, Clarke, delivered the 22nd minute corner which Sertori bundled into the net. One foot in the League. Wycombe posed little threat but 1-0 is always a fragile advantage. No-one could relax. Then, 17 minutes into the second half, Casey cleverly opened up Wycombe's defence for Brown to race through and collect his 20th goal of the season. 2-0. Wycombe offered little. Barnet had won 2-0 at Welling but it didn't matter. When referee Malcolm Thompson, from North Shields, sent three sturdy offerings of breath into his small, metallic tubular instrument, the party began. City were back.

Reames lauded the supporters. "All the talk has been about management, about players and directors," he said, "but without the support we have received right from day one of the season we would be nowhere. The supporters have made all this possible."

True, but the board did the business too. They invested heavily behind Murphy. They hired the right man and equipped him with sufficient funds to achieve his target. The cost of the Conference triumph - City lost £134,000 on the season - was to hang heavily over the football club for years, but the potential cost of being stranded outside the League was unthinkable.

And then there was 'Murph.' Since 1988, the maverick Londoner has travelled far and wide. He has achieved plenty in football in locations from Southend to Vietnam and Tottenham to Burma. But he won't achieve anything more special and satisfying than constructing a squad, almost from scratch, to win the difficult, abrasive and gruelling competition that was the 1987/88 Conference.

He reflects upon it still, clearly, with pride. "It was a colossal achievement," he says, "because we won it despite playing our first 10 games with two or three youth players. Really we got promoted on three quarters of a season. The first big step forward was Trevor Matthewson saying he would join us. Then the likes of Clive Evans, Phil Brown and Paul Smith came. Bob Cummins and Steve Buckley were outstanding. I felt that Lincoln had no right to be in that League. The players were tremendous.

"You have to give credit to the board too. They kept the players full-time and that was vital. We were the fittest side in the division and won a lot of matches in the last 10 minutes. The supporters were superb, especially away from home. They knew we were in a battlefield and really built the momentum. I think it was the different circumstances which meant they really got behind us. I don't know whether Lincoln's support has ever been better."

A crazy, nerve-pulverising year ended with a high to match the mortifying low of 12 months earlier. How much did reclaiming Football League status mean to Lincoln City Football Club ? Ask Geoff Davey. "The deaths of my two parents aside," he says, "nothing has ever come anywhere near the sadness and remorse I felt when Lincoln went out of the League. And nothing has ever come close to the joy of getting straight back in."

20.
The managers' merry-go-round.

AS WYCOMBE slid off silently south towards Buckinghamshire - their bit-part fulfilled to perfection - Lincoln City set about celebrating, long into the night. Triumphant songs were sung. Handshakes were exchanged. Backs slapped and lager supped but even as the revelry was swinging into top gear, Colin Murphy was pondering his future.

"My first feeling was happiness," he recalls. "Happiness for the team, the staff and the supporters. And satisfaction of a job well done. But then, even that night, I was thinking 'right, what shall I do now ?'

"Really, I had gone back to Lincoln on a one-season mission. But now I was thinking 'Do I stay or do I go ?' I was far from sure but, in the end, I got caught up in all the emotion and was lured into staying."

The climax to the Conference season was so ebullient, so perfect, it was impossible to follow. From being the centre of attention throughout a boisterous, emotion-juggling, ultimately glorious season, City returned to life as just another honest trampler of the Fourth Division treadmill. Their first fixture - at home to Hartlepool - provoked much less intrigue than the opener at Barnet a year earlier.

The Imps took to the treadmill with a different goalkeeper, Mark Wallington, signed from Derby for £20,000. At 35, Sleaford-born Wallington made his City debut 19 years after being on the club's books as a schoolboy. Nigel Batch joined Darlington, at first on loan, then permanently. Graham Bressington, a rugged midfielder, joined from Wycombe and utility player Darren Davis arrived from Notts County but no fanfares accompanied City's return to the League. They lost 1-0 to Hartlepool, then 3-0 at Wrexham.

Gordon Hobson rejoined, for £60,000, from Southampton. He scored four goals in three games, all of which Lincoln won, to kick-start the season, but consistency was elusive. The Conference bit back when City were dumped out of the FA Cup, 3-2 at Altrincham, and while there was never a threat of that dreaded 24th place, the Imps never rose above mid-table. Most entertainment came from Murphy's increasingly bizarre "Message" in match-day programmes.

When Tranmere visited on March 1, the Imps' play-off hopes were wearing thin. "We cannot expunge the last 30 games," warned Murphy. "What we can say is as a result of the last 30 games, whatever the variables, excuses or praises one wishes to implicate, our position is as it is. All we know is that there have now been two thirds of the season elapsed and hopefully if we are to remain very settled in the last third and be in a position which we have not been all season to use competition, by virtue of injury-free circumstances, as a norm then we shall want our arses kicking if we do not run the situation very close or as close as can be considered very close. We are in a quick-fire explosive results business and as far as we are concerned as players and managers I have always felt there can be no better test than increasing the heat in the kitchen, we are all on simmer."[Sic]

City's simmer failed to come to the boil. They finished 10th and when Leyton Orient arrived for the last home game, there was more than a tinge of world-weariness to Murphy's notes. "For two seasons," he wrote, "you, me, we all of us have been forced to breakfast on travesty, lunch on objection and insult, dine on inflicted pressure. High tea we daren't sit still long enough to take and by supper we were still expected to have been victorious.

"In all cases," he added, concisely, "there are four ways to do a thing, which are, the right way wrongly, the wrong way rightly, the wrong way wrongly, but as I think you will agree in the last two years as we have attempted, the right way rightly then I am sure you will come again in these numbers again if we are to give you the good commencement."[Sic]

As Murphy passed his 100th month as City manager, the familiar financial pressure was severe. City sustained another substantial loss - more than £100,000, year-on-year. Lincoln had been on the back-foot with the bank manager virtually ever since that decision, in 1892, by the club's committee to double the players' wages. Almost a century later, pinned on the back-foot they remained. While more cash than ever, from sponsors and TV companies, showered down upon English football's top clubs, little trickled down to those in the lower divisions. More than ever, Lincoln were a 'sell-to-survive' club, always hunting a young player or two to cultivate as the next cash lifeline. During the 1988/89 season, central defender Tony James filled that role. The Sheffield-born 21-year-old had impressed Murphy for Gainsborough against City in a pre-season friendly. Lincoln signed him for £6,000 and what a shrewd investment that proved. Despite starting only 23 League games, James earned the supporters' player-of-the-season award in his first season. After playing in the Imps' opening game of the 1989/90 campaign, he joined Leicester City for £150,000. Linked to the same deal were the arrivals of defender Grant Brown and midfielder Paul Groves with Lincoln on extended loans.

Sunderland-born Brown slotted straight into the first team alongside Steve Thompson, now back at the Bank after spells with Leicester and Sheffield United. Lincoln started well. They conceded only one goal in the first seven games to move top of the table. Murphy's magic, maybe, was working again. Alan

Roberts arrived for £60,000 from Sheffield United but the unlucky winger collected a serious knee injury in a 1-0 FA Cup win over Billingham Synthonia. He was forced to quit after just 11 games for the Imps. City stayed within reach of the play-off spots and the board freed cash for signings. In came midfielder Steve Stoutt (£9,000 from Grimsby), winger David Puttnam (at first on loan, then for £35,000 from Leicester) and striker Tony Lormor (£25,000 from Newcastle). Another midfielder, John Cornforth, joined on loan from Sunderland. But just as the season reached its nitty-gritty, City's form got bitty. A position of strength in mid-March was squandered by just two wins from 10 games. On the final day, to reach the play-offs, City had to beat champions Exeter and hope that results at Aldershot, Maidstone, Chesterfield, Peterborough and Halifax all went their way. Exeter won 5-1 and City again finished 10th. Murphy did what he increasingly felt he should have done two years earlier. He left.

June, 1990. Presidents George Bush and Mikhail Gorbachev ratified a new round of arms reductions. British actor, Rex Harrison, died. So did the Social Democratic Party, officially disbanded by Dr David Owen. Pat Eddery, on Quest for Fame, won the Derby and the Imps' board drew up a short-list of three potential managers. Barry Fry (last seen at Sincil Bank being escorted from the pitch during the furore of Barnet's Conference visit), Graham Carr (manager of Northampton when they coasted to the Division Four title two years earlier) and former Leeds United and England striker Allan Clarke. All were interviewed at John Reames' house and Clarke impressed most. City's previous experiments with former top-flight players - David Herd and Willie Bell - had brought limited success but Clarke's credentials were more relevant. He had starred in a great Leeds side, played 19 games for England and scored the winner in an FA Cup final. But he also boasted 11 years' experience as a manager in the lower divisions, including three promotions with Barnsley and Scunthorpe.

Clarke was the board's unanimous choice but Reames soon picked up some negative vibes. "We went out for a meal - all the directors and their wives and Allan Clarke and his wife," he recalls. "We went to a Chinese restaurant and as soon as we sat down Allan informed me that he never ate foreign food. He absolutely insisted on English. That immediately set alarm bells ringing that maybe here we were dealing with an inflexible mind." Clarke was equally forthright about style of football. He denounced Murphy's long-ball approach. "I intend to work round the clock to make things work," he pledged, "and I intend to play attractive, entertaining football."

On the eve of the 1990/91 season, Sincil Bank's renovation advanced a step. Before a Yorkshire and Humberside Cup match against Leeds United, the new Stacey-West Stand, named in honour of the two Imps fans who died at Valley Parade in 1985, was opened at the northern end of the ground. A tidy, if small, structure, it took some getting used to by fans accustomed to the old, much-loved Railway End terrace. City held Leeds until just after half-time but then, driven by Gordon Strachan and Gary Speed, the First Division side eased to a 4-0 victory.

Led by a man of Clarke's pedigree, promising to attack, attack, attack, the Imps' pre-season hopes were sky-high. "There's a buzz about the team," said the new boss. Lincoln started well enough with a 2-2 draw at Burnley and a 1-0 home win over Halifax but the third League game, at York City, was invaded by tragedy. In the 42nd minute, York striker David Longhurst collapsed on the pitch. The nearest Imps player, Paul Casey, raced over to the stricken player but Longhurst, aged 21, was already dead of a heart attack. The match resumed in unreal, stunned fashion until half-time but was then abandoned.

City seemed to go into shock. They won only two of the next 11 games. Clarke would not compromise his free-flowing football philosophy - admirable, up to a point, but it asked a lot of Fourth Division players. The manager's frustration grew. The players that were so recently "buzzing," he now lambasted, particularly those Colin Murphy had recruited from non-League. "Seven have come from non-League," said Clarke. "That's too many. We are trying to get players to play football but there are quite a few players at the club who can't play football. No matter how hard you work with them, they don't come up to the required standard. End of story."

Hardly surprisingly, the players didn't react too positively to that. City lost 4-0 at Stockport - "We were rubbish," said Clarke - and 4-1 at home to Crewe in the FA Cup. Before the next match, at home to Darlington, striker Phil Stant was drafted in on loan from Notts County. Stant, 50 goals from just over 100 League games behind him, was confused by his first meeting with the Imps' boss.

"I was asked to play in a County Cup match against Grimsby," recalls the striker, "but when I got to Lincoln, a real pea-souper had come down so the match was called off. I still had to report, though, so I went in and introduced myself to Allan Clarke. He just turned away. I waited round a bit then went up to him again and said again who I was. 'Oh, right,' he said. 'So, what are your strengths?' The guy had brought me in on loan and didn't know what my strengths were!"

City's strengths were getting hard to spot. After a 3-0 defeat to Darlington, the Imps had conceded 10 goals in three games, scored none in four, won only two of 15 League games and slipped to 22nd in Division Four. Next came a 2-0 Leyland Daf Cup defeat at Birmingham, to which only 59 Lincoln fans bothered to travel. After 179 days in the job, Clarke was sacked.

Reames recalls: "Sadly, a lot of the players had lost all confidence in him. Allan tried to do things the way Leeds did them. But he had played in a great

Leeds team. Here he was dealing with Fourth Division footballers and it was a total disaster."

The manager's merry-go-round twirled again. Wallington fancied the job but club captain Steve Thompson stepped up for his first crack at management. Thompson, 35, was always an inspiring on-field presence for Lincoln and, after Clarke's extravagant failure, City fans were happy to have one of their own back in control. 'Thommo' immediately proved he knew his onions. "The objective, " he asserted, "is at the end of the day to score more than your opponents." He was also streetwise, acknowledging, on his first day in the job: "Nothing is more inevitable than that sooner or later a football manager will get the sack."

Thompson abandoned Clarke's intricate passing, played it simple and tightened up defence. The players were instantly more comfortable. There was a big improvement, with three wins and three draws in January. The arrivals of Keith Alexander (£7,000 from Stockport) and Jason Lee (£35,000 from Charlton) added substance to the front line. They helped Tony Lormor relocate his goal touch. Having scored no goals in 16 starts, Lormor harvested 14 goals in 16. City lost only five of 27 games after January 1 to finish 14th. Matt Dickins, a youngster recruited from Sheffield United, got his chance in goal and settled quickly. A stirring revival was rounded off in style by thrashing Carlisle 6-2 at Sincil Bank. Lormor scored four and 17-year-old Dean West one on his debut. Thompson had emphatically turned things round.

The season included one remarkable milestone. At half-time during Blackpool's visit to the Bank, on April 6, Lincoln and District Football Supporters Club handed a cheque for £25,506 to John Reames. It took the total donated to the Imps by the supporters' club to a cool £1 million. In the year 2000, so many million-pound sums are bandied about in top-flight football, it's easy to become blase about them. Multi-million pound transfers, sponsorship and wage-deals are all over the place. But most of that first £1 million raised by LDFSC was generated in the 1950s, 60s and 70s when, to quote the late, great Ena Sharples, "money were money." It was the product of decades of foot-slogging, ticket-selling, door-knocking, canvassing, collecting, bingo-calling - all for the love of Lincoln City. Its equivalent figure today would be astronomical. LDFSC is still going, in its 49th year. It's more of a struggle now, with the fund-raising market-place more competitive then ever, but take the £1,398,615 they have raised to date out of Lincoln City and you probably take Lincoln City out of existence.

In 1991, as always, the Imps were grateful for every penny. A record annual loss of £268,000 meant Thompson was unable to enhance his squad for the 1991/92 season. After a stylish opening-day 2-1 victory at Cardiff, they proved erratic. Home form was wretched as Rotherham (2-0), Barnet (6-0), Chesterfield (2-1), Burnley (3-0) and Scarborough (2-0), all won at the Bank before

Christmas. The Imps failed to score in 16 of their first 25 games as Lee struggled to win the fans over. But City rallied, first with a gentle recovery, then an explosive burst. Confidence soared as City compiled a run of one defeat in 18 games and ended with seven successive victories. Away form, impressive all season, ended lavishly with a 5-1 win at Chesterfield and 4-1 victory at Halifax. A remarkable recovery, achieved despite the sales of Dickins, to Blackburn Rovers for £250,000, and Shane Nicholson, to Derby for £80,000, lifted City to a final placing of 10th. Thanks to those sales, the Imps also made a profit for the first time in five years.

City became a Division Three side again for the 1992/3 season, with the divisions renumbered to accommodate the Premiership. Sincil Bank became three-sides rebuilt with the opening of the new South Park Stand. Executive boxes, 17 of them at the rear of a small stand, were introduced to the Bank, with the Centre Spot bar down below. In that bar, confidence was expressed about the approaching season. City's blistering finish three months earlier saw them installed as joint promotion-favourites. Those credentials were enhanced by a pre-season 5-1 friendly win over Middlesborough, inaugural members of the Premiership.

On August 15, 1992, City opened their Fourth Division campaign with a 2-1 defeat at Colchester. Same day, back in Lincoln, another windfall-in-waiting tiptoed into the pipeline. The Imps' youth team beat Port Vale 4-0 with 16-year-old Darren Huckerby scoring twice on his debut. Keith Alexander, youth team coach, said: "Young Huckerby looks to be coming to terms with the demands of full-time training."

Three straight defeats - to Colchester, York and Carlisle - was not the anticipated start. City gave Premiership side Crystal Palace - including Nigel Martyn, Gareth Southgate and Stan Collymore - a worthy battle, going down 4-2 over two legs in the Coca Cola Cup but embarrassment followed in the FA Cup. Conference side Stafford Rangers, managed by former Imp Dennis Booth, held City 0-0 at Sincil Bank and Jason Lee's missing of the king of all sitters was fully punished when Stafford won the replay 2-1 at Marston Road.

Hampered by Tony Lormor's absence for the whole season with a knee injury, City were always just off the play-offs pace. The team included some effective players - Mike Pollitt, Paul Smith, Matt Carmichael, Grant Brown, Jon Schofield, Ian Baraclough, David Puttnam - but the killer touch was missing. Just one win from eight attempts in March and April sent City towards their last match, against Darlington, needing to score eight to reach the play-offs. Three days before the game, Thompson departed after the board decided not to renew his contract.

Geoff Davey, then managing director, recalls: "Steve Thompson had some potential as a young manager but he wasn't sacked for footballing reasons. Steve never used to show up in the boardroom after a defeat. After a few wins, on the other hand, he was incredibly upbeat, sometimes not treating the directors with much respect.

"Thommo took us to the brink of the play-offs and was confused and livid when he was sacked. Maybe he had a point. He had done OK and maybe we should have sat him down and had a word with him, not sacked him."

Youth boss Keith Alexander was given control for the final game. He gave full debuts to two of his youth products, Matt Carbon and Ben Dixon, and Lincoln won 2-0. They finished eighth - their highest since returning to the League. Thompson had every right to feel football was a strange, cruel, old business.

Alexander wanted the manager's job long-term and, 13 days after the season ended, he got it. It was a gamble by the board. Alexander was a popular bloke and, under his control, City's youth set-up was well-run and respected. But, as a manager, he was totally unproven. "Alex" had arrived late in senior football after an extensive tour of East Midlands non-League football. He passed through Worksop, Ilkeston, Kimberly, Alfreton, Stamford, Boston United, Kings Lynn, Spalding, Grantham, Kettering and Wisbech before stepping up into the Conference with Barnet. Even then he retained his East Midlands links - Barry Fry once fined him two weeks wages for playing for Washingborough, in the Lincoln Sunday League, while with Barnet. Alexander finally reached the Football League, aged 28, with Grimsby and then Stockport before joining Lincoln for £7,000 in December 1990. Fifteen months later he became youth team coach. Now, in May 1993, he was the gaffer.

He brought in experienced centre-half Mark Smith, from Notts County, and two wingers; David Johnson, for £32,000 from Sheffield Wednesday and Steve Mardenborough, for £10,000 from Darlington. In, too, came squad numbers. Mike Pollitt found himself with GK on his back while David Johnson had the honour of becoming Lincoln's first number 20.

The first six League games brought just one win and three goals. Again, City lifted themselves against Premiership opposition in the Coca Cola Cup. Against Everton, the Imps lost a thrilling first leg 4-3 in front of almost 10,000 at Sincil Bank. In the second leg, at Goodison Park, they twice trailed but fought back to equalise through David Johnson and an Ian Baraclough penalty. They entered the closing minutes at 2-2, but, pouring forward for the goal to force extra time, were caught by two late goals from Tony Cottee. Everton won 8-5 on aggregate.

An advocate of passing-based football, Alexander provided some stirring early-season fare for the fans. City scored 18 goals in seven games, only two of which (against Everton) they lost. Sky TV cameras discovered Sincil Bank and beamed the Imps' FA Cup 3-1 defeat to Bolton to a grateful nation. As winter deepened, though, Lincoln's form and confidence evaporated. Nine games in January and February brought just one victory. After two seasons when supporters looked at the League table from the top downwards, suddenly the reverse was true.

On a dark February night at Shrewsbury, Huckerby made his first team debut and scored with a crisp shot after a jinking run, four minutes after coming on as a substitute. Experience arrived in the shapes of goalkeeper Andy Leaning, striker Tony Daws and defenders Nick Platnauer and Alan Johnson. The £180,000 EGT Stand, was opened at the south-eastern corner of the ground but, with City languishing 18th in Division Four at Easter, there were a few grumbles that stadium improvements had advanced to the cost of team improvements. After City's best finish since returning to the League, came their worst - 18th. The consequence was the same: exit the manager. Reames' reputation, as the Fred West of Football League chairmen, was growing. Alexander, ever civilised, acknowledged: "I have to admit that in the second half of the season in particular things have not gone well."

Next came Sam Ellis, the 26th manager - and ninth in 10 years - of Lincoln City. An Imps hero of the Taylor era, Ellis had since added some managerial success to his CV. In seven years in charge of Blackpool, he steered them to promotion despite the tightest of budgets. After a brief spell at Bury, Ellis then spent three seasons as assistant manager to Peter Reid at Manchester City. A boardroom cataclysm at Maine Road moved him on and, toward the end of Alexander's season in charge, Ellis had coached City on a casual basis. Now he got serious.

Ellis' teams were built in his own mould. Solid. Gritty. Few frills. The epitome of those attributes, centre-half Colin Greenall, was lured from Chester while former Coventry and Sheffield Wednesday playmaker Garry Bannister, interested in coaching, also arrived. Again, City under-achieved in the League. The best moments were reserved for knock-out competitions. Yet again there was a resolute Coca Cola Cup second-round display. Crystal Palace were forced to extra time in the second leg at Selhurst Park before two late goals took them through 3-1 on aggregate. In the FA Cup, Lincoln won 1-0 at Hull (Bannister) and at home to Huddersfield (David Johnson) to earn a third round visit to - guess who - Crystal Palace. This time the Imps were well-beaten 5-1. In the Auto Windscreen Shield, they emerged from a group containing Hull and Doncaster to visit Huddersfield in the second round. In extra time at the McAlpine Stadium, City became the first team in senior English football to lose to a sudden death goal. Huddersfield won 3-2.

The League season meandered tamely into spring. On March 4, the crowning jewel of Sincil Bank's reconstruction was unveiled. Where, for decades, the Sincil Bank terracing stood, now there was the Linpave Stand. The 7,700 capacity, pillar-free structure offered an excellent view and took the total coast of rebuilding the ground to around £3 million, to which the Football Trust and Lincoln City Council had contributed plenty. In front of 6,477, City celebrated the opening with a 3-0 win over Hartlepool but the season never got exciting. Lincoln finished 12th and sustained a massive loss of £464,000, the fifth time in seven years a substantial deficit had been reported. This time, the Imps' manager survived the summer - but not much longer.

City started the 1995/6 season with a 2-1 win at Preston, emphatic defeats to Gillingham and Colchester, and a home draw with Scunthorpe. Then they lost 3-1 at Barnet, a poor performance having squandered a first-minute lead supplied by Huckerby. After the match, Geoff Davey recalls, "We were in the boardroom and John Reames called all the directors into a corner. He said 'the new manager of Lincoln City is sitting in the stand.' That came as a surprise because we didn't even know that the old one was going." Ellis, and his assistant Frank Lord, were sacked. In, not as manager but as head coach, came Steve Wicks.

Wicks had been recommended to Reames by Bradford City chairman Geoffrey Richmond, under whom Wicks had been manager at Scarborough. Richmond assured Reames that Wicks was the best young manager in the country. Reames believed him - but not for long.

The new man was unveiled as a part of a revolutionary new set-up. Reames said: "By appointing a head coach we are giving Steve total control of team selection and style of play but removing from the job all the pressures of having to deal with financial matters. They will be dealt with at boardroom level.

"We accept that there has not been much stability but now we want to make sure the managers' merry-go-round at Lincoln comes to a halt. In that respect there is no point in just changing a name. We will be changing the way the whole club is run." City's supporters waited and wondered.

Wicks was a smooth operator. A slick, well-groomed son of the Home Counties, he had played First Division football with Chelsea, Derby County and Queens Park Rangers. An accomplished centre-half he certainly had been, though he was another rookie team boss with less than a year's experience at Scarborough to call upon. Intelligent, confident and populist, he launched an immediate charm offensive but some of the players, particularly some of the northerners, were unimpressed. Greenall lodged an immediate transfer request. Experienced striker Joe Allon, signed by Ellis during the summer, did the same, then withdrew it but hardly radiated joy at being at Sincil Bank.

Wicks began with two home games, a 2-1 defeat to Rochdale and a 2-2 draw with Bury: one point out of six but the performances were not that bad. Then the Imps got bad. They lost 5-1 at Chester and 3-1 at home to Cambridge. A 4-3 Auto Windscreen Shield victory over Rochdale provided a grain of hope. It was crushed, three days later, with a dreadful 3-0 defeat at Plymouth. Despite bad results, and woeful defending, the supporters still viewed Wicks as a potential saviour. He talked a good game and, like Clarke and Alexander, wanted to play attractive football, but if he was going to turn Lincoln round it had to be in alliance with Reames. Instead the two fell out big-time.

Wicks brought in Darren Davis, Matthew Bound, Michael Appleton (on loan from Manchester United), and Kevin Hulme. Hulme, a hard-working but limited midfielder, arrived from Bury, swapped for the popular and versatile Dean West. It was a move which puzzled supporters. Another was the departure of David Puttnam to Gillingham. In from Gillingham came veteran defender Shane Westley and striker Steve Brown. They both made their debuts in Wicks' sixth League game, at home to fellow-strugglers Darlington. After Darlington's 2-0 win, City were five points adrift at the bottom of the League. The merry-go-round was cranked up again.

Professional respect between coach and chairman totally disintegrated. Wicks accused Reames of blocking his transfer deals. Reames believed Wicks' lenient coaching methods were "unprofessional." City fans had mixed feelings. There were bits and pieces of attractive football but large tracts of bad defending. With the Conference still a fairly recent memory, the big question was: how much more time can Wicks expect?

Reames had already decided. Believing that Wicks had let the players become soft and disorganised, he searched for a disciplinarian. Former Swansea manager Frank Burrows - about as disciplinarian as you can get - was asked to take over but joined West Ham's coaching staff instead. City's next fixture - at Scarborough on Saturday - was looming. On Thursday and Friday, former Cambridge and Preston boss John Beck was interviewed for - and accepted - the manager's job. On Friday October 13, Reames called his fellow City directors to confirm that Wicks would be sacked after the Scarborough game.

This development was all over the Lincoln grapevine by the time City reached the East Yorkshire coast on Saturday lunchtime. At City's pre-match meal in a Scarborough hotel, City's directors dined together at one table. Wicks, already sentenced, sat confused, angry and sullen at an adjacent one. The players munched their spaghetti. Everybody knew the situation but no-one mentioned it. It was a tense, bizarre lull before the storm.

At the McCain Stadium, City's travelling supporters made their feelings known. They chanted Wicks' name throughout the match. His record at Lincoln was poor - and it was hard to say things were getting better - but there was genuine sympathy for a guy who came with such a big build-up and was now going so fast, so ignominiously. Ironically, aided by Grant Brown's return from long-term injury, City fought out a goalless draw. At the final whistle Wicks, close to tears, waved to the Imps' supporters then hurried away without speaking to any City director. Reames telephoned him at his Berkshire home on Sunday morning to confirm what everyone knew. The whole mess had been dreadfully handled by the club. Wicks was hurt and angry, but not for long. He was a survivor. He had plenty of contacts and he'd be OK. Soon he was scouting for Kevin Keegan at Newcastle, then back into management in Singapore and Malaysia.

Back at the ranch, a torrid week concluded with Lincoln City four points adrift at the bottom of the Endsleigh League Division Three. Many supporters called for Reames to go. Some fans thought he was a fool for appointing Wicks. Others felt he was culpable for not giving Wicks enough time. Either way, the chairman was about as popular as a wasp up a trouser-leg. The supporters were militant. The players were confused. Into this nest of strife and recrimination landed John Beck.

21.
Power struggle

ON his first day at Sincil Bank, John Beck told supporters: "I can't guarantee to keep Lincoln City out the Conference. But I can guarantee to give them their best chance of staying out of the Conference."

He did keep them up. In fact, during the next two seasons, Beck achieved a great deal more than that. He built a squad which earned Lincoln City's first promotion within the Football League for 17 years. The Imps enjoyed one of their most vivid cup runs. Several quality players arrived at bargain prices. The match atmosphere at Sincil Bank, buoyed by a Beck-instigated supporters' band, was its best for years.

Beck followed Graham Taylor's precedent in sending players out into the community. They attended schools, factories, fairs, pubs, condom awareness promotions and 100th birthday parties. Beck went into the bar before home games and told fans the team. He went into the stocks on gala day and took wet sponges (many thrown by the players) in his face.

Beck turned a sloppy and disorganised City team into one that was mean, proud and difficult to beat. He galvanised the football club and hoisted it from adrift at the bottom of the League to the brink of promotion. Yet his last match in charge was conducted to vociferous chants of "Beck Out." Most of the fans wanted him sacked. Few players, manacled to his singular style of play, leapt to his defence and the chairman who hired him couldn't wait to get rid. John Reames and John Beck are two strong, stubborn, volatile men, used to getting their own way. Their 29 months working together began as a functional liaison, drifted into mutual suspicion and soon developed into a full-blooded battle for control. It was never going to conclude peacefully. It ended in the bitterest acrimony.

John Beck was the Imps' 11th manager in 10 years and their fourth in 18 months. He was hired with the most specific target in mind. When he arrived, Lincoln's squad was demoralised, tactically confused and full of strangers. They were four points adrift at the bottom of the Football League. City had visited the Conference before and hated it. Murph's mission had been to get them out of that dungeon. Beck's was to keep them out.

His track record was impressive. A playing career, as a polished midfielder, began at Queens Park Rangers, then spanned Coventry City, Fulham and

Bournemouth before ending at Cambridge United. There he joined the coaching staff and, in 1990, replaced his mentor Chris Turner as manager. Beck immediately guided Cambridge to successive promotions from Division Four to Two and a sensational rise straight through to the Premiership was only thwarted by a play-offs defeat to Leicester City. He also took tiny Cambridge to two FA Cup quarter-finals. This unfashionable club, as poor as it was new to the Football League - they only replaced Bradford Park Avenue in 1970 - he turned into a feared terrier. Also an unpopular, much-vilified one.

As a player, Beck was a midfielder of guile and craft yet his philosophy as manager was the antithesis of guile and craft. Get the ball forward, fast and high. Win set-pieces. Put the ball into "quality street:" Not the goalmouth, but the channels between the touch-lines and the sides of the penalty-area. Long-throw alley. Beck, the player, would have been swiftly offloaded by Beck the manager. The game-plan was specific, direct, aggressive and inflexible. To deviate from it risked immediate substitution. The purists hated it but, for several seasons, hardly anyone could combat it.

Beck's approach was rooted in discomforting the opposition and this extended, at times, off the field. The away team's dugout at Cambridge was moved along the touchline to provide a restricted view. Tales of inhospitability towards visitors at the Abbey Stadium are legion and not all apocryphal. It was anathema to many people but what Beck was committed to, 100 per cent at all times, was winning. He hated losing and with Lincoln City in their king-size pickle at the bottom of the League, they simply had to stop losing.

When interviewed for the Imps job, Beck had been out of football for 11 months. After leaving Cambridge, he spent just over a year at Preston. They reached the Third Division play-offs but the Deepdale supporters abhorred "long-ball" and Beck was sacked after an FA Cup home defeat to Walsall. Next, he ran a business in Southport while watching plenty of football to keep informed until another chance came along. When Frank Burrows turned Lincoln down, that opportunity arose.

Beck impressed the chairman. Reames recalls: "We were four points adrift at the bottom and the prospect of going back to the Conference was unthinkable. We had to do something. John had a great track record and made a very good impression at interview. He had a very clear idea of the what he wanted to do."

Beck knew all about Reames' track record of hiring and firing. He insisted on a two-year roll-over contract with some powerful clauses. One guaranteed him a year's salary - in the region of £50,000 - if he was sacked. Others entitled him to attend all board meetings and appoint his own assistant. Had he demanded the installation of life-size marzipan statues of Demis Roussos behind every corner flag at Sincil Bank, the board, terrified by the prospect of relegation, would have got right onto it.

Beck was told he had up to £70,000 - supplied by Reames out of his own pocket - to spend. He spent quickly and by his third game, five new players were in the team. From Preston came goalkeeper Barry Richardson, defender Steve Holmes and right-winger Gareth Ainsworth. Jason Barnett, a versatile 18-year-old, was plucked from Wolves' third team. From Huddersfield came Jon Whitney, a left-back of little elegance but chilling tackles and huge personality. Ten weeks into the season, City had used 32 players, 11 of whom had already left.

On October 16, 1995, Beck started with a 1-0 home defeat to Cardiff. "There's no such thing as losing," he declared, "only learning." That made City, with nine learning processes in 13 games, the most educated team in the League. They began to move forward. Points were extracted from each of the next five matches, including three awkward away games. Barnett scored on his debut in a 1-1 draw at Exeter. Holmes fired his first City goal, a late winner in a 2-1 victory at Mansfield, and Ainsworth hit his first - and second - in a 2-0 win at fellow strugglers Torquay. That victory lifted Lincoln off the bottom. Beck got the Manager of the Month award for November. "I don't want that thing," he said. "It's a ******g jinx." Next day, City lost 2-1 at Cambridge.

Beck talked up "Team Lincoln." The we're-all-in-this-together theory. He invoked the spirit of the blitz. "Little ol' Lincoln" penned in at the bottom of a hostile, big-spending, uncaring League. Only by everyone connected with the club pulling together would escape be possible, he insisted. It was a strategy of broad appeal, immediate success and, as divisions the size of canyons developed within the club, savage long-term irony.

John Still arrived as assistant manager. Rational, intelligent and likeable, Still had enjoyed considerable success in non-League management in the south-east. A much less abrasive presence than Beck, Still provided an important listening ear for unhappy or insecure players. There were a few of these because new men in the team obviously meant others were bombed. Beck set up a new scouting network and, on specialist advice, new fitness and diet regimes. The improvement to players' fitness was irrefutable but these changes all cost money. The board quickly learned that here was a free-spending manager.

Fortunately, in Darren Huckerby, City had a highly saleable asset. At the Mansfield game, Newcastle's three wise men - Kevin Keegan, Terry McDermott and Arthur Cox - all inspected the goods. Just after half-time, they left. They had seen enough. Six days later, as the Imps' team coach, driven by the debonair Nolan Bourke, rumbled toward an Auto Windscreen Shield tie at Darlington, Reames handed a mobile phone to Huckerby. A few seconds later, the 19-year-old handed it back, beaming. He had just spoken to Keegan. Next day, Huckerby joined Newcastle for an initial £400,000 with further £50,000 payments to follow if he made one and 10 appearances for the Magpies. Newcastle would also visit Sincil Bank for a friendly. City's ever-mounting debts were temporarily reduced.

The manager wasn't too sorry to see Huckerby go. The youngster's unpredictable flair was hardly Beck material - he preferred a bit of cash to use. He brought in Terry Fleming - another refugee from Preston. Colin Alcide, an archetypal Beck acquisition of height and strength, joined from UniBond League side Emley. Centre-half John Robertson moved across from Wigan. In two months, the side was totally rebuilt. Beck brought in fighters. Ainsworth, Holmes, Whitney, Richardson, Fleming, Barnett and Robertson showed a passion that Lincoln needed after some vapid displays under Ellis and Wicks.

Ainsworth was a real bonus. Hurt by his release as a youngster by Blackburn Rovers - his home-town club - the winger had under-achieved at Preston. Now he blossomed, adding to his strength and pace on the right wing an alertness in the box which brought 12 goals from 31 games. The supporters loved Ainsworth's wholehearted approach on the field and his bright, open personality off it. No offered autograph-book went unsigned. No request for a PR visit was resisted. Karaoke night in the Centre Spot was flagging until Ainsworth stepped up to belt out Pulp's "Common People." He established a mighty rapport with the fans, always first to acknowledge them, home or away. Here, for just £50,000, was a gem.

City were safe by March and finished 18th. From the chaos of October, that was highly acceptable. Mission accomplished. But Beck's relationship with Reames had already started to deteriorate. In February, the manager received a written warning from the board after some doctored expenses-claims were discovered. The seeds of distrust were sown. Beck's regimes, meanwhile, while thorough, well-researched and innovative, were also dangerously expensive. Lincoln were losing £10,000 per week. Beck believed in spending every penny, stretching every budget, to build a successful team. It was up to the football club's hard-pressed board and commercial staff to keep the debts manageable.

Reames says: "John Beck had the same attitude to money as some supporters. 'You've got to find the money,' he'd say. But you can't find the money if there's no source ! Obviously, John had a reputation in football but I naively believed I could control him. Most people learn by experience and I thought maybe he'd have changed slightly. In that first season, he achieved everything he said he would achieve - but then nothing developed."

Just before Beck's first full season - 1996/97 - came the final instalment of Huckerby's transfer deal. Lincoln got lucky. Two weeks before Newcastle's August 9 visit to Sincil Bank, they bought Alan Shearer from Blackburn for a world record £15 million. The most expensive footballer in the world played his first game, on British soil, in a Newcastle shirt, at Sincil Bank. For a couple of hours, English football turned its gaze on Lincoln. Most importantly, the friendly yielded maximum revenue from a 10,000 crowd. Injury prevented Huckerby from playing but Keegan, Shearer and Co conducted themselves superbly. The national press got the story they wanted after 32 minutes when Holmes handballed a cross and Shearer tucked home his first goal for Newcastle from the penalty spot. Philippe Albert also scored in Newcastle's 2-0 victory.

Beck did a bit more building. He spent £30,000 on defender Kevin Austin from Leyton Orient. Experienced trio Tony Dennis, Worrall Sterling and Mark Hone arrived on free transfers. Young winger Jae Martin joined on loan from Birmingham. At 2.55pm on August 24, all five recruits were happily warming up on the sunlit Sincil Bank turf before Lincoln's first home game of the season, against Leyton Orient. Beck was in his office, ready to head for the dug-out, when the door opened. In walked a delegation of burly officers from HM Customs and Excise who promptly arrested the manager. Still in his shorts and football boots, Beck was handcuffed and escorted from the stadium. While City and Orient fought out a 1-1 draw, Beck was driven over to Leyland, in Lancashire, for questioning about an alleged fraud in connection with a whisky business in which he was a partner. He was released without charge - and never charged - but again where Beck went, controversy and complications seemed to follow. By now, Beck and Reames were clashing more and more. The chairman re-examined the small print on the manager's contract and came up with a plan.

On September 17, Manchester City visited Lincoln in the Coca Cola Cup second round. In the throes of boardroom and managerial upheaval, the First Division side were vulnerable and Lincoln had high hopes of building a lead to protect in the second leg at Maine Road. After 41 seconds, Uwe Rosler headed Manchester City in front but Lincoln first scrapped their way back into the game and then overwhelmed their fragile visitors. Fleming's volley and Holmes' header sent City 2-1 up by half-time. Gijs Bos (a striker signed from Dutch amateur champions Yseermeervogels) and Jon Whitney made it 4-1 after the break. Driven forward by Ainsworth and Fleming, City supplied the best night at the Bank for years. The players received a standing ovation. Two days later, Beck received two years notice.

The board had given themselves a get-out, albeit a distant one, of the compensation clause in Beck's contract. To dismiss him in contract would cost £50,000. Now, when the manager's notice elapsed, two years down the line, City could simply not renew it. Beck was told the development didn't necessarily mean he wouldn't get another contract, two years on - indeed, the door was not closed on discussions over a new deal before then. But it was a demotivating blow for the manager. He felt "shocked and shattered" that such jockeying for position was taking place. Battle was now joined.

Lincoln completed the giant-killing with a 1-0 win at Manchester City. Two thousand Imps fans richly enjoyed the night but as they departed, delirious, for home, up in the Maine Road boardroom, the edge was taken off the celebrations for Lincoln's directors.

Geoff Davey recalls: "John Reames commented on what good sports Manchester City were and Francis Lee [their chairman] said 'that's more than I can say for you lot.' We asked him what he meant and he unleashed a tirade about the game at our place. He said none of their players had ever been treated so badly.

"He said the toilets in their dressing room were all blocked and in a disgusting state. No tea was provided and when they asked for some, they were told it was on its way but it never came. As Lincoln's players walked past the visitors' dressing room they hammered on the door and howled. John Reames and I felt absolutely astonished and ashamed. It was not until I left the club that I realised how despised Lincoln were under John Beck."

If Beck was up to his old tricks off the field, he also still knew how to prepare a potential giant-killer, fully fired up. In the Coca Cola Cup third round, Lincoln visited Southampton and again rose to the occasion. They matched the Premiership side all the way as the Saints were confounded by one of Beck's key ploys - the long throw. One was tattily defended in the 22nd minute and Mark Hone pounced to put Lincoln ahead. Spectacular goals from Matt Le Tissier and Ulrich van Gobbel, straight after half-time, appeared to have stilled the Third Division upstarts but Lincoln fought and fought. Alcide sent a header against the bar then four minutes from time, from another long throw, Hone's chip to the far post was met by Ainsworth's looping header. 2-2. Another magnificent night for City's travelling fans. A "momentous performance" said Beck.

The cup glory trail went on but, before the replay with Southampton, the Beck/Reames rift came to a head. Beck recalls: "We had a lad from Birmingham called Jae Martin whose loan was due to expire but I felt we needed his pace up front for the replay. I asked the chairman to buy him or extend his loan but he said no.

"He then told me that he had received about 20 letters from fans criticising our style of play and saying they would never come to watch Lincoln again while I was manager. I asked to see the letters and in fact there were four. I pointed out of the window and there was a mile-long queue for Southampton tickets !

"I said if you're not going to back me, I might as well go. The chairman said OK, but then I thought wait a minute, we've got something going here. I'm not going to see it go down the drain. I said I'm gonna stay and fight you."

Hardly the ideal chairman/manager scenario. Next day, back in the Third Division, Lincoln beat Colchester 3-2 and Martin scored. At the final whistle, Beck rushed onto the pitch and extravagantly hoisted the youngster toward the Linpave Stand crowd who responded with "Sign him up, sign him up." Reames signed him up.

A week later, 10,523 people were inside Sincil Bank for the Southampton replay and for a long time it was momentous again. From yet another long throw, Ainsworth prodded City into an early lead which they held until 15 minutes from time. Then Egil Ostenstad tumbled in the Imps' box. Jason Barnett, the nearest defender, turned in disbelief as referee Terry Heilbron pointed to the spot. Jim Magilton converted the penalty and City buckled. Two late goals sent Southampton through 3-1.

A serious hangover followed - six weeks without a win, including a 7-1 defeat at Colchester - but a Christmas arrival re-ignited the season. Veteran striker Phil Stant joined from Bury for £40,000 on Christmas Eve, his second coming after that unfruitful month's loan at the Bank in 1990. He scored on his debut on Boxing Day - in a 2-1 defeat at Hull - and netted four goals in the next three games, all of which City won. By now, Ainsworth's pace, crossing and attitude on the right were terrifying Third Division defences and in Stant, he had a perfect foil. To the supporters' relief, a £400,000 bid for Ainsworth from Wigan Athletic was resisted, despite Reames insisting the club needed "an immediate cash injection of £250,000." A dodgy February - one win in six attempts - dropped City to 14th place in early March. But a 3-1 Easter Monday win at Cambridge - Beck orchestrating City from the inconveniently-sited dug-out - triggered a haul of 13 points from five matches. On the last day of the season, Lincoln could still squeeze into the play-offs if they beat Rochdale at home and Northampton or Cardiff lost. Cardiff were beaten at Darlington but City froze and Rochdale took advantage to win 2-0.

Still, a final position of ninth was acceptable progress. Ainsworth, ever-present, had scored 22 League goals, the first Imp to top 20 since Derek Bell, 14 years earlier. He was definitely City's next lucrative sale. Kevin Austin, converted from left-back to left-sided centre-back, was getting better all the time. "Team Lincoln" was gelling. City fans spent the summer thinking: "Next season is our season."

Though tension was never far from the surface, Reames and Beck co-existed. They had to. Beck wasn't going anywhere. Reames couldn't afford to shell out £50,000. It hardly made for a great atmosphere within the club and the departure of John Still, to manage Barnet, was a grievous loss to any hopes of peace breaking out. Soon after the start of the 1997/8 season, there was another skirmish. City youth boss Ian Whyte asked Beck to talk to the club's trainees after one or two disciplinary problems. The youngsters were lined up and Beck delivered some ribald and forceful opinions. When he got to young striker Danny Lynn, he went too far, grabbing the young player. Lynn's father was quick to complain. Beck got another written warning.

Young striker Lee Thorpe, freed by Blackpool, was signed after impressing in a pre-season friendly against Nottingham Forest. Ainsworth, however, having served Lincoln brilliantly, now wanted to go. Except for a hat-trick against Scarborough, his early-season displays were lack-lustre. His memorable, uplifting Imps career ended in the least glamorous circumstances. On a chilly September night at Rotherham, Lincoln played poorly and lost 3-1. Many of the 250 travelling fans were through the turnstiles within seconds of the final whistle. Only a few lingerers saw Ainsworth trot towards them and signal that it was all over. One last mutual wave of respect was exchanged. Next day, after 37 goals in 83 League games for City, Ainsworth joined Port Vale for £500,000.

Deprived of their star asset, Lincoln dug deep. They responded with a 2-0 win at Hull and set off on a bristling 16-match unbeaten run. Having lost their main man in attack, they defended brilliantly, conceding two goals in 10 games. Richardson unveiled the best form of his career. At the heart of defence, Kevin Austin formed a formidable partnership with Dean Walling, bought for an Imps record £75,000 from Carlisle United. Another centre-half, Steve Holmes, patrolled in front of the back four.

Beck's private life hit problems. He split from his long-time girlfriend, arriving at the ground one morning with his clothes in the back of his car. For a while, his office became his home. Troubles were crowding in on the complex Londoner but that's when he's at his most dogged. City stayed organised, stayed - on the pitch - "Team", stuck to the ever-familiar method and gritted out result after result. On December 2, a 2-1 win at fellow high-fliers Exeter City took them top of Division Three.

The achievement appeared to overwhelm them. Lincoln had needed a replay to scrape past UniBond League premier division side Gainsborough Trinity in the FA Cup first round. Now Emley, of the same division, visited Sincil Bank in the second. The west Yorkshire village side led 2-1, seven minutes into injury time, before Fleming scrambled an equaliser. Next day, the stakes were raised by the third-round draw - a money-spinning visit to mighty West Ham.

The replay, on a snowy Wednesday night at Huddersfield Town's McAlpine Stadium, was a match few supporters of either club will ever forget. Lincoln were hit by a goalkeeping crisis. Richardson had a thigh problem and deputy John Vaughan was definitely out with a back injury. Phil Stant, who had once kept goal for the reserves in an emergency, was put on standby. In the end, Richardson was risked and for more than an hour, there was stalemate. Then Jon

Whitney (former Huddersfield) and Colin Alcide (former Emley) put Lincoln 2-0 up. With 10 minutes left, the electric scoreboard shone brightly through the murk: Emley 0 Lincoln City 2. Bring on West Ham and associated revenue. But no. The part-timers fought magnificently and hauled it back to 2-2. They took the lead in extra time only for Hone to stab in an equaliser in the dying minutes. Penalties. Emley knew Richardson was hampered and put all their penalties high to his right, to his greatest discomfort. Barnett and Stant missed for Lincoln. A six-figure payday and an afternoon in the spotlight at Upton Park were snatched away. The silence of Lincoln's dressing room, post-match, contrasted agonisingly with the revelry in Emley's a few yards down the corridor. Three days later, shell-shocked City were thrashed 5-1 at Peterborough. Young goalkeeper Simon Brown, on loan from Spurs, had a 'mare in his only game for the club. Five more games without a victory dropped Lincoln out of the top eight.

John Beck is the first to admit that if a side, playing his way, is not winning, then it's poor to watch. He pins his reputation on results. Few people like his long-ball style but few complain if it's put their side top of the table. Grumbles grow quickly, though, when it's not going to plan. Now the grumbles grew. Lincoln were still within reach of promotion but won only two of nine home matches. About the same number were entertaining. Season-ticket holders, having spent their hard-earned dosh on this, were not amused.

Discontent peaked in March when Swansea City visited the Bank for a midweek fixture. The drab 1-1 draw was accompanied by prolonged chants of "Beck Out". The manager was at his most bullish after the match. "Beck out, Beck out," he chanted, smiling, as he entered the press room. "I don't think this football club can afford, financially, professionally or in football terms, to sack me," he asserted. It was outrageous brinkmanship and, 48 hours later, he toppled over the brink.

Reames finally decided he had enough on Beck to warrant dismissal on disciplinary grounds, obviating any compensation payment. Citing serious breaches of discipline, he suspended the manager to allow Beck, as stipulated in his contract, to instigate internal grievance procedures. The final straw, it transpired, was a five-day holiday Beck took after a Friday night game at Cambridge in February. Straight after the match, he left for Switzerland, having informed only his assistant Shane Westley. None of the board were told so it was, they felt, an "unauthorised absence from the club," a "serious breach of contract" and "wilful neglect of duties."

On March 11, 1998, at Sincil Bank, Beck's lawyer Mark Morrison delivered his client's appeal against dismissal. In a 100-minute meeting he told the board that Beck's getaway was a recharging exercise, necessary after a distressing break-up with his girlfriend.

"He has been prescribed medication and received stress counselling," Morrison told the City directors. "He took the break to get away with the intention of clearing his mind and restoring himself in order to commit himself to the club." This, the board rejected. They reaffirmed that, along with the Danny Lynn incident and some dodgy petrol expenses submitted by Beck, there were sufficient grounds for dismissal. As the appeal was heard by the directors who had sacked him in the first place, the whole procedure seemed a tad pointless. Once and for all, Beck's explosive Sincil Bank reign was over. The rancour bubbled on for a few months as Beck pursued a claim for unfair dismissal. His claim was rejected by an industrial tribunal.

John Beck has not been back to football management. And he insists that, after his experiences at Lincoln, he won't go back.

"What happened at Lincoln City turned my whole life around," he says. "I was quite happy running my business at Southport but they begged me to come in and keep them out of the Conference.

"I did that. I got a half-decent squad together and turned things round. Not just on the pitch. The players understood that being a footballer wasn't just about playing football. I got them out in the community, into schools, set up the "adopt-a-player" scheme, got the supporters' band going. I talked to the fans - the Lincoln fans hadn't been listened to for years.

"But as soon as we were safe from relegation in that first season, everything changed. From then on, everything I set out was questioned. At every board meeting, before we got round to discussing important things, there had to be two hours of me justifying my style of play."

The circumstances of his sacking, particularly his "unauthorised absence" after the Cambridge game, have left Beck with a bitter taste.

"Sure I went skiing," he says. "But I told Shane Westley that I was going and I was contactable on my mobile all the time. I'd had one or two problems in my personal life so I went to the Alps to get away for a couple of days. Then I got back on the Thursday, spent a couple of days training with the players and on Saturday we beat Barnet 2-0. What's the problem? But they saw the chance to get rid of me and save themselves some money.

"I won't go back to football," he says. "I like supporters and I love getting teams organised and working with players, making them better. There's nothing else like it. But then there's the other side - the media and the club politics and I hate that. I've got my marketing business now and I'll work hard at that and hopefully make a go of it.

"A lot of people don't want me to go back to football. They hope I never go back. And I don't care."

***

When Beck was sacked, City sat eighth in the Third Division, outside the play-offs zone only on goal difference. Control for the rest of the season passed to Shane Westley, assisted by reserve-team boss Phil Stant and physio Keith Oakes. Westley's elevation completed an unlikely rise through the ranks. An experienced central defender, he arrived in Lincoln two weeks before Beck in 1995. After just 11 games he was banished to the reserves. Beck saw no playing future for Westley so, to get some value out of his three-year contract, switched him to coaching duties. A year later, Westley stepped up to assistant manager. Soon he became a disciple of Beck's on-field style.

As caretaker boss, Westley stuck rigidly to the system that had got Lincoln into the promotion race. Notts County and Macclesfield stretched clear to secure two of the three automatic promotion spots but six other contenders seemed to be battling against promotion. City travelled to their penultimate game, at Darlington, still with a sliver of a chance of going straight up. A 2-2 draw, secured by an injury-time goal by on-loan striker Dennis Bailey, secured a play-offs place and took the automatic promotion dream into the last day. Torquay were favourites. If the Gulls collected a point at Leyton Orient, they were up. But if they lost - and Lincoln beat lowly Brighton at Sincil Bank - the Imps would sneak into Division Two.

Inside a packed Sincil Bank, Brighton, backed by 2,000 travelling fans, declined to roll over. City toiled in vain during a tense and even first half but chants of "1-0 to the Orient" then "2-0 to the Orient" from the Linpave Stand, informed the players that, down in east London, half the equation was falling into place. Orient were helping. Could Lincoln help themselves ? Yes. Ten minutes into the second half, Terry Fleming poked home one of the scrappiest goals ever seen at Sincil Bank. Off-balance, eight yards out, he stuck out a toe and sent the ball wobbling apologetically into a net deserted by goalkeeper Mark Ormerod. So scrappy, but priceless. Three minutes later Lee Thorpe hooked home a second goal. Brighton scored deep in injury time but there was hardly time to restart. City had won 2-1. Thousands of fans charged on to the pitch to celebrate.

Wait a minute. Torquay had pulled back to 2-1 and their game was running late. They were still playing, one goal from promotion. Just like that cataclysmic day, 11 years earlier, the Imps' fate hinged on Torquay. In the dressing room at Sincil Bank, Lincoln's players prowled, desperate for news, refusing to celebrate too soon. Even as the supporters chanted and sang, Torquay were camped in the home box at Brisbane Road. Six minutes into injury time, they hit the bar. The ball was scrambled clear. Finally, confirmation came through. This time the agony was Torquay's. City had done it. The Imps had held their nerve. The players headed into town to join the supporters in celebration. A few days later came an open-top bus parade through the city centre. A string of mundane, middling, mediocre seasons had been terminated, despite all the upheaval.

"To gain promotion was a great achievement by a very small squad of players," said Reames. "And, of course, John Beck takes some of the credit. He has got some very good points as a manager and a lot of what he put in place at Lincoln was extremely effective. But I don't think the club would have got promoted if we, as a board, had not acted when we did to dismiss him. When discipline at a football club goes, then everything goes and we had three rock-solid, disciplinary reasons to sack him - as the industrial tribunal later agreed."

Westley's hold on the manager's job was firmed up. To assist him for the challenges ahead, in came Wally Downes - a tough, uncompromising Londoner and member of the Wimbledon squad which rose through the divisions in the 1980's. Downes was enlisted to add experience to the management team. It didn't work. Much to the players' dismay, Westley remained committed to predictable pressure-football. Downes preferred a mixture, so conflicting messages reached the players. The two men had little in common other than that, on November 10, 1998, after steering Lincoln City to just three Second Division victories in three months, they were both sacked.

22.
Love story

PROMOTION to Division Two in 1998, while a great achievement by the team, only increased the financial pressure on Lincoln City. Players' bonuses had to be paid out while the wage-bill, adjusted to a higher level, rose by a third. Squad strengthening was essential if Lincoln were to survive in the Second Division, so a joint club record £75,000 was somehow found to buy striker Tony Battersby from Bury. That bust the transfer budget in one go, with other arrivals - defender Jason Perry, winger Lee Philpott and striker Leo Fortune-West - all joining on frees.

To help meet increased expenses, the board hiked up season-ticket prices by almost a third. Match-day admission rose to £13. That's not a cheap afternoon's entertainment and the first home game, against Wigan Athletic, attracted only 3,355 people. A week into the new season, John Reames put Lincoln City Football Club up for sale.

"The situation is critical in all respects," he said. "This football club is in real danger. Only because most of our creditors have been extremely sympathetic have we been able to carry on. We are only just managing to pay the wages every month. We are getting very, very close to the point at which the club is handed over to the administrators."

For years Reames had pleaded for major investment alongside him at boardroom level. No-one, of the requisite financial weight, responded. Perhaps because football is a risk, often a bad one. Perhaps because accountants turn pale at the prospect of clients investing in a business with such a phenomenal appetite for capital. Maybe because Lincolnshire, principally a farming county, had seen more prosperous times or perhaps just because, after 14 years in control, Reames loomed too large over the club. A major investor, surely, would want control. If that was the obstacle, the chairman now sought to remove it. "If my presence is the problem," he said, "then it needn't be. If me being here is all that's stopping somebody coming in with enough money to make this club safe, then let them come. I'll go."

Still, a queue of investors failed to form. Only American sports entrepreneur Terry Smith expressed realistic interest. Smith, formerly coach to Great Britain's American football squad, was keen to turn his attention to association football but negotiations did not get far.

"Only Terry Smith came in and I got the impression that he didn't really understand the level of investment necessary to keep this football club going," recalls Reames. "Apart from Terry, there was no serious interest at all and I do find that amazing. We're only talking about, say, £300,000. I know, to a lot of people, that's a lot of money but, in football terms, it's chicken-feed."

While Smith bought into Chester City instead, in Division Two, the Imps found themselves competing with clubs of incomparable spending power. City had stretched every commercial sinew to find £75,000 for Battersby, yet 11 of their Second Division rivals had, at some point, spent at least £500,000 on a single player. The roll-call for the 1998/99 Second Division included some illustrious names - Manchester City, Stoke City, Fulham - alongside well-resourced clubs like Wigan, Preston, Gillingham and Reading. The standard was probably the highest ever at that tier of English football. The step-up would have challenged even Bill Anderson's talent for turning sows' ears into silk purses. The most proven, sagacious, experienced manager would have found it daunting. For a rookie like Westley, it was impossible.

Four points from the first three games was promising enough but five successive home defeats plunged City down the table. After a ragged 3-0 defeat at Chesterfield in early November, the Imps landed bottom of Division Two. A difficult Tuesday-night visit to high-flying Walsall was next, followed by an FA Cup first round trip to Conference leaders Cheltenham Town.

At Walsall, Battersby prodded Lincoln into an eighth minute lead but they folded in the face of late pressure and lost 2-1. It was the third time in five games they had surrendered an early lead and it was their 12th defeat in 14 games. City had won just three of 20 League and Cup matches. As the team coach nosed its way home, out of misty Staffordshire, Westley and Downes turned their thoughts to Cheltenham. Lincoln needed an FA Cup run - in terms of finance and morale - more than ever before. "We've got to beat Cheltenham," Westley muttered, almost to himself. Downes knew that. Westley knew Downes knew. Downes knew Westley knew he knew and the players knew too but what none of them knew was that, as soon as the final whistle had sounded at Walsall, John Reames reached a decision. Next day, Westley and Downes were sacked. And team-matters passed to......John Reames.

Reames was the third chairman in senior English football to cross the line into team-management. Michael Knighton at Carlisle and, more successfully, Ron Noades at Brentford were already having a go. It was an adventurous move and a brave one. Or foolish and desperate, depending on your point of view. The Imps' supporters were split. Some, already convinced the chairman was a control-freak, believed he now had the total control he always coveted. Others, aware of the club's grave financial circumstances, appreciated the logic of saving a manager's salary. They knew that Phil Stant and Keith Oakes, having played well over 1,000 Football League games between them, were there to advise Reames, and said: "Give him a chance."

The players' immediate response to Westley's departure was to go and have a few beers in town. They had felt ever-more trapped and frustrated by the style of play. Then they beat Cheltenham 1-0. City's players and supporters alike relished a freer, more attractive style with Reames choosing the team and its formation while Stant supervised training. Behind the refreshed philosophy, however, remained defensive fallibility. Reames was kept waiting for a League win. Despite a curious two-match cameo from 41-year-old former Liverpool goalkeeper Bruce Grobbelaar, Lincoln were five points adrift at the bottom by Christmas. The advocates of the "foolish and desperate" theory shook their heads sadly and knowingly.

A Boxing Day 1-0 victory over Macclesfield triggered a revival - just two defeats in 10 games - but injuries to key players Kevin Austin and John Finnigan overstretched City's small squad. Hit by a string of tough away games - at Preston, Fulham, Gillingham, Stoke and Manchester City - in spring, City lost them all and were sucked back into the bottom two. On the final day of the season, an elaborate plot had to unfold for the Imps to avoid relegation.

First and foremost, Lincoln had to beat Wycombe at Sincil Bank. Most of an 8,145 crowd willed them forward but the atmosphere soon ebbed as results elsewhere quickly went wrong. Oldham, who had to lose to give Lincoln a chance, led 2-0 after 27 minutes against Reading. Lincoln scrapped hard but so did Wycombe, who would, themselves, be relegated by defeat. Into the closing minutes, it was still 0-0. City had to score and hope late goals arrived at several other locations to complete a miraculously escape. Instead, seven minutes from time, Paul Emblen's header looped over John Vaughan into Lincoln's net and, beyond all doubt, the Imps were down. At the final whistle, supporters gathered on the pitch to applaud the team. Player-of-the-season Steve Holmes - no-one could have given more for City's cause - took the warmest ovation. Lincoln had fought hard and acquitted themselves honourably but the jury was still firmly out on Reames as manager - with a sizeable majority against. Nevertheless, he stayed in charge.

In the summer of 1999, John Reames became Lincoln City's longest serving chairman, overtaking Pearce Milner's 14-year hegemony which bridged the First World War. Reames' leadership has not embraced a golden era for the Imps. The stadium has been developed into one of the best in the lower divisions. There have been three relegations and two promotions. There's been a soupcon or two of cup glory but mostly, increasingly, it has been a scramble for survival. Lincoln City Football Club, a lurker close to the brink for most of its 116 years, remains there. At the start of the 21st century there has never been more money in English football - almost all directed towards the top end. While the likes of Manchester United and Chelsea juggle their multi-millions, the likes of Lincoln City agitate over every penny. For them, every season survived is an accomplishment in itself. When the weekly wage of one Premiership player is equivalent to the transfer fee for two or three Third Division players you know something's gone badly wrong.

Life's always been hard for Lincoln City and recently it's been as hard as ever. For more than a decade, Reames has played a substantial part in keeping the Imps alive, yet he evokes deeply divided emotions from City fans. His forceful style and itchy trigger-finger have made him enemies. For every Lincoln fan who admires and respects Reames there are two who are resentful and suspicious of him. He's made mistakes and is the first to admit it. After taking over, in 1985, he "ran the club like a business" and City tumbled into the Conference. But then he backed Colin Murphy to the hilt as the Imps bought and fought their way back into the League.

There have been too many managers. Allan Clarke; "a total disaster," said Reames. Steve Thompson; "real ability but impossible to deal with after a few wins." Keith Alexander; "great potential but I let him down by not insisting on an experienced assistant." Sam Ellis; "our most disappointing manager." Steve Wicks; "A great publicist - but that wasn't what we needed. We needed a coach." John Beck; "I was naive enough to think I could control him. I failed abysmally." Shane Westley "Tried to run it exactly John Beck's way and the players didn't accept it."

Yes, some mistakes among that lot. Next: John Reames. The chairman was still picking the team as 1999 finally gave up the ghost, ordered one for the road, held up its hands and, with a plaintive cry of "it's a fair cop, guv," surrendered to the year 2000. Reames the manager. Mistake ?

"By the nature of football," he says, "Lincoln City have always had one of two types of manager. Either a manager who has failed somewhere else or a player who has spent all his working life playing football and now suddenly is asked to take responsibility for running a fairly large business. Neither of those make the greatest sense to me. I have watched some managers at work and thought 'well I couldn't do any worse.' I would never get involved in the training of players. That's Phil Stant's domain. But if we all do what we are qualified to do, and pull in the same direction, it can work." Midway through the 1999/2000 season it was working effectively enough. Reames collected the Third Division manager-of-the-month award for October and, despite a frightening injury-list, Lincoln were still eyeing the promotion race as winter deepened.

So, into another millennium go the Imps, still struggling, still battling, still surviving. City lost more than £1 million during the last five years of the 20th century - how many businesses could survive that ? But, then, Lincoln City have been losing money almost every year, almost every week, for more than a century. Penury has been a constant companion, crisis a regular visitor. Lincoln - a small city in a rural area, with a relatively small fan-base at its disposal - charged into the Football League at the first opportunity, 108 years ago, and found the terrain hostile. But once in, it was damn well going to stay in. Or, if squeezed out, get straight back in.

In 1954, John J Sawyer wrote a brief history of the Imps, "Down the Years with Lincoln City." It was produced during City's Second Division days - happier times - but Sawyer still concluded by focusing on the struggle rather than the triumph. "No doubt the days ahead will bring their grey skies and chill winds," he wrote. "Yet we may rest assured that, as always in the past, adversity will weld players, officials and supporters still closer together. And, who knows, bring to our aid and inspiration those spirits who, still watching now from that strange and silent Neutral Ground, launched the good ship Lincoln City upon the perilous deeps of English League Football."

Lincoln City has survived those perilous deeps because generation after generation of supporters, from the city and the county, have stuck with the club through thick, thin and thinner. Turnstile-clickers doing their vital bit while someone - Robert Dawber, Pearce Milner, Frank Eccleshare, John Reames - has injected more serious money at vital times. In 2000, never mind all the hype that propagates the Premiership, supporters turn up at Sincil Bank and travel country-wide with the Imps, resigned to the struggle but all the more determined because of that. Proud of Lincoln City. A club steeped in history, bristling with identity.

On match days, in the year 2000, you see supporters, hunched into the icy winds, fists burrowing deep into pockets, eyes rheumy to the freezing rain, trudging along Cross Street, down High Street, up Newark Road or beside the Sincil Drain, towards Sincil Bank, just as their predecessors have done for more than 100 years. Doggedly, fiercely, unflinchingly loyal and that's why, for all the turbulence and crises, for all the aggravation, all the body-blows sustained and the conflict weathered during decade after decade in the brutal, dog-eat-dog industry of professional football, the story of Lincoln City is essentially a love story. The Imps are still around because there have always been people who loved the club enough, even in the darkest storms, to keep the red-and-white striped flame aglow. Long may it burn.